MY LIFE IN ARCHAEOLOGY

C.W.P. in 1940

MY LIFE IN ARCHAEOLOGY

CHARLES W. PHILLIPS

ALAN SUTTON
1987

First Published in 1987 by Alan Sutton Publishing Limited
30 Brunswick Road
Gloucester GL1 1JJ

British Library Cataloguing in Publication Data

Phillips, C.W.
  My life in archaeology.
  1. Phillips, C.W. 2. Archaeologists—
  Great Britain—Biography
  I. Title
  930.1′092′4   CC115.P4/

ISBN 0-86299-362-8

Cover Design by Martin Latham
Typesetting and origination by
Alan Sutton Publishing Limited, Gloucester.
Printed in Great Britain

CONTENTS

LIST OF PLATES

Preface

Archaeology, to a larger degree than most historical or scientific disciplines, has for long been advanced by amateurs. We in England have been especially fortunate in this respect and our subject boasts a long and very distinguished line of men and women who devoted their leisure to the study of the material remains of the past. Charles Phillips was for half his life an outstanding example of the great British amateur archaeology tradition.

From the time he took his degree in history in Cambridge in 1922 until the outbreak of war he was a history don, Librarian and Fellow of Selwyn College: *all* his spare time was spent in field archaeology especially in Lincolnshire and the Fens. He excavated in Wales, in the West Country and Lincolnshire: the Skendleby dig was the first modern scientific excavation of an earthen long barrow – a landmark in British archaeology.

In 1939 he was put in charge of the excavation of the ship burial at Sutton Hoo – the richest, most spectacular and most important find ever made in British archaeology, and that work, done quickly but with consummate skill, as the shadows of war darkened that late summer, and its subsequent quick publication, *alone* are enough to justify his assured place in the hall of archaeological fame.

He worked on the Fenland Research Committee and together with his colleagues and friends Grahame Clark, Christopher Hawkes and Stuart Piggott turned the Prehistoric Society of East Anglia into *The* Prehistoric Society of which he was Secretary for ten years. It was good that he was able to be in Norwich when the Prehistoric Society celebrated its fiftieth anniversary and that though unwell he was able to visit the new excavations at Sutton Hoo.

Then, after the war, in mid life, he became a professional archaeologist: from 1947 to his retirement he was Archaeology Officer of the Ordnance Survey. He had achieved what he once described as 'a long and oblique progress to what seemed an unattainable end'. He reformed the Archaeology Section of the Survey and by his tact and good sense achieved, in a way, even more than had his predecessor and friend O.G.S. Crawford. They were both doughty, determined and sometimes difficult men but the cartographical excellence and eminence of British archaeology is entirely due to these two men.

It is unusual for anyone to have first a distinguished career as an amateur archaeologist and then a distinguished career as a professional archaeologist but Charles Phillips was an unusual man: he was also a kind and generous man: his bluffness and apparent brusque manner covered his goodness, warmheartedness and friendliness which so many of a younger generation remember with affection. I certainly do, and I remember with special affection his days in the Central

Photographic Interpretation Unit at Medmenham in the war. He was a pillar of strength to all of us studying on air photographs the German occupation of Europe. When we had problems we invariably went to him. He became a myth at Medmenham and the rumour went round that he was omniscient. On one occasion a WAAF officer trying to plot a town in Czechoslovakia asked him if it had two railway stations – one each side of the river. He was a railway buff among other things. 'No', he said firmly without consulting a map, 'If it had I should have known'. He wore his learning with modest and engaging assurance. On another occasion while studying air cover of the west coast of Normandy I thought I had found a prehistoric village now under the sea, and excitedly took my discovery to Charles. He looked at the photograph for a while and then said, 'My dear sir, I thought you were supposed to be knowledgeable about the human geography of France: these are modern oyster beds'.

In August 1939 I drove from Cambridge with Hector and Nora Chadwick to see the Sutton Hoo dig. Phillips and Chadwick had never met and both were slightly apprehensive. The encounter turned out to be a great success. As we were leaving Chadwick said to Charles 'It's the grave of King Redwald you know. I've no doubt of that'. And when we got back to Cambridge Chadwick said to me 'That was one of the most memorable days of my life. I think Phillips is a great man'. And indeed he was – a great man. Future historians of British archaeology looking back at what was achieved in the twentieth century and remembering, as we do today, Charles Phillips, might well say in the words of Genesis iv 'There were giants in the earth in those days'.

Professor Glyn Daniel
address given at the funeral of Charles Phillips
at Teddington on 2nd October 1985

Foreword – A complete life

The present book is one of three accounts written by CWP, as his friends affectionately called him. Of the other two, one is more personal and the other much less so. He wrote a private autobiography based on memories of childhood and youth, marriage, family life, travel, told with the aid of a tireless memory and a love of topographical detail. He also wrote the story of his forbears, farmers working mainly in Essex, whose claim on his interest was that for three hundred years their life and background had remained constant, giving an historic picture of rural England.

The sense of history prompted the pages which follow. He was fully aware of the place he occupied in the development of archaeology, standing between the pioneering activities of earlier generations, to whom it was the interest of gifted and wealthy amateurs, and the professionalism and technical elaboration of the science of today. For this reason, his memoir is directed to illustrating the stages of archaeological discovery with which he was acquainted, speaking with the single-mindedness of one to whom knowledge of the past was a passion.

But he had many other interests and pleasures which rounded his life, and which do not appear in this book. The memory of them endears him to those who knew him best. To his family he was an unfailing source of varied lore. His encyclopaedic memory and steady powers of observation combined to give us understanding of the past and eyes for the present. We remember his flow of wide-ranging talk. He loved so many things: wild flowers, – he hunted for orchids and recorded the finds in his botanist's handbook, and made a rejoicing list of the seventy-five species of wild flowers to be found in his suburban garden; his observant eye watched the earth and the pond-surface for small creatures, with a curiosity carried on from childhood, and was equally open to the glory of a starry sky. Music was his special delight. He enjoyed working in wood, carving and painting toys for his children; stamp-collecting held him since boyhood and his collection was rare. He had loved railways from the days when he stood on a box at the end of his father's Wimbledon garden to watch the trains go by. It was remarkable how many of his interests had begun in early life and continued without abatement to his last days, fructifying into adult preoccupations. One of his marked characteristics was the power to take up and make good a long slow task which flowered under his hands, – making a European gazetteer for a beleaguered Intelligence unit during the war, cataloguing an art collection for his son, helping his daughter with clerical work for a charity, indexing my books, carrying on with undaunted patience and pleasure work which others might have considered dull. But needless to say, he took the same zest to tasks which were far from dull, like his masterly reports of field-work and excavation.

Above all he had brought from childhood a strong love of the landscape of England. It was an education to travel with him through the countryside, where every slight variation in contour, every rise or hillock, revealed itself for what it was – a precisely-recognised vestige of the past. He had a meticulous knowledge of these traces, mapping them in his mind as he took care to map them for the Ordnance Survey. Nothing was too small to have its significance, and at the same time he loved wide spaces, long views, the great perspective of the physical landscape, the meaning of place.

Though he lived most of his life in towns, Cambridge or the Thames Valley suburbs, it was as a countryman that he felt and thought. He was wary of sophistication, impatient of pretentiousness, sturdily independent in mind, and ready to speak out with bluff candour when need arose. But to the unfortunate, the crippled in life, he was tenderheartedness itself. Many will remember him as the one who helped them on their way, gave them the start they needed, cared for them in calamity. An American professor, an old friend, spoke of Charles one day to me. He might have mentioned the intellectual qualities he admired, the scientific interests they shared, but what he said was, 'The reason why I like Charles is that he's *good*. But you don't need telling that, do you?' No, indeed.

Margaret Mann Phillips

Introduction

The active career in archaeology described in this book has extended over half a century, during which period I have been involved in most of the significant developments in field archaeology and intimate with many of its most distinguished practitioners. The recorded history of my family extends back over some 350 years and a strong predilection for maps and topography has been displayed by the more recent generations, markedly so in my father's case. When I was a schoolboy one of my favourite pastimes was drawing maps of imaginary areas of country fully provided with correctly symbolised features. To me maps have always been an open book, a characteristic which has been repeated in my children.

This childhood pastime developed into an urge to explore any new region in which I found myself, and just as I was beginning in the 1920s to realise the defects of our national map system, in correctly presenting the visible relics of the past, I made the acquaintance of O. G. S. Crawford. When this gifted man joined the staff of the Ordnance Survey he opened a new era in our archaeological topography and also, by virtue of his journalistic flair as the founder and editor of 'Antiquity', became a world force in the promotion of archaeological studies.

I had already learned something of system in archaeological work through membership of the University of Bristol Spelaeological Society and Crawford confirmed and extended this knowledge by introducing me to the Curwens of Brighton, who taught me much about excavation. Among my new friends at this time of rapid expansion in archaeology were Stuart Piggott, Grahame Clark and Christopher Hawkes. I carried out an overhaul of the 6 inch scale maps of Lincolnshire for Crawford and was involved in his period map programme. In due course Piggott, Clark and Hawkes were promoted to Chairs of Archaeology at Edinburgh, Cambridge and Oxford respectively.

In the mid-1930s prehistoric studies were put on a sound basis in Britain and in the same period the problems of the Fenland as revealed by air photographs were dealt with by a committee at Cambridge, using new botanical and geological techniques. The Fenland Research Committee's approach to its task anticipated the present inter-disciplinary attack on archaeological problems.

In all this I was essentially practical, getting things done and not prone to theorise. In 1939 I was put in charge of the first Sutton Hoo excavation, but when the 1939–45 war broke out I was still without any official employment and did not expect any. After the war years (spent in service with the Royal Air Force) my prospects were not bright, but in 1946 an unexpected series of events gave me the chance to succeed Crawford as Archaeology Officer at the Ordnance Survey at a crucial moment when the long overdue general revision of the country's map system was put in hand along with a new scheme of staff deployment. The creation of an effective archaeological service for the Survey was not easy but it was achieved and the topography of British archaeology was accurately surveyed and fully represented. As a result, existing period maps received new editions and the list of new ones published grew longer.

An important innovation was the establishment of a non-intensive record of archaeological data from the earliest times to 1851. This was carefully maintained and based on National Grid references and was a continually developing archive from which the Commissions on Ancient Monuments, other interested bodies and members of the public could draw at will.

When I retired in 1965 this scheme was working exceedingly well, but in its wisdom the Government has since decided to dismantle it and map users are beginning to complain that important sites and monuments no longer appear on the maps.

This is a blow to good archaeological field work in Britain because good scale maps with up-to-date records of sites and monuments are indispensable tools for the archaeologist. Time will show whether this situation will be allowed to continue.

Perhaps the happiest days for archaeologists are now over and today archaeology is almost assuming the character of an industry. Reports of excavations are almost unreadable because an extremely wide technical knowledge is required to understand what has been written. To people of my generation this is admirable, but quite daunting, and it is seldom that I read a major report except to learn its overall conclusion.

I belong to a generation which, in excavating a site, often had to do its own digging and no bulldozers were brought in to remove unwanted deposits in the course of a few hours. Today's archaeology is no longer quite the one we knew but it is certainly something of which to be proud.

Chapter I

As I mentioned in the foreword, I was born into a family which can trace back its origins with certainty for nearly 350 years, a rather surprising circumstance since none of them ever had any pretensions to gentility or culture until quite recent times. In fact they were entirely concerned with the land as tenant farmers and, in the case of my great-great-grandfather, with auctioneering and land valuation as well. One of them, my great-grandfather, was a notable hop-grower at Hadlow in Kent near Tonbridge in the last quarter century of his life, but otherwise they were all confined to the parts of Essex lying in the neighbourhood of the towns of Thaxted, Dunmow and Chelmsford.

The first Phillips of whom we know came from the tiny village of Berden a few miles north of Bishop's Stortford, close to the boundary with Hertfordshire. This family intermarried with a farming family called Green of Thorley, south-west of Bishop's Stortford. My great-grandmother on my father's side was a Taylor, a member of a farming family at Welwyn in Hertfordshire and herself a practical farmer for many years after her husband's early death. Various members of these families emigrated to Australia and New Zealand. By the beginning of the nineteenth century the boys of the family were being educated at 'Mr Hayon's Academy' at Bocking. Only one member of the family, my great-great uncle, the Rev. George Bull Phillips, born in 1799, was a professional man trained at the Newport Pagnell Congregational College, and for much of his life he was Minister of the Congregational Church at Harrold in Bedfordshire. He fortunately took the trouble to write an account in 1851 of all that he had heard from his forbears about his family when young; research and the possession of seventeenth century heirlooms in the family today, confirm the accuracy of his memory and that of his informants.

There is nothing to show that any of my Phillips antecedents took any interest in history or antiquity, and I am quite sure that my paternal grandfather was never aware that the line of the Roman road from St. Albans to Colchester formed the southern boundary of his farm at Mardleybury near Welwyn. As a boy my own father was a serious collector of the shells of the land *mollusca* to be found round his home, but this is the only sign of this kind of activity which I have detected in my father's family.

In general they were a sober and God-fearing lot, members of the Church of England but not without some leanings towards Dissent, which is not remarkable considering its great strength in most of those places where they lived. I have been able to identify nearly one hundred members of the family and have only come across one case of dipsomania. There was also one case of death from scalding while brewing at the farm.

So much for my father's family. My mother came from a Berkshire family with a very modest background. They lived at Ardington, two miles east of Wantage in the Vale of White Horse, now, alas, incorporated in Oxfordshire by Whitehall decree. The Williams reputedly took their name from a Welsh cattle drover, who is said to have settled at Wantage some time in the later eighteenth century eventually becoming the local overseer of roads. His son, William, set up as carpenter and small builder in Wantage and married a woman named Howse whose father was a keeper of the Rising Sun at Abingdon, now long demolished. At least two other members of the Howse family kept inns, one the Fox Inn at Steventon and the other the Blue Boar in Newbury Street at Wantage. By 1834, William Williams the builder already had three children, two girls and a boy, and his wife was expecting a fourth child. The wife was a very temperamental woman and she frequently quarrelled violently with him. One morning in 1842 she sent him off to his work, saying in the hearing of witnesses that she never wished to see him alive again. She did not, for when he was looking over the work that he was doing at the Leather Bottle Inn on the road to Faringdon, at the point where it crossed Brunel's new Great Western Railway, he forgot where he was, stepped backwards off the scaffolding, fell, and died while they were carrying him back to Wantage. The child who was born not long afterwards was my maternal grandfather, another William Williams, and the melancholy temperament which plagued him all his seventy years was attributed to the effects of this tragedy on his mother who was very loth to let him work away from Wantage. However, he became very efficient in farriery and blacksmithing and after a spell at a racing stable at Chilton near East Ilsley he settled down to work for the rest of his life at the estate yard of Lord Wantage, which was situated in Ardington, one of the 'improved' villages redeemed from squalor by the Wantage philanthropist.

In due course he married Jane Bosley, who was of pure peasant stock and from a local family which had had some difficulty in living through the Hungry Forties. William and Jane had five children, two sons and three daughters, the youngest of whom was my mother, Mary Elizabeth, born in 1881. Owing to my own father's untimely death in 1907, I had to spend most of that year and part of 1908 with my grandparents at Ardington. I had a good deal of contact with William in my seventh year and even at that early age I could recognise that my grandfather had a keen, if uninstructed interest in the past. He told me all the local legends about King Alfred, the Uffington White Horse, and the Blowing Stone, all of which is set out in Hughes' *Scouring of the White Horse*.

He was also very concerned about the history of the Jews and I think that he would have profited very much from a formal education, a luxury not available to him. Three of his children, my uncle George, my aunt Emma and my mother were of well above average intelligence and my mother, who wrote a beautiful hand and was very good at figures, declined to stay in the village atmosphere although she had begun to train as a pupil teacher. Instead she went to London, where she lived with cousins and was employed as a cashier at some good shops. It was in one of these that my father saw her and later married her, much to his family's displeasure, on 14 October, 1899.

My paternal grandfather had retired from farming six years previously, discouraged by the effects of the great depression in agriculture and unable to see any long-term improvement in farming prospects. He encouraged his sons to look for alternative careers and so Wilfred became a pharmaceutical chemist and Harold, my father, was apprenticed to the milling trade and had experience in wind, water and steam mills.

It was round about 1893 that my father began to have occasional attacks of depression. He did not continue with milling but was established in a corn, forage, straw and coal business in Wimbledon, where my grandfather had retired. It was not a fortunate choice because the world was about to feel the effects of the invention of the internal combustion engine and the demand for most of these things would soon begin to decline.

When the attachment between my father and mother became apparent no attempt seems to have been made to warn my mother of his growing disability. This was a delicate matter, but in accordance with the social prejudices of the day his family certainly regarded his intended marriage as a mis-alliance, and it might have been expected that an opportunity was thus afforded of preventing it. In spite of the fact that my father had several crises during a short engagement, the wedding still took place at Ardington, but with none of his relatives present.

Between that time and my father's death early in 1907 three children were born, myself on April 24, 1901, my brother Harold John on September 3, 1903 and my sister Helen on December 23, 1906. Our early life was punctuated by a succession of collapses and recoveries by my father, during the course of which he made short therapeutic visits to Canada and New York and gave up living at Wimbledon in favour of a farm at Henley-on-Thames. His business was put into the hands of a manager, who cheated him when he tried to exercise some supervision by visits from Henley. This phase of our family life was brought to an end by his suicide on January 30, 1907. His trouble was almost certainly one which could have been controlled and even cured by the right medical treatment, but this was unknown in his lifetime.

For the time being our family life was completely disrupted and I was sent to Ardington for a year. I was a forward child and learned to read very early and I have no doubt that it was contact with my Ardington grandfather which first began to kindle the interest in history which was to develop in the next ten years. My awareness of archaeology was very much in the future and was still embryonic in my later teens.

My mother was a brave and resourceful woman and, after we had found our feet again as a family and been reunited in a little house in Vicarage Road on the west side of Henley, she boldly went to work to acquire a skill. As a part-time farmer's wife she had picked up some knowledge of dairy work for we had kept a few cows, and now she resolved to add to this by taking the short course in dairying at nearby Reading University. She secured the diploma, and almost at once learned of a vacancy involving charge of the Duke of Norfolk's estate dairy at Arundel Castle in West Sussex. She applied for this, got the job and, at the end of the summer of 1908 moved into the attached house at Arundel. I had a rather difficult time at the rather decayed Henley grammar school. While there, I lodged with an old friend of my father and then joined the others at Arundel at Christmas.

I now found myself in a very historic background in which I was to remain, at least for the school holidays, until 1917. One of the few fortunate circumstances about my father's former connection with Wimbledon was that he had become a Freemason and the Craft is active on behalf of the widows and orphans of the brethren if they are in need. So it was that during the early months of 1908 an effort had been made to secure as many votes as possible within the Craft as would give me a place in the Royal Masonic School for Boys at Bushey in Hertfordshire. Our case was a particularly sad one and I was elected. During the period of waiting for admission which lasted until I was nearly ten years of age, the Freemasons paid for my schooling at home.

Thus from the spring of 1909 to the end of 1910 I attended a small private school of unusual character called Littlehampton Commercial School in the neighbouring seaside town, which could be reached by a short railway journey. This did not contain more than about twenty or thirty boys of all ages between eight and fifteen and it was conducted by a queer little Norfolk-jacketed man called Edmund P. Toy who must have been in his late sixties. He was a sort of polymath and though he did not attempt to teach us Greek and Latin or give us religious instruction there was little else that was not touched on in the course of a week. It would be a lengthy business to give an adequate description of this school and I have attempted it elsewhere, but all I can say here is that Toy was a born teacher and did not hesitate to include natural history in his work and we were encouraged to bring specimens to school for comment. Curiously enough he never dropped a hint about local archaeology and history, though he had a lot to say about the ancient cultures of the Near East and even introduced us to cuneiform and hieroglyphics as early modes of writing. But what he most certainly did was to widen my mental horizon at an early age; the experience of Littlehampton Commercial School had its rough side but it also gave me a measure of self-reliance which was valuable to a small boy who was about to spend the greater part of his time away from home.

In due course the summons came for me to go the Masonic School at Bushey in January 1911, and as I was very big for my age I found myself the only new boy in one of the two junior Houses. This might have operated to my disadvantage but this House was very well run, while the other was under a housemaster who was a sadist and was compelled to leave two years later after a scandal. We were soon in the period of the 1914–18 war and the latter part of my stay at the school was a time of some difficulty, even privation, but the school was excellently managed.

In 1917 our life at Arundel was ended when the Duke of Norfolk died and a policy of retrenchment became necessary, leading to the closing of the dairy. At school I did well in my Cambridge Local examinations and was steadily taking a greater interest in history, which was leading me to hope that perhaps I might yet get an award at a University.

There can be no doubt that the experience of Arundel with its dominating castle and almost feudal atmosphere could hardly fail to stimulate this interest in history. Archaeology was yet to come, even though the wide spaces of Arundel Park over which we ranged in our holidays could show at least one area with plain signs of Romano-British cultivation and peasant settlement. This was recognised as being an example of some kind of human activity in the past by its name, 'Shepherd's Garden', something which today I should regard as significant and requiring further exami-nation.

However, the influence which edged me in precisely the right direction were some of the works of Hilaire Belloc, whose mother lived at the nearby downland village of Slindon. He was a great lover of Sussex, a love which I was growing to share, and I eagerly read his book *Hills and the Sea*. In this he writes of his walks and rides to the

Gumber and Nore Hill, places near the crest of the Downs behind Slindon, and he talks of the Roman Stane Street. This ancient route from London to Chichester, still used as a modern road in a number of sections, mounts the escarpment of the South Downs near Bignor as a green track and continues on its way to Chichester past the spots mentioned above. Belloc was a man of vision and through his writing he made me aware of this aspect of the past, and when I became possessed of a bicycle I began to look around for myself. The archaeology bug had taken its first bite.

At this time my mother moved to Plymouth because she was now working in the Women's Services there. This opened up a new area to me and I now made the acquaintance of the 1 inch scale Ordnance Survey maps. I bought those which covered Dartmoor and the eastern part of Cornwall and began to spend much of my holidays in long cycle rides based on Plymouth which took me over the nearer parts of Dartmoor and the Cornish lands across the Tamar. I examined many hut circles and other ancient relics on the Moor and wondered how men could ever have lived in such inhospitable surroundings.

By midsummer in 1918 it was clear that the war was drawing to a successful close but the general shortage of man- and even woman-power outside the armed forces, and the industries directly supporting them, led to a great shortage of workers on the land. The services of older schoolboys were required to get in the harvest and so it was arranged that I and some thirty other senior boys of the Cadet Corps from Bushey should spend the last week or two of our holiday under canvas at Stourhead in Wiltshire. At the last minute the plan was changed and we went by train to Amesbury and marched west from there a mile or two to a small tented camp at Countess Farm. As we came up the road out of Amesbury a vista opened up westwards and I was astonished to see something about a mile away on an opposite slope which proved to be Stonehenge. It was quite unguarded, open to anyone who cared to stroll among the stones and, at this time, on the edge of a wartime airfield whose perimeter came close to the monument. Even as we watched, Handley Page bombers, forced to take off into the wind coming from the east, only just staggered into the air before they reached and passed over it.

We worked at picking up potatoes and camped amongst a large, straggling clump of trees, in which stood a group of sizeable round barrows. But our camp did not last long, for all the boys except myself and one called Simmonds caught a widely prevailing kind of summer diarrhoea which was afflicting the troops present in their thousands on the Plain. Apart from making the acquaintance of Stonehenge and noting the numerous burial mounds clustered within view of that numinous spot, I also had an important first experience of the nature of chalk, important because so much of my work in later years was to be done in chalk country. Owing to the nature of their affliction we had to have a number of latrine pits ready for the convenience of our sufferers, but, apart from an Army cook, Simmonds and I were the only people in our party left on their feet. For several days we had to dig one pit after another and I soon got to know all about digging chalk. Fortunately the situation improved when the worst of the sufferers were removed by ambulance to Salisbury for hospital treatment. The archaeology bug had taken its second bite.

At Christmas 1918, I went home not to the far south-west but to the east coast because my mother, now in the Womens' Royal Naval Service, had been posted to

Great Yarmouth. It was here that I made my first leisured examination of a dramatically obvious and complex archaeological site and got my third bite from the bug. This was Burgh Castle, the Roman coastal defence fort, set on the bank of the Yare, known in Roman times as *Garianonnum* and only a couple of miles south-west of Great Yarmouth. Quite a large amount of its massive perimeter wall still stands but that part near the bank of the Yare has fallen outwards in a single mass. I was much excited by finding that in one of the corner towers there was a large square socket surviving in the centre of its solid top which may have been part of the emplacement for a piece of artillery. The area inside was under cultivation but bare of crop during my visit and I was thrilled to pick up my first pieces of Romano-British pottery – rims, bases and body pieces, some with scraps of barbotine decoration. Of course it was very commonplace stuff but I carefully collected a quantity. I did not know that later work on this site would not only show that it became the site of an early Anglo-Saxon monastic house with its associated inhumation cemetery, but also that when the Normans took over the area of the old fort it was used as the outer bailey of a motte and bailey castle and that a castle mound was raised in the south-west corner to carry a keep. This has long been reduced by cultivation but it is still possible to note the spread material from the motte which permanently raised the level of that part of the interior.

When I got back to Bushey at the beginning of my last term I wished to share my excitement with others, for at this stage of my career I must have been touchingly naive. I labelled some of the more attractive pieces of pottery I had gathered and put them in a case in the school library which they then shared with a few other unrelated and incongruous objects.

Although I had now tried and failed in one attempt to get a scholarship award at Lincoln College, Oxford, on the strength of my knowledge of history, I was still to be allowed one more chance before leaving school. Meanwhile, as a precaution against failure I had a wild idea that now the war was over and the British Museum was restoring its treasures to public view from the places of safety to which they had been committed in the war years, there might be a need for active young persons to help in this work. Perhaps if one could get taken on for even a short time as a manual worker it might not be impossible to work one's way on to the permanent staff.

The chairman of the school's board of management was Charles E. Keyser, a prominent business man I knew to be interested in the past because he had given an evening lecture to the whole school not long before on Romanesque Architecture. This subject was his hobby. He really knew quite a lot about it and at the lecture I was not bored by the subject or his presentation of it. I therefore wrote him a letter asking if he could exercise any influence on my behalf at the British Museum. The next monthly meeting of the board came round and I was bidden to attend when it was over. Keyser spoke to me quite kindly but then he asked Attenborough, a famous pawnbroker board member who was standing by, 'What do boys from the Masonic School normally do when they leave school?' Attenborough grunted out that they went into business, which was true, and they often got a good start from board members. But I had no desire to follow that line, and so that avenue to archaeology was closed. Of course Keyser, although he was a great business figure, had no influence at the British Museum which, in any case, was quite adequately supplied with the necessary manual staff. The truth was that, admirable as the Masonic School was in many ways, it was not geared to produce professional men though it widened its field quite soon after I had left it.

My luck now changed for, greatly to my surprise, I was awarded an exhibition in history by Selwyn College, Cambridge. It was only for £20 per annum but the Freemasons could be relied upon to supplement this and they were the more able to do so at the time because an American Freemason called Vandusen had just given a considerable sum to be used for educational purposes by the Craft in England. During the ensuing years a steady trickle of boys from Bushey went to universities on the strength of this endowment.

Although there was a recently established Faculty of Archaeology and Anthropology at Cambridge, in 1919 it was still limited to little more than palaeolithic studies on the archaeological side, while anthropology attracted more takers because the famous A.C. Haddon was on the staff and the Colonial Service now sent its entrants for training in this subject.

I have already said that in my Plymouth sojourn I had become aware of the Ordnance Survey 1 inch to the mile map series with its large number of indicated antiquities. At this time I came to learn by experience that some were not very accurately described. I worked hard at the requisite subjects for the History Tripos, but although I was either at lectures or at private study during the mornings and evenings, I kept the afternoons free and, having my bicycle with me, I spent most afternoons cycling about the district with the relevant 1 inch map and examining the various antiquities shown. My normal range in an afternoon was between twenty and thirty miles out and back depending on the time of year and the weather; in this way I would get as far as Huntingdon, St.Neot's, Ely and Saffron Walden at the different points of the compass. All the areas within these general limits were very thoroughly looked over and at weekends when conditions were favourable I would rise early on Sunday and go even as far as Norwich, King's Lynn or Bury St. Edmunds. I was a good cyclist and could keep up a speed of twelve miles an hour in the mainly flat country round Cambridge but had many a tough struggle with headwinds. It was not till my fourth year that I managed to acquire an old second-hand Rudge-Multi motor cycle, but it was not a very reliable mount.

In general such archaeological activities as there were at Cambridge were in the hands of a little clique of men of substantial means headed by T. C. Lethbridge of Trinity, who was an able enough man but unpredictable and often uncooperative. A notable exception to this clique was a young man named Cyril Fox, who was quietly carrying on, from Cambridge, a programme of field work which was soon to be published as an archaeology of the Cambridge region. This was to be an epoch-making book, but unfortunately at this time of his career I did not meet him. Our first meeting did not occur until some years later, when he was already director of the National Museum of Wales at Cardiff and had been knighted.

There was a museum in Downing Street which contained a fine collection of material, particularly from Anglo-Saxon cemeteries which had been found in the Cambridge area, as well as the almost sensational Romano-British material (including a good deal of iron work) excavated by the Hon. Richard Neville early in the nineteenth century at the small Roman town of *Iceanum* (Great Chesterford) in Essex.

It also contained a good deal of valuable Central American material and a collection from the plains of Hungary which had been brought together by the Curator, Mr L. C. G. Clarke, who was a man of wealth and taste, much more in his element when in later years he became the director of the Fitzwilliam Museum.

I visited the museum frequently during my first three years at Cambridge and looked carefully at those exhibits which were of local provenance in order to get hints which I might follow up in my field work, but I did not become a member of the group which met regularly in the Museum for mid-morning coffee. I had no great faith in the situation there and this was borne out shortly after my fourth year, when I had acquired a motorcycle, and made my first run up the Great North Road with a particular desire to look over the site of the pottery-making and iron-smelting Roman town of *Durobrivae* (Water Newton and Castor) at the point where Ermine Street crosses the River Nene. I noticed an abandoned gravel pit outside the walled part of the town and I could see that its working face had not yet collapsed. There was a dark area on this face which proved to be a section of a rubbish pit still standing with its contents in place. Many fragments of pottery were visible, but what I specially noticed was what appeared to be a lump of mineral coal embedded in the pit's bottom. I extracted this and there was no doubt that it was coal which must have been thrown into this pit in Roman times. Where had this coal come from and how had it come to *Durobrivae*? The nearest source available without mining in Roman times was probably the Barnsley Main Seam outcrop in South Yorkshire.

When I got back to Cambridge, full of excitement about my find, I hastened to tell Mr L. C. G. Clarke about it. He showed no particular interest in the probable significance of this find and how it implied the transport of a heavy material over more than one hundred miles, possibly utilizing Foss Dyke and the Car Dyke, two ancient watercourses strongly suspected to be of Roman origin, which would link the southern terminus of the Car Dyke with the river Nene and so provide a continuous line of water transport from South Yorkshire via the Humber river system, the Trent and the Car Dyke. I was disappointed by this rebuff, but someone suggested that I should take the coal to the Botany School and tell my story to the Professor, Sir Albert Seward. He showed the greatest interest and sent a piece of this coal to the appropriate authority, where it was confirmed by palaeobotanical examination that it certainly came from the Barnsley Main Seam, which would still be outcropping in Roman times. Later I was to find mineral coal on a number of Roman sites and, so far as Lincolnshire was concerned, it always told the same story. It was from experiences of this kind that, at this stage of my life, I found the Downing Street Museum disappointing.

At the end of 1922, my mother went to live in Bristol, and it was then that my beginnings as an archaeologist received their most powerful boost. Bristol was to be my home base in my vacations till the late 1930s and I was to prolong my residence in Cambridge as history teacher, minor lecturer, librarian and fellow of Selwyn through the same period.

I had not been long in Bristol for the Easter vacation of 1923 when I met a certain John Davies, I do not recall how, but it was he who first set me on the way to become a field archaeologist. His background was very modest. His father had a small and not very successful tailoring business in Clifton. The Davies family came from Presteigne in Radnorshire and they had that tubercular tendency which was just beginning to diminish in Wales as a whole. Great ability often accompanies tuberculosis and both John Davies and one of his sisters, who had become a pioneer woman engineer, were examples of this.

Bristol had a very reputable University and John Davies took a science degree there at the time of the 1914–18 war, when he already had the seeds of tuberculosis well established in him. In due course he was called up and joined the 8th Gloucesters. It was a measure of the manpower drainage of that war in its last stages that a fairly obvious tubercular case should be called up for active service, but so it was. The war was nearing its end and his length of service was short, but he and his 8th Gloucesters were among those who had to withstand the last great German effort on the Western Front. Gas was used and under locally overwhelming pressure Davies and his comrades had to make a fighting retreat till the enemy were in sight of Amiens. When it seemed that the Channel ports must be lost, relief came in a great flanking attack on the Germans. Their front began to collapse and their forced retreat out of France and Belgium followed, ending in the Armistice of November 11, 1918.

This terrible experience broke John Davies' health and he was soon in a tuberculosis hospital, from which he emerged after about a year and was advised to live as much in the open air as possible. Bristol University had a Spelaeological Society and John had joined it when he was a student at the University. It was a unique society for its time. It had two main aims. The first was the thorough investigation of the geological, hydrographic and archaeological features of the caves and rock shelters of the Mendips in Somerset and in the lower Wye Valley. The second was a general investigation of the surface archaeology in the same area and south Gloucestershire generally. The leading figures in this society were professors, mainly from the University medical schools, and others well forward in their courses and, in a number of cases, destined to become professors themselves. Their work, whether in caves or in the open air, was meticulously organised and the society regularly published all its results in its *Proceedings*.

The general competence of the Bristol society became so generally recognised that it was invited to investigate caves in Ireland and I went with it to one such investigation, but although I helped in the often dangerous and uncomfortable work of the exploration of sundry caves in the Mendip area, such as Aveline's Hole, and was later entrusted with the direction of the excavation of a cave in the lower Wye Valley of which more anon, I spent far more time in the investigation of surface features ranging in age from Neolithic long barrows and Early Bronze Age 'henge' monuments to various aspects of the Roman and later periods in the region. Here I worked quite closely under the direction of John Davies and it was he who gave me my first experience of open-air excavation in May 1926, at the time of the General Strike. This was at Bury Hill, a small single bank and ditch, circular fort of Iron Age type at Winterbourne, overlooking the valley of the river Frome north of Bristol. We cut sections across the tumbled rampart and the ditch, but did not know enough in those days about structures of this sort to look for signs of former wooden reinforcement. There was nothing obvious to give a date for the ditch and the traces of one or two round huts noted inside gave us nothing beyond some scraps of common Romano-British pottery, possibly belonging to squatters long after the site had been slighted and abandoned – not a very exciting start.[1]

In the time between his discharge from the tuberculosis hospital in which he had to spend a year and the time when he first met me in 1923, Davis had not obeyed the hospital's injunction that he must live an open air life, but, after a very short time, he had gone north to Teesside where his scientific qualifications secured him a job in one of the chemical works. It was here that he met his future wife, Jessie Plater. However, regular employment was too much for his health, and, about the time I arrived at Bristol, he was also back in the city with his parents and living the outdoor life in which he introduced me so thoroughly to the field archaeology for which he had such a remarkable flair.

But a longish spell of outdoor life may have deluded him into thinking that he could resume his relationship with Jessie Plater, and by Christmas in 1927 he had married her, a move which was tantamount to signing his own death warrant. He took a house in the Bristol suburb of Fishponds but could find no suitable employment in the Bristol area. The only job he could get was as representative of a manufacturer of leather-sewing machinery used by boot and shoe repairers, dreadfully heavy objects which he had to drag round even the remoter parts of Ireland, a killing occupation for anyone, let alone a sick man.

In 1927, having by this time acquired a car and begun my survey of Lincolnshire, I was able to give him a run to Cambridge and round that county to show how his instruction was bearing fruit, but by the middle of the year the birth of a son put the coping stone on his troubles. His health finally collapsed in a storm of haemorrhages and he died in his parents' home on January 24, 1930.

I had little hope for him when I saw him for the last time in his sickbed early in the month and I felt his death terribly. I hurried down from Cambridge to join a large concourse at his funeral and it was some time before I recovered my usual spirits. After O.G.S. Crawford he was the most important influence on my beginnings in archaeology.

In the late 1920s I did some minor open-site excavation work on my own initiative close to Bristol along the ridge which runs from the Abbot's Leigh side of the Avon gorge as far as Clevedon by the Severn estuary. To the north this ridge overlooks the Gordano Valley while to the south it commands a wide view over the land known as Kenn Moor, which stretches away to the west end of the Mendips as they meet the sea beyond Weston-super-Mare.

The ridge carries an important medium-sized Iron Age hill-fort called Cadbury Camp and most of it from Bristol to Clevedon was pasture field. At the Bristol end lies Ashton Park, a mainly grassy area surrounded by a high stone wall, almost ten miles long, and representing, unchanged, a grant of Free Warren made by William the Conqueror, a fair guarantee that the area had not suffered much change since the eleventh century. Inside this park there were clear signs of ancient agricultural activity, which continued here and there right up to the ramparts of Cadbury Camp. The part of this area outside Ashton Park is known as Failand.

North of the Gordano Valley lies a second ridge which falls sharply to the sea. The western half of this seaward ridge is known as Walton Down and also carries similar

1   U.B.S.S. Proceedings, Vol. 4, 1929–1935, pp. 34–42

indications of ancient agricultural activity, as well as a large ring work, of no defensive value but provided with a wide opening from the ends of which low banks extend outwards to form a funnel for helping to drive in cattle. I made a number of small exploratory excavations in all of these areas and found that the occasional round hut site almost invariably turned out to be Romano-British in date. Sometimes there were small concentrations of iron slag which suggested that here iron may have been smelted almost domestically at need. There was no sign of any plainly Iron Age material or dependence on Cadbury Camp, though no doubt this may have been the local centre when this peasant farming was in progress before the Roman conquest. In two cases I also came on the sites of small farmhouses of much later date, proved by the pieces of broken Bristol delft and of other seventeenth century wares found in their rubbish dumps along with clay tobacco pipes of early form.[2]

With hindsight, I can now see that much of the Romano-British life here may have depended on the enigmatic walled Roman site at Gatcombe Farm at the foot of the more southerly of the two ridges, by Ashton Watering in Flax Bourton parish. Here the construction of the Bristol and Exeter Railway Company's line early in the nineteenth century revealed elements of large buildings including big stone pillars. The whole Gatcombe site is a puzzle, full of traces of buildings and once strongly walled, yet in a totally indefensible position at the foot of a steep slope. But the realisation of this was to come some years later.

Before the end of my 'Bristol' period I had my first experience of appearing before an important audience when, at the Bristol meeting of the British Association in September 1930, I gave a short paper to the appropriate section on my field work between Bristol and Clevedon. It was politely received but the occasion was a little spoiled by the intervention of a notorious crank who took part in the discussion which followed. In 1929 I had an opportunity to show O.G.S. Crawford the Walton Down sites and my confidence was much improved by his general approval of my interpretation of them.

My close connection with the Spelaeological Society lasted from 1923 to 1929, by which time I was making my own way at Cambridge and elsewhere and was less able to spend time in the Bristol area. But before this severance began I had been in sole charge of the Society's excavation of Merlin's Cave at Symond's Yat in the lower Wye Valley and had published the results in the Society's *Proceedings*.

In the archaeological sense, this work was disappointing. It was a cave with a mouth only about about twelve feet square which opens in the face of a sheer limestone cliff. The height above the natural foot of the cliff must have originally been as much as thirty feet but there was an old, rather overgrown talus below its mouth which showed that a lot of material had been thrown out of it in the past. Once one had scrambled up this talus the vertical distance to the cave mouth was about ten feet and the final climb up into the cave was made easier by a number of very rough natural steps and hand-holds in the rock face. Inside, the cave rapidly narrowed to a dead end after about twenty feet. The floor was very rough and did not contain much earthy matter before the solid rock was reached. On the left side, as one entered, there was what appeared to be a long natural bench of rock. When this bench was examined more

2   U.B.S.S. Proceedings, Vol. 3, 1926, pp. 8–24

thoroughly it had more of the character of a rough natural trough and it contained a large quantity of dusty matter in which an occasional small bone could be seen.

It should be said at once that during the latter half of the eighteenth century and for some while in the nineteenth century the area on both sides of this part of the Wye Valley had been heavily prospected for useful iron ore. Most of the area is densely wooded today, and moving through these woodlands must be done with caution because of the number of entirely unfenced prospectors' shafts of considerable depth which remain as relics of this search. The prospectors also broke up the stalagmitic floors of local caves in the same quest, and any contained relics of human occupation were disturbed and the stratigraphy destroyed.

This was certainly the case at Merlin's Cave. The objects with a human provenance which we found jumbled up in what remained of the deposit on the floor of the cave, included a pair of unhafted axes or adzes, similar objects, probably of Neolithic age, made from pieces split out of very large bones with the medullary cavity showing clearly on one side, and a large quantity of sheep bones from animals which had been skilfully butchered into joints and chops with sharp knives. A lot of them showed the light cuts made by the knives of those who had sliced off the meat while eating it. The most probable explanation of this phenomenon was that these bones were relics of the feasts of sheep stealers in relatively modern times. No deer bones were found.

Between these extremes occurred a miscellaneous collection containing a forged silver coin of Claudius, bone pins whole and broken, some coarse Romano-British pottery sherds and trodden and abraded scraps of prehistoric pottery of various periods back to the Neolithic. No doubt if the trouble were taken to sift through the large talus of material below the mouth of the cave many more bits and pieces of various periods would be found, most of them thrown out by miners in their search for ore.

But by way of compensation, the zoology of the cave was of exceptional interest. The natural trough full of dusty matter, mentioned above, was emptied and it was found to contain a vast quantity of small bones belonging to birds and mammals. Large samples of this deposit were sent to South Kensington for examination by E. T. Newton and Martin Hinton. It proved to come mainly from a Pleistocene fauna containing the Arctic whistling hare (*Pika*) and the pygmy vole (*Arvicola Abbotti*) along with a great range of birds, most of them small, but ranging up to larger birds such as swan, pelican and eagle owl. The verdict of the zoologists was that the condition of the deposit suggested that it was the product of the decay of a vast number of owl pellets.

When the side of the cave which was immediately above the trough was examined, sure enough, there was a long ledge on which owls could have perched so that any pellets they ejected would fall into the trough. E. T. Newton was of opinion that the producers of these pellets were eagle owls.

When it was clear that this material was almost entirely an assemblage brought together in the Pleistocene period the collection provided one more surprise. There were a great many ptarmigan bones present, the bones of mature individuals, but they were always distinctly smaller than those of the modern bird. Newton was disposed to think that they represented a ptarmigan which has become extinct.

This was my first complex excavation and an excellent experience because of the variety of factors involved in an understanding of the history of this obscure cave, and the one really novel contribution was the massively represented Pleistocene rodents and avifauna.[3]

Before I ceased to be able to take part in the Spelaeological Society's work in the Bristol area, I had experience helping with long and round barrow excavation in the central Mendip area round Priddy. The most important open-air work which the Society undertook in the late 1920s was the excavation of an abnormal small ring work not far from the western edge of the deepest part of Cheddar Gorge. It was called Gorsey Bigbury, a name which would seem to imply some sort of defended site, but its location did not support this interpretation. It was not large and an excavation began which was a sort of 'side dish' among the Society's activities for a number of years. The site proved to have a much-spread outer bank, with an internal ditch surrounding an oval area of flat ground. The ditch turned out to be quite wide and deep, painstakingly cut in the underlying rock. The filling of this ditch, which was largely a sticky clay, contained many sherds of Early Bronze Age 'Beaker' ware, especially towards the bottom and it became clear that here was a small type of 'henge' monument and as such an important addition to the other 'henge' monuments of the district at Priddy Circles and Stanton Drew. These small henges are now recognised in many parts of Britain. It became an open question whether the element Gorsey in the name could be a corruption of the Welsh *gorsedd*.

I have said above that the Spelaeological Society was sometimes invited to work outside Great Britain and in August 1928 I accompanied an expedition of the society to the Cappoquin district of southern Ireland, near the little town of Dungarvan in West Waterford, where the excavation of a cave was to be undertaken at Kilgreaney, to look for evidence of Palaeolithic Man in Ireland. This was an important question which required to be settled. In fact, we found nothing older than the Bronze Age during the partial examination which proved to be possible. The coming years were to see the arrival of a powerful and liberally financed expedition from Harvard University which included the completion of our work at Kilgreaney. Its programme was extensive and very successful, but it also failed to find any traces of Palaeolithic Man. It would seem, therefore, that this question has been answered.

But to return to our own experience: we camped in a field at Whitechurch, close to the railway line from Rosslare and Wexford to Cork, and when we wanted some rather more substantial fuel for our camp fire we used to throw various missiles at the passing railway engines. Of course we never aimed to hit them but the firemen replied by pelting us with coal which we carefully collected.

In that part of Ireland the echoes of the 'Troubles' had not yet died away, and when our advance party arrived to arrange a camp site it was quietly visited by one or two leading local men who wanted to know which cave we wanted to excavate. It had been our intention to work in the cave of the Two Brothers, but we were warned not to attempt this and no explanation of the warning was given. Eventually, our camp site landlord, a local squire called Ussher, (a descendant of the archbishop of the same name who worked out that the world was created in B.C. 4004) explained that during the 'Troubles' not only were the bodies of persons who had been killed sometimes buried in caves and that to disturb their remains would cause trouble,

3   *U.B.S.S.* Proceedings, Vol. 4, 1929–35, pp. 11–33.

but also that it was certain that some of the caves contained secret caches of arms and ammunition which it would be equally tactless to find. We were therefore directed to the Kilgreaney cave and worked there with the negative result mentioned above. Our work was not made easier by incessant rain and I managed to work up a short but sharp attack of lumbago, which is not funny when one is under canvas in any weather.

While at Kilgreaney we made a short expedition under the guidance of Praeger, the distinguished Irish paleaeobotanist, up into the nearby Comeragh mountains where we inspected the corrie lake and climbed to the top of the range at Coumshingaun to see the still-surviving cover of forty feet of peat, testifying to the intensity of the wet climatic phase which set in during the last millennium of prehistoric times. I was to get to know much more about the archaeological possibilities of peat in coming years in the English Fenland.

I am rather ashamed to say that when we were prevented by the rain from working I would sometimes seek a quiet form of entertainment by going to the nearby small railway station at Cappagh, which was the nearest one to the great Mount Melleray monastery, a few miles away on the lower slopes of the Comeraghs. Amongst other activities (like keeping a school for boys) the House also contained a home for inebriate clergy, not uncommon among the parish priests of that time. The train would discharge the new arrivals and also take away those who were judged to be cured. The new arrivals provided a spectacle which was both ludicrous and painful, as they were helped into the conveyances which were to take them up the hill to the monastery.

I started back to England by myself and found that I had half a day to wait at Waterford before I could get from there down to Rosslare and the boat for Fishguard. The weather was uncertain and my first idea was to while away the time in the cinema at Waterford, but I was discouraged from taking this course by a native who told me that I should not be able to see the picture for 'the leppin'o the fleas' between myself and the screen. So being an enthusiast for exploring odd little railways, I contented myself by making the six mile journey to Tramore and back in an old open-sided carriage drawn by an engine of an 1837–39 vintage, itself a piece of industrial archaeology.

Chapter 2

By the summer of 1928 my association with the Bristol Society was drawing to a close; I have acknowledged my debt to this society, which was not confined to the example of its sound and scientific methods of work. The society was also visited from time to time by leading archaeologists and one event which decisively changed the course of my future career was my meeting with O. G. S. Crawford. In 1927 I had already become a subscriber to his new periodical *Antiquity*.

Crawford was an outstanding figure among those responsible for the phenomenal rise in the status of archaeology in Britain between the end of the 1914–18 war and the middle of the century. The son of an Indian High Court judge and born in 1886 in India he had a difficult early life, left a complete orphan almost in infancy and brought up by a number of aunts. He was fortunate in having all his early education in the antiquity-rich areas of Hampshire, Berkshire and Wiltshire. He hated much of his period at Marlborough College but it is difficult to think of a school in England which is in an area richer in ancient monuments of many kinds and periods. It was in this area that he also met with and was inspired by the pioneer archaeologists Dr. J. P. Williams-Freeman and Harold Peake of Newbury.

In due course he proceeded to Keble College, Oxford with an exhibition, but as an undergraduate he wasted his energy in non-academic pursuits and achieved only a third class – no measure of his real abilities. As in my case, but almost two decades earlier, he was faced with the problem of obtaining gainful employment in archaeology, a pursuit which was now becoming an obsession. The archaeological establishment was only just getting into its stride, but required academic qualifications which he did not possess and the most he could hope for was museum employment. He was all for fieldwork and ultimately he achieved this by becoming a demonstrator in the recently founded University Department of Geography under the pioneer Herbertson. The idea of the distribution map was already forming itself in his mind and with it the germ of a map of Roman Britain.

But first he had to pass through many vicissitudes between 1910 and 1920, including membership of an abortive expedition to Easter Island, excavation under Sir Henry Wellcome in the Sudan, and then, in the 1914–18 war, service in the front line, work with the Ordnance Survey, the Army's map service in war, trench photography, survey and map making and finally joining the Royal Flying Corps as an observer. During this last, although it led to a short period as a prisoner of war, he became aware of the potentialities for seeing archaeological features from the air and saw the whole enormous future of aerial photography, a field in which he was to become the most notable and successful pioneer.

Contacts which he had made during the war with Sir Charles Close, then

Director-General of the Ordnance Survey, finally brought him to the post of Archaeology Officer to the Survey and to work totally concerned with cartography and field archaeology. But this was a meagre affair with no staff and a minimal salary. The post-war economy campaign of the next few years was gravely to reduce the whole of the Ordnance Survey staff and almost halt any progress with the now very necessary revision of the maps of the whole country. However, this did not limit Crawford's activities because he could continue with a campaign of progressive investigation of field archaeology to gather accurate information for use on the maps as and when the pace of revision revived; for this he was already recruiting the voluntary services of well disposed and qualified observers in whatever areas he could find them. Hence his visit to the Mendips, riding his bicycle and loaded with the 6-inch maps of the district. I was to become one of these observer-correspondents.

I first met him at the Bristol Spelaeological Society's hut at Burrington at Easter 1929 when I was introduced to him, but on this occasion we had no opportunity to exchange more than a few words. Next day I was in the same area on business which required me to drive to the top of Mendip by the long climb up Burrington Combe. I had recently acquired a three-wheeled Morgan runabout. I had only just started up the Combe when I saw a figure ahead of me pushing a bicycle and as I came nearer I saw that it was Crawford. I pulled up and offered him a lift to the top of the hill and he got in beside me, balancing his bicycle on its side over my back wheel. Thus we reached the top of the long hill and stopped for him to get off.

The view was very far and clear over all the country towards Bath. We sat and admired it for a short while and then, drawn by some sort of natural affinity, began a long conversation about field archaeology which lasted for the best part of an hour and ended with my enlistment among his local correspondents for the Cambridge area. He also spoke of the great work that the two doctors Curwen, father and son, of Brighton were doing to put the archaeology of Sussex on a sound footing and he promised to introduce me to them. There was something infectious about Crawford's enthusiasm for his work and this roadside conversation completed my conversion to field archaeology, if it required any further stimulus. From this time forward I was resolved to overcome all obstacles between myself and this aim. The main course of my life was fixed.

Upon my return to Cambridge I began a close correspondence with Crawford. Much of my time was now fully occupied by supervision and coaching for both the History Tripos and the Ordinary Degree and I was now giving lectures for the history part of the latter. I was soon to add the reorganisation of the College library to my tasks. Crawford plied me with a stream of field problems for solution and I should have been quite unable to cope with them if I had not motorised my transport for these forays, which took place on one or two afternoons and the weekend in each week.

Antiquity-wise, the Cambridge area was in fair order on the published maps and Cyril Fox's classic *Archaeology of the Cambridge Region* was now available, but there were large areas not too far away which cried out for investigation. Crawford was always particularly interested in long barrows and had already published a book on the numerous examples in the Cotswolds. In view of their prevalence on the Yorkshire Wolds, he thought it probable that they were also 'present on the Wolds of Lincolnshire.

I was now to concentrate all my spare time efforts on this county for most of the next four years. Up to this time knowledge of the archaeology of Lincolnshire was slight. Although this very large county had produced one of the fathers of British field archaeology, William Stukeley, who was born at Holbeach in the fenland area in the south of the county in 1687 and later in life Vicar of Grantham, yet he had made little contribution to the knowledge of the archaeology of his own county.

Lincolnshire lies almost entirely to the east of the Great North Road and has been a backwater for centuries without deriving any benefit from its relative isolation. Henry VIII called it 'the most brute beastly county in Our Realm,' under the stress produced by the Rising of the North.

Crawford considered that it was high time that the whole county should be perambulated and its archaeological potential established. In 1928 there were only four museums of any consequence in Lincolnshire. The oldest was that belonging to the Spalding Gentlemen's Society, a body founded in Stukeley's time with a small but very valuable library which had been put together in the early days but in which the Society, though surviving as a body of local worthies, had no particular interest. As far as local archaeology was concerned, its museum was of little account. Next came the County Museum at Lincoln, housed in an old monastic building and containing material from most periods, particularly Roman and Anglo-Saxon, quite well arranged and kept so by its curator, Arthur Smith, who was near retirement and seldom went far from the museum. A small museum at Grantham was an adjunct to the public library and was maintained by Mr Harry Preston, the manager of the town water-works, who was well-informed about the Grantham district and particularly interested in the Roman site at Saltersford south of the town in the valley of the river Witham. The latest addition to the list was the museum at Scunthorpe, the newly-developed iron and steel town in the north-west corner of the county. Alderman Mr Walshaw, one of the leading figures in local industry, was the force behind its foundation and it enjoyed the active and well-informed care of Mr Harold Dudley as curator, equally competent in the local geology and archaeology. Scunthorpe is close to Risby Warren, a large sandy area on the greensand ridge east of the town, where the scour of wind and rain continually revealed a remarkable wealth of flint microliths and ample evidence of the former presence of Bronze Age folk. The whole of this north-western corner of the county was rich in archaeological sites and contained the point where the Roman road from London to York, Ermine Street, reached the south bank of the Humber and, presumably, a ferry across to Brough, the site of the small Roman site of *Petuaria* on the north bank where the line of the road to York was resumed.

A thorough perambulation of Lincolnshire was a tall order. The county is one of the largest in England, roughly oblong in form, 70 miles long from north to south and about 45 miles wide at the level of Lincoln between the Trent to the west and the North Sea to the east. Its northern boundary is defined by the estuary of the Humber and the western boundary is mainly determined by the course of the Trent; on the east side the North Sea and the western side of the Wash supply a natural limit, and to the south the circuit is closed by an arbitrary line from south of Stamford across the Bedford Level to a point north of Wisbech.

The outstanding physical features of the county are the Jurassic Lincoln Edge and the Wolds, in effect an extension southwards of the Yorkshire Wolds across the gap made by the Humber outfall.

The Edge runs from the bank of the Humber past the Lincoln Gap, down as far as Grantham and then south-westwards out of the county into Leicestershire, and its moderate elevation commands wide views over the Vale of Belvoir. But it hardly attains more than 300 feet south of Lincoln and through most of its length its form is that of a narrow ridge dropping by a steep escarpment into the valley of the Trent, and on the east side sloping away very gently towards the much steeper escarpment of the Wolds. Its total length in the county is fully 70 miles.

The wolds are mainly capped with chalk, with outcrops of greensand at their western and south-western edges. They run southwards for some 40 miles to end abruptly overlooking the East and West Fens and the distant prospect of the Wash. They are markedly higher and wider than the Edge and reach a maximum height of 540 feet just south of Caistor. Their western escarpment, which is very steep in places, looks over the valley of the river Ancholme to the Edge. Eastward they slope away to the plain bordering the sea. Before the agricultural improvements of the late eighteenth century much of the surface of the Wolds was uncultivated heath, as also was the large area of the eastern slope of the Edge which extends south from Lincoln to Sleaford. It is here that the Dunston Pillar now stands beside the roadway between the two towns. Today it carries a statue of King George III at the top, but before the heath was brought under cultivation and the road improved, it carried a light to guide travellers at night; in fact it was a land lighthouse.

The wide valley which divides the Edge from the Wolds is crossed by an east to west ridge of land which divides the river Ancholme flowing north to the Humber from the river Witham which, after coming through the gap in the Edge at Lincoln, turns south-eastward to enter the Wash at Boston. The southern part of the county east of Stamford consists very largely of reclaimed fenland with centres at Spalding, Boston and Holbeach, much of it only a few feet above sea level in the silt areas nearest to the Wash, and often actually below sea level on the reclaimed peat lands.

As I anticipated carrying on most of this work from Cambridge, and most of it at weekends in term time, it would be impossible to do this without motor transport and it was for this reason that I bought a Morgan three-wheeler in 1925, a speedy and economical type of vehicle with ample weather protection on the unencumbered roads of those days. A further and unusual advantage to a budding archaeologist was that the Romans had already created a remarkably direct route to the southern limits of Lincolnshire and then, once in the county, an even more direct route to its furthest limits on the Humber shore by a road which passed through Lincoln city.

From Cambridge the first stretch followed the fifteen miles of the Roman road, the *Via Devana* from Cambridge to Godmanchester, precisely as straight as a die. At Godmanchester one joined the line of the Ermine Street, the Roman road from London to York, the 'Great North Road', and remained on it as a modernised road, with only a few deviations, through Stilton to Stamford where Lincolnshire was entered. From there onwards to near Colsterworth the Roman line, known locally as Horn Lane, was strictly followed, and it could be quickly regained close to Great Ponton railway station and then followed for an almost unbroken stretch of fifteen miles through Ancaster to Byard's Leap. The last twelve miles of Roman Ermine

Street are green track into Lincoln. At this point the straightness of the Lincoln Edge makes the road along its crest also a very direct route into the city. Before the 1939–45 war the line of Ermine Street north from Newport Arch, the northern gate of Roman Lincoln to the Humber, was thirty-two miles long, dead straight and viable as a good road for fully sixteen miles with a quite unbroken stretch of twelve miles out of Lincoln. All together, from Cambridge to the Humber shore, the distance was about 115 miles. In those days this could be travelled comfortably in three to three and a half hours, allowing four to five hours of work before starting back.

I labour this point about the roads of the later 1920s and early 1930s because this fortunate situation made travel to and from field work very much easier than it would be today. I have described what would have been involved with work at extreme range in the north of the county, and the large tracts south and east of Lincoln were much closer and could be worked with greater ease. This proved to involve one of the most important areas, the central and southern parts of the Wolds.

I have mentioned the museums in the county and I could rely on them for active co-operation, especially in the case of Scunthorpe museum under Mr Harold Dudley. Harry Preston at Grantham was very helpful to the limit of his local knowledge, but at the time that I began Mr Smith at the Lincoln Museum was elderly and sedentary. He knew the collection in his charge but otherwise he sat at the receipt of custom, surrounded by clouds of tobacco smoke in his little office, and only emerged from it to go home. There was very little activity in the very important Roman city site of Lincoln, although sections of the puzzling Roman pressure waterpipe in the gentle slope of the Nettleham Road on the north-east exterior of the town kept turning up in the new front gardens of the houses being built up that road. It was not till Mr Tom Baker came to the museum on Mr Smith's retirement, and a young civil engineer called Graham Webster joined the city's staff from Canterbury, that the secrets of Roman Lincoln began to be examined by deliberate excavation and a tradition was begun which has had great results. It was also during this period that Mr J. W. F. Hill, a leading solicitor in Lincoln and later to be knighted, was beginning his magisterial study of the history of Lincoln city.

The county could not boast an effective archaeological society. There was a Lincolnshire Archaeological and Architectural Society of long standing, but its published reports dealt mainly with the ecclesiology of the area and archaeology received little attention. However, a Lindsey Local History Society was coming into existence at about the time I began work and it published a Lincolnshire Magazine which began to penetrate into places not reached before. By far the most scholarly influence was wielded by the Lincoln Record Society, which was then under the able direction of Canon Foster of Timberland.

In the late 1920s and for much of the following half century, as far as the parts of Lindsey and Kesteven were concerned, the person who had the widest knowledge about the field situation of archaeology and bygones generally, was Mrs E. H. Rudkin. She died in 1984 at the age of 91, then living at Willoughton, a village at the foot of the escarpment of the Lincoln Edge or 'Cliff' as it was generally called, about half way between Lincoln and Scunthorpe.

Her husband, a member of a farming family at Sapperton, between Ancaster and Bourne, had been severely wounded in the 1914–18 war and had not survived it for long, after which she fell back on her parents' home at Willoughton. Their name was Hutchinson and I understood her to say that they had migrated into the county from Nottinghamshire and were of the same family as the well-known Colonel Hutchinson of Civil War fame.

From this base she would sally forth to follow up and investigate any kind of positive information which she received from any source in the county, and she was quite a well-known figure at county fairs, sales and other occasions at which the folk who worked the land assembled. If, when going round farm buildings she noticed interesting out-of-date farming tools and equipment, she would try to rescue them. A remarkable collection of agricultural 'junk' thus came into her possession, with the aid of which she would mount exhibitions of farming bygones at county fairs, a practice which produced many other discarded examples. This far-seeing activity was a big factor in making possible the opening of a richly-stocked permanent Bygones Museum in Lincoln in after years.

But although this was a most commendable activity, with which I was in full sympathy, my purpose was a survey of field archaeology with the immediate aim of making it available to Crawford for application to the 25 inch to the mile scale maps of the county when they were revised. In the existing climate of economy, that day might be a long way off but, meanwhile, a good deal of evidence which would inevitably be destroyed by the ordinary processes of rural and urban life, would be saved from oblivion.

Mrs Rudkin was also an indefatigable field walker and it was quite remarkable what could be found on the fields of Willoughton alone, most of it inevitably bits and pieces of different periods right back to Mesolithic times, especially on the plough soil after frost and rain had broken up the surface and washed off any earth liable to mask objects when the soil was freshly turned. I vividly remember that once, when a piece of land was ploughed after being down to grass for an indefinite time, she noticed pieces of the local Jurassic stone which were disposed in a rough circle about six feet in diameter. Examining the ground inside this circle she made the very unusual find of a coin of William the Conqueror. There were a few scraps of nondescript coarse pottery and the whole thing was probably the last traces of a small round shelter of the eleventh century in the fields of Willoughton. This was only a minor field walking find but it demonstrated the importance of this branch of field archaeology, particularly in areas where there is much cultivated land. Even on pastureland the activities of moles, rabbits, badgers and foxes, can throw out buried objects, showing the former presence of human beings. Finds in newly-ploughed earth are unpredictable and no one can say that he has a good knowledge of the potentialities of any area who has neglected the field walking factor: wet, wearisome and cold though it often is.

On each of my weekly forays into Lincolnshire I tried to follow a regular procedure. I visited those archaeological features already on the 6 inch maps in the particular area that I was checking. Then at the same time I looked everywhere for such features as were not shown on the maps, determined the category they belonged to, and made any necessary measurements. Then finally I looked for features our honorary correspondents had told us about. Having completed these three investigations, I drove back to Cambridge.

In the case of the first investigation, an antiquity shown on the map had to be correctly named and 'supplied'. Proper names might raise queries about correct spelling and punctuation. Giants' Hills, the Neolithic long barrow in Skendleby parish of which we shall hear a lot more later in this account, is a good case. It was given the right place, form and dimensions on the map as it appeared in the 1920s, but the name as printed would suggest more than one long barrow. Long barrows have a tendency to occur in pairs, not necessarily very close together and when I began my work in Lincolnshire I did not know this. I had already seen most of the examples on these Wolds when I first came to Skendleby and should have been impressed by this pairing habit, which I had seen in other places on the Wolds. Also Mr Gainsford, the young landlord, who was later to permit me to excavate this barrow in 1933–34, was fond of shooting and told us that there was a largish area some way down the next field where the partridges were to be found because they prefer better drained ground to damp land, and that part of the field seemed to have a higher proportion of chalk on its surface.

As we found out later, there had been another long barrow much the same size as the one I excavated, but it had been completely levelled at some earlier time and its chalk content spread over the plough soil round its site, thus producing more dry and comfortable sitting for the partridges. The name as given to the Ordnance surveyors during the first 1 inch survey, when the barrows both stood intact, was in the plural but now the name of the survivor should be corrected to 'The Giant's Hill' and the other site, when we recognised it at last, as the 'The Giant's Hill, site of'.

Last, 'supply' must be accurate, i.e. the necessary slopes must be given to show the true shape of the item, man-made banks, ditches, pits and so forth.

In the second class the more obvious antiquities like round barrows were as well shown on the Lincolnshire maps as in other counties, but often the enquiry would show that the feature had a name like Cock Hill or the Butts and so on, which would be a further and sometimes very significant addition when printed in the Old English type. These were collected and noted for application to the map at the next edition.

Sometimes an odd name like Magotty-pagotty would already have been applied to spots where nothing very obvious was apparent, but a close look at the place in the field might show the reason for the name. In the case of Magotty-pagotty, which, incidentally, is a place near Aller in the Somerset Fens, local peasants in past ages had been puzzled by casual finds localised at this place. Here careful inspection showed that these were probably traces of a Roman building, possibly a Roman villa with a mosaic pavement, now deep in a thick woodland.

Another better known example is Cold Kitchen Hill, a high wind-swept spot near Warminster in Wiltshire. Here three ridges of chalk down meet and there is a shallow bank and ditch earthwork across each spur just before it reaches the junction area. In contrast to the rest of the surrounding downland the ground is much disturbed, and not by rabbits. The tumbled and exposed chalky soil contains a high proportion of animal bones and a close look at some of these will show that they belong to animals which have been cooked and eaten. These are obvious, but less so are occasional scraps of metal.

This place was one of the native shrines of pre-Roman and Roman times where the local peasantry gathered to worship the native gods. These were literally feast days, at which much food was eaten, hence the bones, and it is certain that hucksters came and set up their stalls to sell trinkets and fairings to the crowd. For centuries past this area on the hill has been known to be worth forking over for items like coins, brooches, bone pins and other minor objects which had been dropped and lost by the holiday crowds which once visited the place. Local swains would come here to hunt for articles to present to their sweethearts, and girls might be seen wearing burnished-up brooches found at this place – antiques in very truth. In my younger days there were 16,000 items from this site in Devizes Museum and the number which have been found over the recent centuries must be very great. The food remains explain the name 'Cold Kitchen'.

A third side to the first round of visits to different parts of Lincolnshire was to make oneself and one's mission known. Leaving aside for the moment the special job of revising and generally improving the antiquity position, there was everywhere at this time a growing unrest among local government circles and map users in general at the long time, sometimes as long as thirty years, which had elapsed since the last revision of the existing 25 inch maps. In the meantime a great war had occurred which had created large topographical changes. The post-1918 house building campaign all over the country had made it the exception rather than the rule if the large scale plans of a town matched up to the facts in the field. Faced with no apparent hope of getting official revision, local government bodies set their own surveyors to work to supply the deficiency.

Lincolnshire contained a severe case of this failure of the Survey. The new steel town of Scunthorpe was still coalescing from a group of villages which had contained windmills and other rural features when the Ordnance Survey last passed that way. The steel needs of the war effort of 1914–18 hastened the process of topographical consolidation, and in 1927 the only available 25 inch maps of the area were of little more than historical interest. The experience of Lincoln and Grantham had been the same to a much lesser degree.

I had to get to know those likely to be interested in the past of their own locality. Here one could be on dangerous ground but I do not recall meeting with any out-and-out cranks. They were mostly like Mr Charles Carter of Louth, a sort of cobbler-philosopher who chatted with the local clergy and farmers when they brought in their footwear for repair. A number of hints of what was turning up on farms and in gardens and elsewhere found their way into his little shop and sometimes the objects themselves; there was usually a group sitting gossiping while Carter worked, an informal club and extra busy on Market days.

A local worthy in a more aristocratic bracket was old Captain William Cragg of Threchingham. His grandfather, John Cragg, had been factor to the Ancaster estate and in the late eighteenth and early nineteenth centuries he was overseeing a considerable area between Bourne and Sleaford. He had an eye for antiquities and noted what was found and where. Later he wrote this up in an alphabetical list of parishes and places, with a statement of what he knew about each. This MSS was in the possession of his grandson, who kindly allowed me to examine it and now it is safely in the Lincoln Record Office. The old Captain had some rather fanciful notions about the ancient routes which had a crossing in Threchingham, and considered it to be the site of a battle in Danish times, but he was very helpful and saved some interesting objects from being lost.

There was also Miss Gibbons of Holton Hall near Caistor, who knew quite a lot about the past of the Ancholme Valley and was also a keen botanist, with the record of the find of a lizard orchis in the county to her credit. Her brother, George Gibbons, was Secretary of the County Architectural and Archaeological Society, but was not helpful. Aside from Mr Harry Preston of Grantham, I did not encounter anyone of any value in the south of the county, and over towards the south-west Mr Smith of Lincoln's son at Newark-on-Trent Museum had nothing to offer.

So the preliminary stage ended and it was time to look more closely at the county's archaeology. Since the ghost of Roman Britain appears very strongly on the map, and I had to use the Roman road system in a big way to arrive at and move round a good deal of the county, the Roman period was made the starting point.

A number of factors entered into the recognition of Roman roads and their former courses. Much of the preliminary work for any area can be done in the study with the aid of large and small scale Ordnance Survey maps. Naturally, within that part of Great Britain which the Romans effectively occupied, they are still the basis for many modern roads. Their lines are also preserved in the boundaries of many ancient units of our countryside, such as parishes; a remarkable example is Watling Street, where a Roman road has not only been used over many miles as a basis for a modern road, but also as a lengthy boundary between the kingdom of Wessex and the Danes in the ninth century A.D. Later it became the boundary between a number of Midland shires. In the case of the two great roads, Watling Street and the Fosse Way, the rather unexpected discovery of pagan Anglo-Saxon burials made in one or two places in the actual crown of the Roman road requires some explanation. It must suggest that, at least in some cases, the 'agger' of the Roman road had already ceased to be used by traffic though, in general, its trace must still have indicated the normal route through the area of these occurrences.

In the case of a third Roman road with which I am familiar, Ermine Street, I know of no burials in the crown of the road, but the motorist who travels along its still well-preserved section from Colsterworth north to Ancaster will find himself running along either on one side or the other of the well-preserved high 'agger' but not along the 'agger' itself. If he is not familiar with this stretch of road and goes along it in the dark he may expect a sudden shock more than once as the modern road heaves itself over from one side to the other over the 'agger'. Otherwise, along the run from Ancaster into Lincoln as far as Byard's Leap near Cranwell, the modern road and the Roman 'agger' seem to be congruent but after that, Ermine Street is a green track at best for the last dozen miles into Lincoln city.

North of Lincoln the marriage of the two roads, modern and Roman, has been more consistent. The Roman road keeps an almost mathematically straight line from its emergence from the Newport Arch at Lincoln till it reaches the bank of the Humber and the ferry across to Brough. Unfortunately, wartime necessity in 1939-45 made the construction of an aerodrome runway across the line necessary and so the modern road diverges to the east to join it again after little more than a mile.

The straightness of the road is so marked that, when at Fox Wood, seven miles from Lincoln, the road wavers from the straight for two or three hundred yards and then resumes its rigid course, one seeks a reason. In fact it is passing through the site of the Ownby Cliff posting-station, for which there is ample evidence in the Romano-British rubbish in adjacent Fox Wood and in the ploughed field of the east side of the road. This field also contains a lot of scattered stone from long-collapsed buildings. Continuing its northward course the road comes to the place called Six Wells in the parish of Hibaldstow, fourteen miles from Lincoln. This spot was viewed with suspicion by Abraham de le Pryme, the seventeenth century antiquary, for here again there were traces of buildings and Roman structures have been found in modern excavations. The name is perhaps significant along a naturally dry tract of country and no doubt wells were sunk here to provide water for traffic on the road. At this point also the modern road bends eastwards to throw a branch out to Brigg at the crossing of the Ancholme, but bends back again to rejoin Ermine Street seven and a half miles further on at Broughton. Here one might also expect a posting station but no traces have yet been found. The remaining ten miles to the Humber seem to have been through much more settled country in Roman times, judging from the numerous finds, and so perhaps there was no other staging point till the Humber and the ferry terminal was reached.

There were two other Roman roads of importance in this area which branch off from Ermine Street. The first ran north-westward from a point two and a half miles north of Lincoln towards the Trent, which it crossed at Littleborough. Here there was a settlement, *Segelocvm*, an artificial ford over this large river. From the other side, the road went on to *Danvm* (Doncaster) and the north and it provided an alternative route between Lincoln and York. The other set off from Lincoln's north gate, the Newport Arch, and made its way eastwards past Wragby and across the southern edge of the Wolds by Belchford and Tetford to Ulceby Cross, where ample signs of roadside settlement have been found. The road then wheels slowly south-eastward to Burgh-le-Marsh, which might well have been another posting station, overlooking the coastal plain. After Burgh all trace of the road is lost towards the Wash, where it has been reasonably regarded as reaching some long lost ferry station, from where a crossing could be made to meet the Roman Peddar's Way, which also comes down to the beach opposite Holme-next-the-Sea in Norfolk. The fact that there must have once been a crossing by sea is inescapable but the terminal sites are gone. The Lincolnshire side is full of traditions of a lost city engulfed by the sea.

The other road which was added to the Roman network was that known as Mareham Lane. It led almost directly north from the urban and industrial site of Water Newton and Castor (*Durobrivae*) on the Nene and continued to the important tribal centre (for which we have no name) at Old Sleaford. Whether the road then branched, with the western fork leading straight on to Lincoln, or whether an eastern fork made the very much more difficult run to Horncastle, possibly crossing the Witham at or near Tattershall, remains unproved at present, but both are quite possible.

However, it is fully established that, a short distance north of Bourne, a road diverges to make a straight run to Ermine Street at the top of the slope overlooking Ancaster from the south. On this road from Water Newton to Ancaster, known as King Street, ample signs of settlement occur at Stainsfield. Seven miles north of this there are more indications of settlement at Sapperton, and seven miles from there the road reached Ancaster. About seven miles south of Stainsfield the road crosses the river Welland at Lolham Bridges, where nothing has been found, though it might be expected, and a further seven miles south of the Bridges the road runs into Water Newton.

The main route along the eastern escarpment of the Wolds in Roman and earlier times was the trackway known as the High Street, which not only provides a good route between the south bank of the Humber at South Ferriby, a ferry terminal since remote times, but it also gives dry land passage between the two small fortified Roman towns at Caistor and Horncastle. In fact, a route from Old Sleaford's Mareham Lane, even if not made up to full standard, must have been a necessity in late Roman times. In the same way, a connection between Ermine Street and Caistor was desirable and must be represented by the piece of road running with Roman directness west from Caistor but not apparently beyond the river Ancholme to Ermine Street. Significantly, the two roads would meet at the site of the Six Wells (Hibaldstow) posting station.

Further south on Ermine Street, the Ownby Cliff posting station seems to have been the point of departure of another similar road across the Ancholme valley, at least to the foot of the Wold escarpment. There is no decisive evidence that the 'Sea to Sea' policy represented by the Fosse Way was ever carried beyond Lincoln and over the Wolds to the North Sea shore.

We have been discussing Roman roads which have made large contributions to the modern road system, but there were a great many secondary roads which require more detective work to restore them to the map today. Where an air-photograph taken at the right time of year is available, the failure of a crop in a line where it is growing in the shallow earth conditions created by a hard underlying Roman road surface is an obvious clue. An aerial view of grassland under conditions of low sun will also show a continuing line of shadow caused by the slight elevation of the grass-covered road surface, while a light fall of wind-driven snow can also gather against and make conspicuous a slight linear obstacle of this kind. In looking at a large scale map it is also possible to see sudden, not obviously accounted for zig-zags in an otherwise straight country lane or field boundary. These may be traces of some otherwise unseen linear feature and, lined up by a ruler, the zig-zags can tell their tale. Sometimes Roman road builders have met a linear obstacle like a small rock escarpment across their intended line. Where a re-routing of the road would have had to adopt a much longer line round this, the road-builders have not hesitated to make a short cutting even if the material they had to remove was rock. Today, the line of the Roman road from Silchester to Chichester preserves a beautiful example of a road cutting of this kind in the parish of East Worldham, near Alton. There is still a rough track approaching this feature from the north and the cutting might easily be taken for a quarry.

Sometimes the building of a Roman road will lead to tell-tale obstructions of drainage. In crossing slight dips in the ground which carry water, where the modern road would have a culvert the Roman road builder was satisfied by putting in a bush drain. But in the course of time, that drain will become choked and its materials rot, so that the roadbed will subside and water pond against its up-slope side. It sometimes occurs that a succession of these little swampy places or ponds will give the clue to the line of a lost road.

The behaviour of flood water can reveal the former existence of a Roman road under the right conditions. I am reminded of an experience which I once had in Sussex while with the Ordnance Survey. There is a secondary Roman road which runs along the base of the northern escarpment of the South Downs from the Lewes area and it passes through Storrington and crosses the West Sussex golf course, where it leaves its trace in the form of a number of short cuttings through some narrow ridges which run across its path. It is obviously making for the posting station at Hardham on Stane Street, the road between London and Chichester, but before it could reach that point it would have to cross a good half mile of Amberley Wild Brooks and then the river Arun. The Wild Brooks are flooded by the Arun in the early part of each year and are a feature which must have been present and even more difficult in Roman times. It would always have been possible to skirt round this area when affected by flood, as it is today, but in fact the road arrives at the present eastern edge of the Wild Brooks and there is even a hint that it may have gone straight on to the posting station, because that part of the river which it would have to cross to keep its straight course is called 'Stony River' by those who fish there, a hint of the former existence of a structure, possibly a bridge.

If there was a direct route into the posting station it must have been on a causeway founded on masses of brushwood, but there was no sign of one along the line. The ground is liable to be very soft here and a causeway not maintained is liable to have sunk in the course of the years. When the spring floods come they spread across the Wild Brooks and I asked a friend living in Pulborough close by to let me know when the floods began their annual rise – by telephone if they seemed to be coming in quickly.

The message came and I hurried down to Pulborough and went to the point where the Roman road met the Wild Brooks. I waited; the water began to cover the dead-flat fields and then, sure enough, there was a short period when the only part left uncovered was a long bare strip of grass dead in line with 'Stony River' and the unseen posting station. In a few minutes it had disappeared under the water. As I thought, there was a causeway once across this bad tract and it had long since sunk out of sight, leaving a very slight elevation across the field which only the spreading water could reveal. We could now put this piece of Roman road on the map with confidence and give good reasons for doing so.

The closest form of investigation in the field short of complete excavation is field walking. Woodland and grass cover defeat this, except where the archaeological features show themselves in the form of inequalities in the surface of the ground, where they may mask wall foundations or the product of one of the activities leading to bank and ditch formation such as defensive works, land boundaries, traces of rig-and-furrow cultivation, mining etc.

The most common objects found in field walking will be stone artefacts, mainly of flint, ranging from the Palaeolithic hand axe to the lost gun-flint. Pottery of all ages from the Neolithic will also occur, but none of this material will be necessarily in situ and every find will have to be considered in the context of the place of finding. Some, like arrowheads, may be losses from hunting or strife. Others, like half-pebbles with the broken face polished smooth, have fallen out of the wooden mould-boards of ploughs, the polish being the wear produced by frequent passage through the soil. Large numbers of struck flint flakes in the soil will show where implements have been fashioned. With the coming of pottery the possibilities are unlimited and the type of broken pottery found will be, in general, indicative of the age of the site, but it should always be remembered that things found on long-cultivated ground may have travelled from former habitation sites with manure.

The writer once had a garden which was at one time part of the West Field of pre-enclosure Cambridge and the very numerous objects I found, almost all quite valueless in themselves, ranged in date from Roman times to the nineteenth century, including small bones from human hands and feet which must have been ploughed out of the large Anglo-Saxon cemetery under the St. John's College sports ground close by.

Because the quarry is elusive some people enjoy field walking over sites where so-called 'pygmy' flints or microliths may be found. These were not made by pygmy people but are fine slivers of flint, triangular or crescentic in shape, which were parts of composite javelins and fish-spears with heads of hardened wood or bone. They belong to the hunting and fishing peoples of the Mesolithic period and the small flints were set with some kind of mastic in grooves on the sides of these weapons to act as barbs. They are often found where the peat cover, which resulted from the wet Atlantic climatic phase, has been removed either by cutting, heath fires or natural wastage. It was open moorland before the peat began to grow and was hunted over by Mesolithic folk. Our Pennine region is a good example.

Lincolnshire contains two classic sites of this period, Risby Warren on the sandy ridge east of Scunthorpe, and the south-eastern summit of Hall Hill at West Keal in the South Wolds. Risby Warren had been famous for years and it had plainly been a favourite camping place of early people who hunted west over the Trent Valley and east over that of the Ancholme. Hall Hill was a new find, its riches having been shown up by wartime ploughing, but here again it was the same story, a dry camping place with springs of water fairly close and a great hunting and fishing area stretched out before it.

Field walking may sometimes produce remarkable individual finds by the merest chance and can show the long distances over which specific objects could travel in prehistoric times. Examples of this are the occasional finds of pendants and perforated beads of jadeite of the rare type known as *callais* apparently occurring only among the igneous rocks of Brittany.

The presence of former potteries will be revealed by a large heap of characteristic sherds and one of the features of Risby Warren was the occasional appearance of large accumulations of much fragmented Beaker pottery of the early Bronze Age. In Roman times, pottery manufacture could be on an industrial scale in many places and each produced its large crop of wasters, as at Water Newton (*Dvrobrivae*).

Similar industrial sites occur in Alice Holt Forest in Hampshire and also at many sites in the New Forest, as well as other places. At all these sites dumps of wasters appear. Pot making was commonly carried out on little more than a domestic scale and each site produced its crop of wasters. Less common, but sometimes large, are the sites where various sorts of tiles of box, roof and common building types were made, as at Ashtead Forest in Surrey and at Holt near Chester.

The Roman Empire was preoccupied with the search for metals, and Britain was in varying degree a source of gold, silver, tin, copper, lead and iron. Lincolnshire was not in a mining area and what little metal extraction there was must have been in the south-west of the county in the Colsterworth area and towards Leicestershire. No certain evidence has been found of this and scatters of ill-smelted slag would be the clue. But there is every reason to believe that iron smelting of a sort could be conducted on an almost domestic scale whenever the necessary ore was available, either from the ground or in the form of the so-called bog iron found in swampy places.

But if there was little metal production, the manufacture of salt along the sea coast and well up into the tide-affected areas of the Fenland round the Wash was an important activity in Iron Age times and right on into the Middle Ages. When air-photographs were available they were, as in so much else, a sovereign aid to the identification of ancient features and sites of activity. One of the methods of production was to leach salt out of saline silt after the water had been concentrated by natural evaporation. But, in Iron Age and Roman times at least, the sea water was boiled down for its salt in rough clay troughs supported on various sizes of squeezed pedestals, also of clay, locally known as 'hand-bricks'. The coast of Lincolnshire north and south of Ingoldmells Point is littered with the debris of this industry. It is revealed right down the foreshore by the tides and it underlies the pasture fields of the plain behind the coastline, where it appears protruding from the sides of the modern drainage channels. This kind of salt-making must be found by ground inspection.

Further up the coast towards Mablethorpe and the Humber estuary the evidence may be plainly seen from the air. It consists of extensive raised areas of silt separated into two or perhaps three or more ranges parallel with the coast line. They were the byproduct of leaching salt out of saline silt, for when the salt had been extracted the silt was dumped by the place of work and so a low raised platform was made which increasingly barred out the sea at high tide.

This industry died at the close of the sixteenth century with the shift to the use of mineral salt from Cheshire and Droitwich. For this late Lincolnshire type of salt production there is ample documentary evidence in the local records of the communities along this part of the coast, and there is also a late sixteenth century map by John Hayward which shows the platforms and calls them 'mavers'.

My handwriting was never very good and it was one thing to examine the archaeological possibilities of an area and another to give the results a more permanent form. It was expected that their final form would be incorporation with the appropriate types and names on the 25 inch scale maps when at last they were revised, and that from these the information would also be carried to the derived 6 and 1 maps. As far as imparting information to the general map-using public was concerned, the 1 inch scale series would be the most important. I therefore adopted a print rather than longhand in making notes on the margins of the 6 inch sheets, placed as much as possible in line either vertically or horizontally with the feature on the sheet and, besides giving reasons for my note which might be understood by the reviser, I also initialled and dated each entry. A pencil line was run across the face of the map from the note and the Archaeology Officer would be the final judge of what alterations were to be made to existing maps. The annotated maps were sent back to Crawford at Southampton where they were stored until required. Crawford had no staff and was very frequently in the field, often in remote parts of the country where he was making a great many discoveries himself. He did all his work as far as possible from a bicycle and he was quite right in this, but work in Lincolnshire was only one of my many preoccupations in the late 1920s and the time available for it made the use of motor transport inevitable.

Thus a great deal of information was gained and stored at Southampton and it was this that made Crawford so active in 1939 in removing all this accumulated record to a safe place in West Wales where it survived while the Office in which it had been stored was burnt out by an air raid on November 30, 1940. The Survey as a whole was not so prescient and was content to let the Name Books relating to the large scale survey of almost all England and Wales stay at Southampton to perish on the same occasion. Historic relics of the early days of the Survey also perished along with vitally important stereo-comparator plant, which was replaced only with the greatest difficulty under war-time conditions.

I need hardly say that I was not paid for this work, but I did receive a useful allowance for petrol, and it and other compilation work on behalf of historical maps were an admirable training for the unexpected day when I succeeded Crawford in his post in January 1947 at a time when general revision had become the order of the day.

Chapter 3

It is now time to change the scene, for while I was taking a decreasing part in the work in the West Country there was a great widening of my horizon elsewhere. A new development was to lead me back to Sussex.

I think that the first time Crawford entered my consciousness was when he had already been at the Ordnance Survey since 1920 and had conceived the idea of a map of Roman Britain, managing to dissuade Sir Charles Close as Director General and Sir Charles Oman of Oxford University from a disastrous historical map plan they were preparing experimentally, in favour of a single-period map printed on an otherwise blank physical base which, if successful, could be followed up by other maps of other periods on the same base.

Close was converted to the idea but the time for his retirement had come. The first of this series of period maps was produced under the next Director General, Brigadier Jack. The project nearly died at birth for Crawford rashly made a model of the proposed map without official permission and was rebuked for this by Jack, but the project was allowed to continue. So the first Ordnance Survey map of Roman Britain was published in August 1924 and sold like hot cakes, as also did an immediate reprint of another 2000 copies. The policy of publishing this kind of map was well and truly launched and it was the first of a long series of special publications carried out by Crawford and also by me when I succeeded to his post.

Crawford's next project was a private one, the founding and publishing of *Antiquity*, of which he was the owner and editor. In 1927 I was one of his original subscribers and have remained one for more than half a century. He put me into touch with the Curwens of Brighton who, since the end of World War I, had been doing remarkable things for the archaeology of the Downland and the coastal area of Sussex.

They were two doctors practising at Hove, Dr. Eliot Curwen and his son Dr. Eliot Cecil Curwen, both enthusiastic workers in archaeology. The elder doctor had been a medical missionary in China and was no longer young; Eliot had been at Gonville and Caius College at Cambridge and had not long completed his studies and qualified when he served in the last stages of World War I. He was now devoting his spare time to what he correctly believed to be the numerous traces of ancient agriculture on the Downs and, fired by the example of Crawford, was applying air-photography to the understanding of many features which appeared obscure on the ground. He was a leading pioneer in this recognition of the traces of ancient farming which might be seen all over the chalk lands of Southern Britain. He was also intrigued by the precise character and function of the chain of hill forts which occurred along the line of the South Downs. In view of the early incorporation of the region in the Roman province after the Claudian conquest, he wished to know how they had fared against the Roman invaders.

Before I go any further, I should say that although Curwen had brilliant insights in his field work there was one serious obstacle to his thinking. The Curwen family were Evangelicals of the strictest sort and as a firm believer in the creation of the world in 4004 B.C., Curwen had no great use for palaeolithic man. In the first chapter of his otherwise admirable book *Prehistoric Sussex* a sense of unease is obviously present and the way in which he so often equated certain phases in the three millennia before Christ with episodes in the lives of the Biblical patriarchs tells its own story. His mother was totally preoccupied with religion, and perhaps it was this trait in the family which led him eventually to give up archaeology and pursue what were for him, less uneasy hobbies like achieving a very high standard as a photographer. But nothing can alter the fact that he was a prime mover behind the great flowering of the archaeology of the chalk country between the two World Wars.

He was kindness itself to me. At Crawford's suggestion he invited me to take part in an exploratory excavation at the Trundle hill fort overlooking the coastal plain of West Sussex, the city of Chichester, and the promontory of Selsey Bill from a bastion of the South Downs 500 feet in height, and commanding the east side of the Lavant gap leading through into the Western Weald.

The work with which I was asked to help in August 1928 was designed to explore the main characteristics of the Iron Age defence work round the top of the hill, a strong single bank and ditch which more or less follows a contour in its circuit and is about 1,000 feet in diameter. It has two entrances opposite each other to east and west and at each the rampart turns sharply inward for some 30 feet. This is not the only feature of the site. Air-photography had shown that there is a much older defensive system, the perimeter of which has been almost completely followed by the Iron Age work except for a short stretch on the north side, and there are three other concentric lines of defence clearly formed by short lengths of discontinuous ditch. We already knew from other examples found and excavated at Windmill Hill near Avebury and another by the bank of the Thames near Abingdon that the Trundle example was Neolithic in age and therefore long abandoned before the Iron Age fort was built. The examination of this was reserved for a later time and in 1928 all efforts were concentrated on the later fort.

The summit of the hill showed signs of the former chapel of St. Roche, which had been a modest place of pilgrimage in the Middle Ages and explains the specific name of the whole hill on which the Trundle stands. The hill was solid chalk so that holes dug in it could be at once revealed by the removal of the thin natural capping of turf and humus. Our objectives were three-fold: to make complete sections through the defensive ditch and bank, to open up the whole area of the entrances and to sample the surface of the enclosed area for traces of hut sites, rubbish pits and the surviving debris of the former inhabitants. There were many rubbish pits and the finds made in them were numerous but not surprising, consisting of the domestic rubbish of the ordinary inhabitants, and Curwen had already examined this situation thoroughly at the hill fort known as the Caburn on the Downs east of Lewes. The defensive bank and ditch were also normal. If there had been a timber palisade along the bank, all traces of it and the holes in which it had stood had long ago slipped down into the ditch.

But the entrances provided much that was novel. The internal ramparts had been heavily revetted with timber on both sides; two great pits in the centre of the approach, an inner and an outer, provided for powerful timber stops against which inner and outer double gates could be secured; and three large pits, ranged on each side and opposite each other at the base of the inturned rampart, provided settings for whole tree trunks from which the inner and outer gates could be hung and which could carry a timber tower overlooking the whole approach to the gates from the outside. The absence of sling stones suggested that the inhabitants did not defend themselves in this way, as they did further west in Dorset and elsewhere.

These great pits contained no traces of wood and were filled up completely with chalk rubble. This showed plainly that the gates and gate defences had been deliberately removed and the defences slighted. The Trundle is in full sight of the Roman walled town and tribal centre of *Noviomagus Regnensium*, now occupied by modern Chichester. It is a matter of recorded history that this part of Britain, ruled by the local king Cogidubnus, made no effort to resist the Roman invasion under Claudius and his restraint was rewarded by his being confirmed as the local ruler and a client of the Emperor. The demolition of the old tribal capital on the hill must have been a condition of this and in 1928 we had proved it.

I had learned much at the Trundle in 1928 and I was to learn still more when invited to help again in August 1930, when the objectives were to find out something about the far older 'discontinuous ditch' features already mentioned above, over the remains of which the Iron Age fort had been built. I was now fast making contact with rising young archaeologists. In 1928 Stuart Piggott had been at the Trundle with his father and he was there again in 1930. Between the two excavations I had found a new friend at Cambridge in Grahame Clark of Peterhouse who was working for a Ph.D. and he joined the Trundle party in the flaming-hot August of 1930. As in 1928 we camped on the site. We did not solve the problems posed by the discontinous ditch features but gained much experience in cleaning out the ditches and made plenty of finds, including some remarkable carved chalk objects.[1]

I must now make some reference to my relations with my family in the second half of the 1920s . The whole process of my education, from the death of my father early in 1907 to the taking of my first degree at Cambridge in 1922, was borne by the Freemasons, and during almost the whole of the period between 1911 and 1922 this involved my food and clothing also. I was used to an impecunious life and till I began to go to Cambridge in 1919 I had virtually no knowledge of my father's family, although my grandfather lived till 1916, my only uncle till 1920 and my only aunt till 1928. As I came into my teens I had a growing conviction that there was something formidable in our Phillips background but it was not till I met my distant cousin, Cheveley Frederick Phillips, at my uncle Wilfred's funeral, by which time I was an undergraduate already in residence at Cambridge, that I began to learn more.

There was no denying that my father's family disapproved of his marriage with a village girl from Berkshire and they demonstrated this by entirely failing to put in an appearance at his wedding in the village church at Ardington. But my father's tragic disability, which progressively unfitted him more and more for a normal life, had given them seven years in which to judge the calibre of the woman he had married. They

1   Sussex Archaeological Collections, LXX, 1929 Curwen, E.C. Prehistoric Sussex, pp. 61–63

still could not bring themselves to admit her beyond my father's own family circle and as we boys got ourselves educated and both entered universities in turn, they saw a new development in the family which had never been matched before.

The Cheveley Phillips I had met at my uncle's funeral was a warm-hearted man who had made a great success of his own career as an ace representative for a leading grocery firm, and had now retired to use his business abilities in managing the very considerable finances of his aunt, my grandfather's youngest sister Eliza. Back in 1878, when she was no longer young, she had married a man much older than herself who did not live very much longer and left her a modest fortune of some £125,000. A stockbroker friend of her deceased husband had proceeded to turn this into a very large fortune and, while making large gifts to charity for the rest of her long and childless life – she lived to be ninety-six – she had also given support to the rather numerous unsuccessful or tragic figures among her nephews and nieces and their offspring. This was the hitherto unknown factor in our family affairs whose existence I was now to recognise.

One of the lessons I learned from my meeting with the other amateur archaeologists of the Cambridge scene in the 1920s was that the possession of financial independence was desirable, if not always beneficial. Men like T. C. Lethbridge and Charles Leaf seemed to be able to do rather second-rate work and get away with it. Leaf was a victim of the late war but Lethbridge, though very able and producing interesting ideas, had no real conscience in his work in the last analysis. He was content to sample many sites and when following his trail years later when I was writing up the Cambridgeshire earthworks for the Victoria County History, I went from site to site and noticed his trademark on many of them in the form of test holes and trenches left unfilled. With him field work could sometimes be a mere pastime.

In 1928 and 1929 we had with us at Cambridge another kind of rich man devoted to archaeology. Hugh Hencken from Harvard spent some time at St. John's and I made his acquaintance without knowing much about him. In my old Morgan three-wheeler I drove him to see Grimes' Graves, the Devil's Dyke on Newmarket Heath, a good slice of typical Fenland and the fine old town of King's Lynn. I did not know that he was a member of the Harvard team then conducting a great programme of full excavation on various Irish sites of first-class importance. He was a rich man and a 'Boston Brahmin', with whom archaeology was to be his life's work, employing all his resources. He was too much afraid of hurting my feelings to suggest that we should visit the sites and East Anglia in general in a luxurious chauffeur-driven hired car. I last met him in Boston in the autumn of 1970 at the annual dinner of the American Fellows of the Society of Antiquaries of London. Sadly, this was only a few months before his death.

Having gained a sufficiently good degree in History and with a natural capacity for teaching which I think I derive from my mother, I decided to set up as a history coach, work hard and save money to get independence as soon as possible. It came about in this way. An emissary had come to Cambridge seeking a lecturer in History for the Episcopal Church of America's College at Annandale-on-Hudson, not far from New York. He applied to Sir Will Spens, the Master of Corpus Christi, who consulted Selwyn as a 'Church' College. They suggested me and when offered the job by Spens I made the probably disastrous mistake of accepting it. The emissary had trustingly given Spens carte blanche and when he saw me he refused to accept the result because I was obviously too young and inexperienced and he was quite right. This left Spens in an embarrassing position and to compensate me for his mistake he gave me some coaching work. The American post was very tempting to a young man, but would have been fatal to my aim of becoming an archaeologist. So the end of 1923 found me in lodgings on Hills Road, looking to gain financial independence, and cheered by a cheque for £500 which I had received from my great-aunt Eliza on the occasion of my coming of age.

There was still an Ordinary Degree at Cambridge in those days and there were many wealthy undergraduates in residence who had no higher ambition than to achieve this, while living the social round of the Pitt Club, the University pack of beagles and so on. There were many quite able people among them who would in due course take their place in public life. There was also a sprinkling of sad cases that would require special attention.

There was a shortage of really competent people to supervise the work of the undergraduates and there were still parents able and willing to pay for their not very bright offspring to be brought to the standard of a modest Honours degree. If a coach was prepared to work very hard, money could be made quite quickly and it was well worth a try, especially if now some money might be hoped for from another source. So I launched out as one of the last of the History coaches.

I have already mentioned the Museum of Archaeology and Anthropology at Cambridge, which was in good order and contained much foreign and local material. The curator was L.C.G. Clarke of Trinity Hall, a wealthy connaisseur who did a great deal to augment the collections with pre-Columbian American objects, and important material from the Danubian lands, at his own expense. But most of the effective work with the archaeological collections was done by his assistant, Miss M. O'Reilly of Girton College, who stood in for him during his frequent travels.

The holder of the Disney Chair of Archaeology at this time was Ellis Minns. This Chair was founded in 1857 and it was quite clearly laid down in the agreement between John Disney and the University in founding it 'that it shall be the duty of the Professor to deliver in the course of each academic year . . . six lectures at least on the subject of Classical, Medieval and other Antiquities, the Fine Arts and all matters connected therewith'. This was not the same thing as the modern definition of archaeology as 'the science of all the human past'.

As an undergraduate I recall seeing the then incumbent of this Chair, Sir William Ridgway, being driven about the town at an advanced age in a four-wheeled cab. I do not know much about him, but I believe that his whole interest was in Ancient Greece and in problems raised by the recognition of the Minoan and Mycenean phases. The archaeology of Britain concerned him very little.

His successor, Ellis Minns, was a likeable man, very learned in the history of calligraphy, the Scythians in southern Russia and much else, but was also quite honest and open in not being interested in the archaeology of Britain. He was quite capable of fulfilling the conditions on which he held his post, but in the post-1915 years Russia was closed to him and his Russian friends were dead or dispersed.

A man who was to be one of the most important figures in British archaeology left Cambridge not long before I became active. He was a young laboratory assistant named Cyril Fox, who had been working independently on the archaeology of the Cambridge region and had single-handedly worked out the factors which had affected human life in the region since remote prehistoric times. He wrote a book called *The Archaeology of the Cambridge Region* which was published by the Cambridge University Press in 1923 and at once was acclaimed as a work of the first importance.

The development of archaeological studies might have been greatly advanced if he had been invited to join the Downing Street establishment, but that was unlikely so long as Miles Burkitt, Minns' chief support and a student of Palaeolithic man, was a leading figure in the Faculty staff and plainly expected to succeed Minns in the Disney chair.

But another and more immediately tempting offer was presented to Fox when the Directorship of the National Museum of Wales was vacated by Mortimer Wheeler when he took over the London Museum. Fox was at once appointed at Cardiff, and Cambridge had to content itself according him a Ph.D. degree.

This left the pursuit of local archaeology mainly to the Cambridge Antiquarian Society, a body with a long record of competent publication of all local work and a membership containing a fair proportion of University folk.

Up to the year of 1928 I had met three out of the four persons who have powerfully affected the developing trend of my life. The first was the Littlehampton schoolmaster, Edmund P. Toy, whose school I had attended in 1909 and 1910. He had awakened my young mind to the world of learning and, however indistinctly, had shown me its vast extent and possibilities. Second came the tragic John Davies at Bristol, and then in 1928 and 1929, I became the firm helper and later successor of O.G.S. Crawford.

I now come to consider the beginning of the fourth big influence in my life as an archaeologist: my lengthy relationship with J.G.D. (Grahame) Clark of Peterhouse, who had gone up to Cambridge from Marlborough School and had achieved a double First in the Historical Tripos. The Marlborough of his time had been very different from that one under which Crawford had suffered and Clark had not neglected the opportunities afforded by free days for visits to the archaeological sites for which this part of Wessex is famous.

He was an orphan. His father, a stockbroker in peace time and a Lieut. Colonel in the West Kents during the 1914–18 war, had died in Malta on his way back from the Mesopotamian campaign. His family had a stockbroking and legal background and his affairs were in the hands of trustees. Although his long-term financial prospects were more secure than my own he was temporarily worse off than I was when we first met in 1929, and was to remain so for a number of years because of the prolonged life of one of his grandmothers. Having completed his Tripos with great success and taken his B.A. he was working for a Ph.D. on a thesis about the Mesolithic period in Britain.

In 1929 there was in Cambridge (and had been for more years past than I knew) a strange character known as N. Teulon Porter. He was a quite good-looking man in early middle age, who had a fearfully deformed but normal-sized right leg. The limb seemed to be bent permanently at right angles to the trunk at the hip and he seemed to have no power to put his right foot down on to the ground at the same level with the left one. I did not know the antecedents of this unfortunate man, but he never seemed to lack for money and I heard it rumoured that he was a native of Yorkshire. By the accounts then current he was one who had made evil his good, and, as he kept open house, he was a natural rallying point for various kinds of male and female rebels, free thinkers and generally unhappy and unsatisfied persons of whom Cambridge had its full quota. At one time he lived in Portugal Place near the Round Church and at the time of the events I am about to describe he had one of the houses in the passage past Little Saint Mary's Church, which looked across the closed churchyard to the north side of Peter-house over the passage through to the river. The house was called the 'Half Moon' and Porter hung out a little cut-out metal sign of a half moon over the entrance; quite possibly it was a former inn, of which there were quite a number in the town.

The house had a bad reputation and there was a time when the authorities of Newnham College put it out of bounds to their undergraduates after some complaints had been received. A friend of mine who moved into the house after Porter had left it told me that the bathroom had suggestive paintings on its walls.

Be this as it may Porter had taken a dislike to the Cambridge Antiquarian Society of which he was a member and he gave notice that on May 14 1929 there would be an open meeting at the Half Moon to discuss the formation of a rival society to be known as the Cambridge Antiquarian Club. At that time I knew little about Porter, although I had wondered who he was when I saw him making his awkward way round the town on a specially built bicycle. The door of the Half Moon was open and I went in to find a small crowd, none of whom I knew and I decided to take my seat next to the most respectable looking of them.

The meeting was opened by Porter and, after I had heard an extraordinary plan outlined for excavating a ruined abbey in Herefordshire and a lot of utterly unpractical nonsense, I noticed that my neighbour was also fidgeting about with disapproval. I caught his eye and we both came to the simultaneous decision to leave the meeting. I heard no more about what happened afterwards; the proposed society that Porter intended to call 'The Young Things' came to nothing.

But something else which arose from this did not fail. The man who came out with me was Grahame Clark and we discussed what we had seen, agreed in our distaste for it, talked about what we ourselves were doing and agreed to meet for tea next day.

From this point on we frequently went on expeditions together. I have already described how he came to the second season of excavation at the Trundle in 1930 because it was concerned with the Neolithic aspects of the site, and it was then that I got to know him more thoroughly partly because we had to put up with the vagaries of a sad youth called Ellis.[1] I was now well started on my Lincolnshire survey and there were two parts of the county which were of particular interest to Clark: the classic Risby Warren area and Manton Warren close by it to the south and the south-west end of the Wolds. Here there were considerable tracts of sandy exposure with southerly aspects which provided very favourable camping grounds for Mesolithic folk, close to tracts of fenland country good for fowling and fishing. It was not till the late spring of 1931 that we began to concentrate on the very prolific site on Hall Hill at West Keal and soon after I was to spend almost the whole long vacation in travel round North America.

1 Ellis, a rather disturbed young man, entered Sidney Sussex College in 1930, but was found dead in his rooms in February 1931, trussed and suffocated. An open verdict was returned.

Meanwhile Crawford had thoroughly made his point about the great value of air photography for archaeological work by publishing jointly with Alexander Keiller the results of an aerial survey of Wessex. Crawford had given a lecture to the Royal Geographical Society on March 22, 1922, in which he showed the results of an air photograph taken in Hampshire north of Winchester and demonstrated how Celtic field systems were perfectly revealed when seen from this angle. The lecture was well received and he followed it up with the wider publicity of an article in the *Observer*, which attracted much attention, not least in the Royal Air Force. But the important immediate result was that Alexander Keiller, who had heard the lecture, suggested that he should provide the flying (he had been in the Fleet Air Arm in the late war), while Crawford should observe and take photographs all over the Wessex area. Keiller was a wealthy but rather erratic amateur, who was intermittently active in important excavation and restoration work between the two wars. He spent much of his great wealth extravagantly but he never spent it to better effect than on this occasion. The Ordnance Survey gave Crawford the necessary leave and in 1928 the Oxford University Press published the result of their joint effort in the book *Wessex from the Air*, lavishly illustrated and well commented, by which the possibilities of the new technique were fairly demonstrated in a variety of contexts.

One of the results was the reporting of new sites seen from the air by R.A.F. officers and an arrangement was made by which Crawford was given facilities at R.A.F. stations to inspect air photographs taken during training, and in particular the aerial mosaics submitted by various squadrons when competing for the Sassoon Trophy.

Meanwhile, important developments were taking place in the Botany School at Cambridge, where the new technique of pollen analysis, which had been developed in Scandinavia and applied to the dating of archaeological deposits and the history of climatic changes since the end of the last Ice Age, had been taken up by the Professor, Sir Albert Seward, and was being applied to the problems of the Fenland by Harry and Margaret Godwin in the Botany School.

Concurrently with this came an opportunity to see and study photographs proceeding from work for the Sassoon Trophy over the greater part of the Fenland in the Counties of Cambridge, Huntingdon, Norfolk and Lincolnshire. In the silt lands directly south of the Wash early in the eighteenth century, William Stukeley had noticed in his native Holbeach area the occurrence of fragments of Romano-British pottery which could only mean some form of settlement, but the matter was not followed up. During the rest of the eighteenth and most of the nineteenth centuries the draining of the peat fens and the large stretches of open water like Whittlesey Mere and Red Mere was carried forward actively and by the 1920s the areas recovered had passed through an initial pastoral phase to be mainly arable land. Once it became arable the peat began to oxidise and shrink and the local practice of enriching the cultivation by temporarily opening and spreading the underlying marine clay over the fields did nothing to retard the slow decline of the level of the arable areas till they were well below sea level.

Before 1914 there were still large areas of pasture, but a lot was ploughed up during the 1914–18 war. In spite of this, before 1939, fair-sized tracts still remained here and there and in particular there were still wide strips on both sides of the thirty mile stretch of the railway line from Ely to Spalding.

The real pioneer of Fenland studies after 1919 was Major Gordon Fowler, the traffic manager of the great Anglo-Dutch sugar beet processing factory which had been built at Ely by the bank of the river Ouse. A large area of the arable fen was now given over to beet sugar growing and Fowler had to arrange for the transport of the harvested beet to Ely by barge and road. In this way he grew to know the Fen people and their way of life. He heard about the huge ancient tree trunks which worked their way to the surface during ploughing and the quantities of broken pottery which could also occur. But what interested him most was the extensive system of meandering banks of silt which crossed the peat areas and which the locals called 'Roddons'. He was sure that they were relics of a pre-drainage situation.

In the late 1920s we were given our first look at the air-photographic cover of the Fenland by the R.A.F. which came to us through Crawford. We were startled to find that almost all of the Fenland, except the Isle of Ely and much of the skirtlands near higher ground at the edges, was covered by an irregular network of settlements, farms, fields, watercourses and droveways amounting to a map of an earlier period and way of life on which the modern scene was now superimposed. There were large whitish tracts where there had formerly been open water and, for good measure, it was possible to see how the drainers of more recent times had laid out their channels and drains sighted on church towers, and other landmarks conspicuous in that flat landscape, belonging to medieval villages which had taken advantage of the few islands like March and Crowland or the higher silt areas along the south shore of the Wash.

We now had the necessary tools. Going into the Fens with 25 inch scale Ordnance Survey maps and these photographs, it was easy to go to all these features on the ground and recognise that most of them were Romano-British in origin by the broken pottery found on them in large quantities.

Parallel with this the botanists and geologists were able to complete the work started by Miller and Skertchley in the nineteenth century and to get a clear view of the natural history of the Fen basin since the end of the last Ice Age. We archaeologists did a good deal of field walking and in one case, Clark found traces of much more ancient human activity on sand hills emerging from cultivated peat fen at Shippea Hill towards the south-east edge of the Fen basin.

It was in the early summer of 1931, before I set off on my protracted journey to North America, that I helped Clark in his important excavation at this site. It was near the verge of the sandy Breckland of Suffolk. In its widest phase of development the peat had spread on to this territory and had covered a number of its sand dunes. Since the drainage, the peat had been in retreat to the extent that the tops of these sand hills began to appear in the cultivated fields as sandy areas which had proved to be rich in a scatter of Bronze Age and Neolithic scraps of pottery, flint arrowheads, flakes from polished stone axes and also a significant number of the 'pygmy' flints belonging to the composite weapons of hunters of the Mesolithic period.

The explanation was that these were the relics of seasonal occupation by hunters of successive periods, who exploited the fish and fowl-rich fens. The signs of successive occupations of the sand hill would accumulate on its top and sides as the peat steadily rose and finally covered it. The period of the latest human artefacts found on the top of the sand hill would be that in which the place became uninhabitable, in this case the Bronze Age.

We saw that if an excavation, following the slope of the hill was made down into the peat we should come to a Neolithic scatter. It was so, and beneath the Neolithic level we found a bed of the so-called 'buttery clay' of marine origin and common all over the peat fens dividing an upper peat from another below it. This was evidence of a great tidal invasion over most of the Fenland with the daily ebb and flow of the tides for a considerable period.

So what about the Mesolithic material we had found on the upper part of the hill with the later material? The excavation was now dangerously deep, but we managed to get through this clay to the lower peat near the hill and there were the tell-tale 'pygmy' flints which showed the presence of Mesolithic folk before the tidal phase turned the Fen basin into a great stretch of mud flats, until at last the sea barred itself out and the peat could resume its growth in the fresh water floods from the land which followed.[1]

Antiquaries' Journal, 1934, XV, pp. 200–319. *Antiquity*, 1962, pp. 10–23.

Chapter 4

I began to travel abroad a fair amount in the 1930s, when I had become sufficiently involved with the general organisation of archaeology and began to attend conferences in foreign places.

In 1929 I went on a Hellenic Travellers' tour in the central Mediterranean and the Aegean visiting, among other places, Athens, Istanbul, Delos, Rhodes, Crete and Sicily. But here my interest was divided between history and archaeology. It was a horizon-widening experience and, as in the least of my travels, satisfying to my strong topographic sense.

When I set out on my long tour to North America in 1931 my first concern was to visit my brother, who was then at Northwestern University in Chicago, and my extended trip to the Pacific was an afterthought. I knew my North American history pretty well and was content to let archaeology take its chance. Frankly, it was a holiday.

Travelling by Quebec, Montreal and Toronto, I went on through Detroit to Chicago, then in the throes of the great depression and plagued by the anti-Prohibition gang wars. After a stay of three weeks, in which I was shocked by the state into which this great city had fallen, I set off on a long trip, mainly by train, to the south-west via Kansas City, Santa Fe and Albuquerque, making a diversion to see the Grand Canyon to be awed by its immensity and then on to the Pacific Coast across the Mohave Desert to Los Angeles, already an awful warning as an example of unrestrained urban sprawl. I took refuge in a short visit to the Yosemite Valley and the giant trees and then moved north to the beautiful city of San Francisco. From here I went up through the Cascades into the states of Washington and Oregon, where I visited 14,000 feet high Mount Rainier, saw a wonderful mountain flora and then ended my northward trek at Seattle, not far from the Canadian border.

From here I made an almost direct journey back to Chicago through Wyoming, North Dakota and Minneapolis-St. Paul. But I made a thrilling diversion to visit the natural wonders of the Yellowstone Park and they exceeded all my expectations; after that the rest of the train journey to Chicago had little interest.

I did not concern myself with American archaeology, but as an inveterate field walker I could not get out of the habit of looking along the surface of the ground. When we were visiting some petrified tree trunks (in which wood is reduced to a sort of chert) we were assured by the guide that the Indians never used this chert for making implements or weapons. Then I asked the guide what these could be, for I was looking down at a quite well-fashioned point and some probable rejects. Further looking about revealed more and it was plain that the Indians had used this material.

Later, on the verge of the south lip of the Grand Canyon, I picked up a well-made arrowhead of some better material. Still later, when we were in the Yellowstone Park and were marvelling at the regular cliff of black obsidian among several now extinct geysers, I wondered why the Indians of the area had never used this very workable material in making blades and points. But I remembered that when the Yellowstone was first organised as a National Park in the 1870s the thermal activity had been vastly greater than it has since become. Impressive as it is now, it must have filled the Indians with dread and they would not venture anywhere near it.

When the Transcontinental railways were being pushed through to the Pacific, beautifully flaked arrowheads and knives of a deep red colour began to make their appearance among the Indians. At the same time there was a plague of thefts of red warning lanterns from the tail end of trains. These implements were made from the stolen red bulls' eyes.

Before I left Chicago for home I made a two-day expedition by car with my brother across Illinois to the Mississippi, crossed that great river and went down to the little riverside town of Hannibal in Missouri, the birthplace of Mark Twain. In 1931 it had not yet become a Mecca for tourists and we meditated on Huck Finn and Tom Sawyer in the little town which in 1931 was probably not strikingly different from what it had been before the Civil War. I understand that today it is quite a boom town with all the trappings of a shrine.

On my way home through Pittsburgh and over the Cumberland Gap to Washington, Philadelphia and New York I was more concerned with the eighteenth century struggle for America between the English and the French and the Revolutionary War.

So home from New York at the end of August and just in time to have a month's exploratory excavation work in an entirely novel area before going back to Cambridge for another bout of archaeology in Lincolnshire and the Fens.

Three years previously, in 1928, as a result of a slashing and fully justified attack by Mortimer Wheeler upon the incompetence of the Royal Commission on Ancient Monuments in Wales and Monmouthshire at the time of the publication of their Pembrokeshire volume, the Secretary had resigned and Wilfred J. Hemp of the Ancient Monuments Inspectorate had been appointed in his stead. This was the moment when the young Stuart Piggott was trying to find his way into an archaeological career. Hemp was entitled to a typist and at the instigation of Crawford, Hemp had offered Piggott this initial toehold and he had taken it.

It soon proved to be an unusual arrangement, for Hemp, although quite able and well-informed, was also rather idle. He really belonged to a type of comfortable antiquarian who was now becoming quite out of date. He took the trouble and expense to provide himself with a coat of arms, the principal feature of which was a hemp-breaking machine, and after his pleasant and modest old minor civil servant father died, had it carved as large as the tombstone could carry on his grave. Hemp was a terrible snob and, as the outcome was to show, his Secretaryship was just as disastrous as that of his disgraced predecessor. That unfortunate's offence arose from undue haste, carelessness and, ultimately, ignorance (he was a political appointee of Lloyd George); while Hemp, who was far better fitted intellectually for the work, took an unconscionable time, eleven years, to produce the report on Anglesey, an island with many antiquities but quite light on the side of secular and ecclesiastical buildings.

The island had an Archaeological Society in which the leading figure was Neil Baynes, the brother-in-law of Lord Boston, who had a modest country residence not far from Benllech on the north-east side of the island, which contained in its grounds the remarkable hut group known as Din Lligwy, built on a scale which would suggest the former residence of chieftains.

One of the big problems in the archaeology of this part of North Wales was the dating of the numerous hut groups and single huts common in the island and in the adjacent mainland. A false start had been made when, a good many years ago, the well-known antiquary St. John Hope, digging among some of the well-preserved groups on Holy Island in the north-west of Anglesey, found an undoubted Bronze Age rapier among them. It was not a very careful excavation and it did not follow that the huts were of the same age as the rapier. The general view was that the huts as a class belonged to a period of more than a thousand years from the Iron Age through the Roman occupation and well on into the Dark Ages.

To contribute to the solution of this problem, and so to assist the Royal Commission to express an opinion in its report, some new excavations were required. It was resolved to make a small beginning and a well-defined single hut in Penmon parish was chosen, which stood overlooking the sea in the direction of the distant Great Orme. It was close to the site of a very big limestone quarry from which stone was being taken in great quantities direct by sea to form a new training bank in the mouth of the Mersey.[1]

Through my friendship with Piggott I was drawn into this new area of work, acting on behalf of the Anglesey Society. I came to North Wales soon after my return from North America and established myself in the Anglesey Arms Hotel at Menai Bridge. There is no need to describe the Penmon hut excavation in any detail here. It was circular and the lower two courses of its thick wall were still mostly in place. The limestone of Anglesey is naturally fractured and can be readily used in drystone walling in blocks of any convenient size. There was an obvious hearth place and right round the foot of the inner base of the hut wall was a bench rather more than one foot high and broad enough to serve for sleeping purposes. It died away flush to the wall on each side as the entrance was approached. This last was wide enough to give easy access to one person and it was directed away from the sea and towards the mainland. The only furniture of any kind surviving in the hut were several fine saddle querns. In cleaning out the accumulation of earth in the hut down to the natural stone floor, the only objects found, besides many limpet shells, were a number of large beach pebbles which had been used as hammers and a few featureless scraps of Romano-British pottery. It was obvious that the inhabitants must have used wooden vessels, as did their successors in Wales almost into modern times.

No animal bones were found but a few yards in front of the entrance the stripping of the turf showed a rectangular pit formed by the removal of the naturally fractured limestone, possibly for the purpose of constructing the hut. The contents of this were remarkable, long columns of limpet shells placed one inside the other and laid in orderly horizontal files. These had obviously come from the beach of the little strait close by, opposite to Puffin Island. While the saddle querns implied the use of grain as

1 *Archaeologia Cambrensis*, Vol. 87, 1932, pp. 247–259

food, it was clear that the occupants of the hut depended heavily on *fruits de la mer* and were fastidious in clearing up after their meals.

Penmon was a useful introduction, but by Christmas in 1931 it had vanished from the face of the earth, the site having been swallowed up in the rapid progress of the big quarry I mentioned above. While there, the work had been frequently interrupted by powerful hourly blasts from whistles which warned that another set of shots was ready to be fired. I then took refuge with other quarrymen in a hut massively constructed of old railway sleepers in which a large stock of dynamite was stored. It was not very reassuring to read the warning to those entering not to have footwear capable of striking sparks when one was accompanied into the hut by a number of heavily-booted men whose footwear certainly did not fulfil these conditions. When the explosions had roared we emerged for another hour's work. Some of these men chatted with me when they lunched on the grass by my little excavation and it was interesting to note that even in 1931 their Welsh was much more fluent than their English. Incidentally, on seeing the great number of limpet shells they told me that the eating of them was a sovereign remedy for constipation.

1932 was to be a very busy year, with the setting up of the interdisciplinary Fenland Research Committee and the first of the resumed series of International Congresses of Prehistoric and Proto-historic Studies being held in London that August, but by now I had broken the back of the revision of the Lincolnshire maps and I agreed to do one more excavation for the Welsh Commission and the Anglesey folk, in an attempt to obtain more decisive dating evidence. This took place at a site known as Pant-y-Saer (The Sawyer's Valley) in the parish of Llanfihangel-Mathafarn-Eithaf, a short way inland from the north-east coast of the island at Benllech Bay. The site is on a low limestone knoll giving a very wide view southwards embracing the whole of the Snowdon range and, to the north, Parys Mountain, the highest ground in Anglesey.[2]

A strong drystone wall made of large natural slabs of limestone surrounded a roughly circular area which tilted towards the east and was, in common with most of the hill top, completely scoured of its light soil cover by the action of wind and rain. One large round hut of considerable diameter stood within the enclosure, similar to the Penmon example, with a stone slab bench at the inner foot of the wall round the greater part of the empty interior and also a hearth. This occupied the upper part of the enclosure, leaving a large open space in the middle, in the lower part of which there were two smaller rectangular huts of a type which can be seen at most of these sites, possibly workplaces, cattle sheds or stores.

It will be readily understood that on a site like this, much exposed to the scour of the weather, there was little accumulation of soil to hide imperishable objects unless they slipped down into the natural fissures in the rock floor. But we were very fortunate in what was found. The only scrap of Romano-British pottery which came to light was a small piece of Samian ware about the size of a Brazil nut which was faceted on several sides by being rubbed on a hard surface, just as a chalk is when used on a blackboard.

The general mode of construction in this limestone area involved an inner and outer wall of horizontally laid slabs, a space of a few inches between them, and then

---

2 *Archaeologia Cambrensis*, Vol. 89, 1934, pp. 1–36.

frequent slabs set across binding them together. The remaining space between the wall was filled up with earth and rubbish, presumably much of it swept up from the interior of the enclosure in the case of these rectangular huts. I thought that the construction of these walls was worth investigating and so a portion of the wall of one hut was carefully taken down. In the fill was found some very coarse fictile material which showed signs of being parts of the sides and bases of crude ill-fired pottery, handmade and certainly not daub, clumsy fired sherds which could never have held together long under the tread of men and animals in the enclosure and could only have survived for recognition built into the wall. Later, some of this crude stuff was subjected to analysis for its mineral content and found to have been made locally. It seems to have been large pieces from easily broken tub-like vessels. Since 1932 other examples of this crude ware have been found elsewhere in Wales.

A clinching find giving a Dark Age date to this isolated farmstead was the finding of a typical well-preserved silver penannular brooch on the floor in the corner of one of the rectangular huts. Its date is not later than A.D. 600.

It is possible that the demolition of what remained of the walls of this farmstead down to bare rock might have produced other surprises but, having begun on September 6 I had to bring the work to an end on September 28 with something achieved. This excavation was later published in *Archaeologia Cambrensis*.[3]

I gave my first public lecture at the Society of Antiquaries about this Anglesey site on the evening of December 14 in the same year. Both Grahame Clark and I had been assiduous attendants at the Thursday evening lectures in Burlington House for a number of years and we were both to be admitted to the Fellowship on February 2, 1933.

I had not yet quite finished with excavation in Anglesey after Pant-y-Saer, because the Ministry of Works were concerned with the condition of a small megalithic tomb chamber near Ty Newydd in the island. The large capstone was showing signs of slipping and as the monument was being stabilised, the opportunity was taken to make sure that no evidence of its former contents survived in the chamber floor. I spent a few days there in September and was able to supply the Ministry with the assurance that they required.

While there I was much impressed by the way in which the Office's foreman for North Wales was able to manoeuvre a heavy capstone with the minimum of apparatus. This was instructive when pondering the problems which must have been encountered by the original constructors of megalithic monuments of all kinds.

There was a pleasant interlude to this occasion. As I was so near to Holyhead, Harold Leask, the Inspector of Ancient Monuments for the Irish Free State, suggested that I should cross to Dublin for a few days when he would show me some of the more important antiquities near that city. I was thus able to see the New Grange complex of great chambered tombs in the Boyne Valley and we also visited Slane and Tara. I had a close look with him at some of the nearly-completed restoration work of the famous Dublin buildings which had been burnt out or otherwise damaged during the Troubles, and I met Professor Sean O'Riordain, whom I was later able to entertain at Cambridge in October.

3   *Archaeologia Cambrensis*, Vol. 91, 1936, pp. 93–99

I had completed the revision of archaeology in Lincolnshire, as it should appear on the Ordnance Survey maps before I went to America, and I had also written an account of the present state of archaeology in the county which was published in two instalments in Volumes 91 and 92 of the *Archaeological Journal*. Twelve long barrows had been recognised, all in the middle or southern part of the Wolds, holding away southwards from the Humber estuary in much the same degree as those of the Yorkshire Wolds also held away northwards from the same feature. This was a time when more certain knowledge of these monuments was needed and, my personal finances having improved, I now decided to carry out as complete as possible an excavation of a good undisturbed Lincolnshire example.[4]

My choice fell on Giants' Hills on the chalk in the parish of Skendleby. This one was aligned along the contour not far below the lip of the valley of a brook which runs south-eastwards to join the Steeping River and enter the Wash at Wainfleet. It formed part of the boundary between two fields, but there was no indication that the body of the barrow had ever been disturbed. The excavation was planned in October 1932 and a careful local survey was carried out in March 1933. The work in 1933 was nearly shipwrecked by my having an attack of appendicitis but I had a successful operation on April 21 and was sufficiently recovered for a month's work to be completed by July 26.

The landlord of the site was a Mr Gainsford, a Sheffield colliery proprietor who lived in the Old Rectory at Somersby, a few miles away. He was sympathetic to our purposes and I found much interest in visiting the boyhood home of the poet Tennyson. In this 1933 season I and my party (whose principal members were Grahame Clark and his future wife, Miss Mollie White of Girton), stayed in the George Hotel at Spilsby and went out from there to the site every day.

In 1933, beyond a contour survey, we made no attempt to examine the barrow but contented ourselves by completely clearing a good length of the ditch on the upper side of the mound. Cultivation of the field uphill from it had long since completely filled the ditch, which proved to be of formidable size, deeply cut into the underlying chalk, its volume giving some indication of the former magnitude of the mound when the barrow was completed. Starting from the bottom upwards there were indications that Neolithic people had squatted out of the wind in the ditch to cook and eat their food. There were ample signs of Early Bronze Age folk in the primary silt at the very bottom in the form of sherds of 'Beaker' pottery, animal bones, hearths and, unexpectedly, the carcass of a young ox. Higher up in the fill there had been a large inrush of soil from the outer side of the ditch which, taken with its associated finds of Iron Age and Romano-British squatters, showed that by that time the ground uphill was being brought under the plough. There was a Romano-British settlement at Ulceby Cross only about half a mile away on the Roman road from Lincoln to the Wash which passed the site only about 200 yards away. The ditch was last used in the mid-eighteenth century, when a shooting party lunched there and left evidence in the form of one or two broken wine bottles from a Wainfleet wine merchant of the period.

A much more extensive campaign was planned for 1934, and the excavation which was resumed half way through June was carried through to mid-September. This time I recruited help for the heavier work from the local unemployed and so was able to

4 *Archaeologia*, Vol. 85, pp. 37–106.

relieve a little of the local agricultural depression. My friend, Mr A.H.A. Hogg, later to be Secretary to the Royal Commission on Ancient Monuments in Wales and Monmouthshire, joined me as a very valuable assistant. A large jointer's tent supplied ample shelter for meals, writing up notes, packing finds etc. and as we could not be quite sure how far the area might have to be explored we avoided possible time- and effort-wasting moving of dumps by barrowing all soil well clear of the site.

This was on chalk that was normally solid, but as the Wolds had been within the limits of the ice it could contain large fissures; pockets of rotted chalk which could be deceptively like pits dug by human agency and filled with fine rubble. A little experience showed that the material in these pits always seemed to be 'mouldy' when dug out, in contrast to normal chalk rubble not produced by pressure *in situ*.

We examined the barrow thoroughly inside and out, and cleared a major part of the ditch which was still very large on the upper side but was much reduced on the lower side where its outer edge had been much eroded by ploughing.

Everything suggested that essentially the barrow had been constructed as a 'house of the dead' in which outstanding leaders of the local Neolithic group could be buried, with the remains of some of their pre-deceased relatives whose bodies had been exposed and their bones duly collected as far as possible.

The group buried here amounted to eight in all: the complete crouched skeleton of a man verging on middle age whose bones showed evidence of great muscular activity, two females, presumably wives; and five other bodies, were represented by bones which had obviously been wrapped in individual packets from which many of the smaller bones were missing, a clear indication that these bodies had been exposed elsewhere. This burial deposit in the barrow was placed on a carefully laid rectangular pavement of chalk across the barrow 70 feet from the east end. On the centre line of the barrow on the right hand side of this pavement, as seen from the entrance to the burial area, there was an unexpected find, a natural more or less cubical boulder of a dull red stone. It is impossible to say what this signified to those who made the burial, but it was shown on examination to have its origin in the Melrose area of southern Scotland and it was a glacial erratic brought down to this part of the Wolds by the ice. No doubt this area was once well sprinkled with them and one such must have given its name to the Bluestone Heath, also in the South Wolds.

There was no sign of an actual or simulated entrance in the centre of the façade at the east end. Access to the burials had been from the upper side of the barrow and was blocked with large pieces of chalk as soon as, or soon after the burial deposit was in place.

The south-western broad end of the barrow had a façade made of split tree trunks set in a curved trench with the flat side facing outwards and at each of the two 'horns' of this façade it was completed by a full trunk. The ditch continued right round the barrow leaving a featureless space between it and the façade and at the smaller end of the barrow it did this again, leaving a still larger unencumbered area. But it was here on the upper side of this turn that the only causeway of undug chalk had been left standing to give access to the barrow enclosure.

On each side of the barrow mound there was a line of holes which carried 6 inch thick posts. These ran from the big posts at the ends of the façade to where they stopped without making junction with eight rather larger posts which had stood squarely across the small end. These side posts, 64 in number, were set in the berm on the inner side of the ditch and would have been good support for a wall of stout hurdles used to give the barrow vertical sides. The façade must have been similar. It is not clear why these posts along the barrow sides do not appear to have married with the eight across the small end to complete the rectangle. We wondered whether the eight posts had any reference to the eight individuals represented in the burials. The fact that the one causeway over the ditch gave access to this area at the end of the barrow and the space in front of the eight posts did nothing to diminish this speculation.

We also ran a trench down the centre line of the barrow from the burial area almost to the small end. We found that when the site of the barrow had been chosen and levelled the builders had erected a strong line of hurdles along the middle line and that, setting off from this at right angles at regular intervals, other hurdles ran out to the other line of postholes along the lower side of the barrow. The compartments thus produced were entirely filled with barrow material on the downhill side of the barrow. Was this a constructional device for giving the barrow greater stability along its downhill side? It would seem likely, as nothing similar was seen on the upper side of the centre line. An exactly similar feature has been observed in some Cotswold long barrows.

Although agriculture was practised successfully in Neolithic Britain it was also a pastoral society and so quite aware of the possibilities of hurdle work. There was none along the 70 feet of the centre line from the burials to the back of the façade, but half way along this stretch was a fair-sized pit, deliberately filled with a darkish soil which had also been heaped up above it and the heap was restrained on three sides by a much lighter type of wicker work which seemed to have no constructional importance. Careful examination in the laboratory showed that this earthy material contained evidence that it might be the sweepings from the hut floor. Had this been piously brought from the home of the deceased?

More sensational and better conducted excavations of long barrows have taken place since the work at Giants' Hills No. I was completed. As mentioned above, the plural nature of the name has been proved quite correct, for the 1825 edition of the Ordnance Survey 1 inch map of the area plainly shows another long barrow lower down the valley in the field below the barrow we excavated. On this map there is the name Giants' Hills to cover both. At some time after 1825 the lower barrow was levelled and the part of the field on which it had been was much whiter than the rest because the chalk from the mound had been spread. We were so pre-occupied with Giants' Hills No. I that we had no time for No. 2, whose site was to be examined for ditch, post-holes etc. a good many years later.

The second season at Skendleby was visited by a number of people influential in the archaeological world including O.G.S. Crawford, Miles Burkitt (secretary of the Archaeology Faculty Board at Cambridge), Stuart Piggott (fast becoming an authority on the Neolithic period in Britain), and Reginald Smith, Keeper of Prehistoric Antiquities at the British Museum.

In excavating this Lincolnshire long barrow I had wanted to find out if they had any obvious affinity with those which Canon Greenwell and J.R. Mortimer had excavated at various times on the Yorkshire Wolds. Instead of being burials by inhumation, the Yorkshire barrows excavated had puzzling features in that they had been used as more or less successful crematoria. Nothing even resembling this had been found at Giants' Hills but the only south country long barrow which had been excavated to date by reasonably scientific methods was the Dorset Wor Barrow examined by the famous pioneer, General Pitt-Rivers, on his own Cranborne Chase property. The Wessex chalk country extended a long finger into East Anglia via the Chilterns to the East Anglian Heights. There were a few barrows along this which had their most easterly surviving example on Therfield Heath where the quite low chalk hills overlook the valley of the Ashwell branch of the river Cam to the north. In 1935 I resolved to make a quick examination of this small example, which had already been opened by a man called Nunn some 90 years before. He ran a trench down the middle line of the barrow and all he found was a secondary inhumation of an Anglo-Saxon warrior, from which he removed an iron knife and a shield boss.

I found no wooden features in the untouched parts of this barrow and there was certainly no sign of a cremation. The Anglo-Saxon's spearhead was still in place in the edge of the trench by his head where Nunn had just missed it. The barrow had been used as a point for a change of direction by an Iron Age ditch system which showed no sign in the existing turf of the hill. It was altogether a very modest affair and with it I retired from any further activity in the long barrow excavation business.

By the mid-1930s I had become better known in the archaeological world. I lectured to the Society of Antiquaries on the Giants' Hills excavation, and the British Museum made and exhibited a model of the barrow showing its various features. Unfortunately this was later destroyed during the 1939–45 war when the Museum was damaged in an air raid.

In 1931 I had been nominated to the Council of the Royal Archaeological Institute, and in 1932 I became Treasurer of the interdisciplinary Fenland Research Committee. In February 1933 I was elected a Fellow of the Society of Antiquaries, in the same year I became a Fellow of Selwyn, and by 1935 I was to be a part-author of a revolution in the Prehistoric Society of East Anglia and become Hon. Secretary of the national Prehistoric Society conjured from its ashes.

I think that the purpose of Burkitt's journey down to Lincolnshire in the summer of 1934, to see what was afoot at Skendleby, was to enable him to judge how far the new people who were appearing at Cambridge such as Grahame Clark and myself could any longer be excluded from the official side of archaeology in the University. Not long after I returned to Cambridge in the autumn I was invited to join the Faculty Board of Archaeology and had an opportunity of judging for myself Professor Minns in action. He was habitually ready to suggest to Burkitt, as Secretary, that he should carry on the real business and this put Burkitt in a strong position to succeed him to the chair. But things did not work out as he had hoped. At this time Miss Dorothy Garrod was carrying out epoch-making excavations in the Palaeolithic field at Mount Carmel and elsewhere in the general Mediterranean area. Unexpectedly, she chose to stand as a candidate when Minns went, and she was appointed.

Little Bardfield Hall, Essex (C.W.P.'s forbears farmed here)

Mother: Mary Elizabeth Phillips (Boyle)

At the Trundle, 1930; centre, C.W.P. and O.G.S. Crawford. Second right, Stuart Piggott and on the right, Piggott's father.

The archaeologist and his work: Trundle 1930

Penmon, Anglesey, 1932

Pant y Saer, Anglesey, 1932

Jubilee Commemoration, Selwyn College, 1933 (C.W.P. at end of 3rd row)

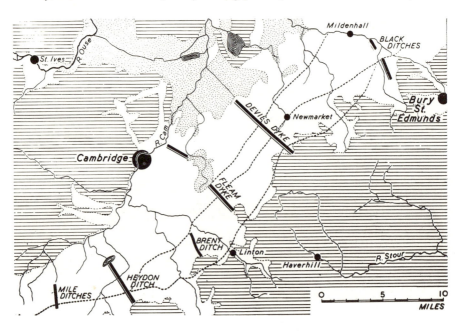

Early Saxon defensive dykes south of Cambridge

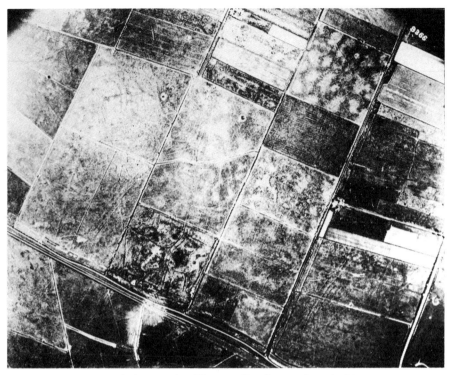

Aerial photograph of Romano-British sites, Lincolnshire

O.G.S. Crawford and Mortimer Wheeler, carrying a crocodile outside the hut at Maiden Castle, 1933 (note by Peggy Piggott: This crocodile was turned out of Dorchester museum by Col. Drew, and we buried it again with red ribbon round its neck and a coin in its mouth)

C.W.P. in the 1930s

Giants' Hills, Skendleby, 1933

Giants' Hills, Skendleby, 1933

Grahame Clark

Drinkthorn, Dorset, long barrow (see Proceedings of the Prehistoric Society, 1935–7)

Chapter 5

I have already mentioned the very important excavation carried out by Grahame Clark at Shippea Hill in June, 1931. But this was only one facet of the work which was now being directed at Fenland problems from the palaeo-botanical, geological and topographic angles, with air photography often an important factor in getting results. In all this, Harry Godwin and his wife Margaret, from the Botany School, strongly supported by Professor Sir Albert Seward, were extremely active and the triumphant results of pollen analysis, still in the flush of its earlier employment in Britain, were being celebrated. W.A. Macfadyen was probing the secrets of the silt, both in the large tract on either side of the major river outfall north of Wisbech and also in the matter of the composition of the roddons. It was possible to study different degrees of salinity in marine deposits by listing the number of different forms of the minute *foramenifera* found in them. It became apparent that the roddons were the beds of the old natural watercourses which carried the land waters of the whole of the Great Ouse Valley and the valleys of all the lesser rivers which had to make their way through the undrained peat to the sea. Their lower courses, sluggish through the peat, had been subject to daily tidal influence almost as far inland as the beginning of the higher land. This meant that twice each day a considerable amount of sea water carrying silt into their beds dropped its burden in the stillness of high water. When the tide went out again, only a proportion of the silt brought in was carried away, and so these rivers flowed through peat and on silt. When at last the peat began to diminish through drainage works, the silt could not shrink and keep pace with the shrinking peat. The result was that gradually these silt river beds began to stand more and more conspicuously from the peat, and the process was well advanced by the time it was investigated. Going round the Fens, one could observe notable demonstrations of what could happen in a comparatively short time. A line of three or four cottages could have been built partly on the peat at right angles to the river bed while the peat was still level with it. This meant that as the peat went down, one cottage would remain anchored on the bank while the others sloped down from it on to the peat, and if the row had been of one continuous build there was grave trouble where the line of cottages sagged. Where the roddon was very wide, as in the case of the Well Stream, which originally carried a great volume of the land waters past Ely and Littleport across to Wisbech and the outfall, long straggling communities like the villages of Upwell and Outwell have grown along its dry edge.

There is one straight stretch of roddon in the March area, and the main Roman road across the north of East Anglia between Ermine Street and *Durobrivae* runs along its edge for the whole of its length.

Working out from Cambridge, several of us visited the numerous Roman-period

farmstead sites and their connecting droveways which were sometimes characteris-
tically straight, but what we did not find time for at this stage was a complete excavation
of one of these farmsteads. What we did was to form an interdisciplinary body called the
Fenland Research Committee at Cambridge on June 7, 1932, under the chairmanship
of Sir Albert Seward. Annual dinners and meetings continued till the outbreak of war
in 1939. Membership was not confined to those concerned with purely Fenland
problems, and there were representatives on it of those concerned with allied problems
on the Essex coast (Mr Hazzledine Warren) and also a newly-formed Norfolk Research
Committee under the leadership of Roy Rainbird Clark, a young Cambridge graduate
now at the Norwich Museum and a native of the county. The Committee had no
publication of its own but a large number of papers proceeded from its members in a
variety of learned journals. There is reason to believe that this was the first example, in
this country at least, of an interdisciplinary body of this kind. The frequent interchange
of views which took place was a powerful solvent of difficult problems.

There was one diverting episode connected with Fenland research which occurred in
the 1930s. A wealthy young American, heir to the riches of the famous Anaconda
copper mine, had become interested in the old story of King John's loss of the Crown
Jewels in the Wash and thought that he might profitably lay out some of his money in
an attempt to recover those jewels. I think he was a simple soul, and he was certainly
duped by one or two aristocratic but shady characters ready to exploit him and aware of
the Fenland Research Committee.

The facts about the last months of the life of King John are that after consenting to
the great Magna Carta agreement he soon repudiated it and, being quite an able and
vigorous soldier, made a great plundering raid into East Anglia against some leading
enemies in the baronial party, during the course of which he not only seized much
valuable property and treasure from castles and noble residences but also did not spare
some wealthy monastic houses. By the time he decided to move into the Midlands he
had accumulated a heavy baggage train, though this did not in fact contain the Crown
Jewels, which had been in pawn for some time.

He wished to take the shortest route out of Norfolk by King's Lynn and cross into
Lincolnshire by the regular ford over the Well Stream estuary north of Wisbech. This
estuary, today a quite minor and canalised affair, was then a wide tidal outfall
discharging the greater part of the higher lands round the Fens and in particular the
waters of the Great Ouse and the Nene. Today the actual site of John's proposed
crossing lies under reclaimed and cultivated land at about the point where Sutton
Bridge now is on the road from King's Lynn to Spalding.

On the crucial day, John seems to have crossed first as soon as the state of the tide
allowed riders to get through and pushed on some twenty miles to lodge at Swineshead
Abbey, leaving the baggage train to follow. In effect, it began its crossing too late after
extreme low tide and some of the carts at the end of the train had to be abandoned to
the returning tide while their drivers loosed the horses and rode to safety. The
American's advisers claimed that when the tide turned, the sands became quicksands
and so would engulf the abandoned carts which tradition holds contained the Crown
Jewels and the loot of East Anglia. When the tide retreated once more, they thought
that the abandoned carts would have sunk out of sight in quicksands and could still be
recovered with their contents if they could be located.

Members of the Fenland Research Committee were invited to give their opinion and the Geological Survey which was experimenting with metal detectors was also contacted. Local men said that there were no quicksands today and that the basic conditions were not likely to have been different in the thirteenth century. The probable truth was that the carts had stuck because of their heavy burdens and were not sunk and therefore were almost certainly recovered at low tide next day. The whirlwind character of John's campaign against his enemies in East Anglia must have exhausted even him, and his death at Swineshead Abbey shortly after the Wash mishap, popularly attributed to the effect of the news of his loss, is not surprising.

There were many arguments whether, even if they had sunk in quicksands, the plunder in the carts, which probably included a lot of silver and gold plate, would long have survived in those saline conditions, to be found in any shape to be worth recovery after seven centuries had passed.

The whole affair ended rather farcically in a court case in the autumn of 1933, in which the American claimed the repayment of the considerable sums he had spent in lavish entertaining, setting up a formal office in Wisbech, and paying travel and other expenses for a number of people, some of them quite well known persons whose advice he had sought. Even the Geological Survey was not spared.

I am glad to say that those people who were really knowledgeable about Fenland affairs like Fowler, Godwin, Macfadyen and Sir Albert Seward, had never given the man any encouragement, but before the case was dismissed by the Court a number of people like Bradfer-Lawrence and Mortimer Wheeler had been made to look rather foolish.

I must now consider another important development in East Anglian and national archaeological affairs which took place in the mid-1930s. Back in September 1930, Grahame Clark had induced me to become a member of the Prehistoric Society of East Anglia. This was a group which had formed in 1906 round some prominent East Anglian personalities, foremost among whom were J. Reid Moir of Ipswich, J.E. Sainty, A. Leslie Armstrong and others, all of whom tended to regard the term 'Prehistoric' in its French rather than its English sense. There were those among them like the active East Anglian journalist, father of the R. Rainbird Clark already mentioned above, and others who were not above concerning themselves with the discovery of Anglo-Saxon cemeteries, but the dominating J. Reid Moir was utterly absorbed in the question of the antiquity of Man in the region. It was true that the late eighteenth century observations of John Frere at Hoxne in Suffolk on the nature of crude flint tools, in fact handaxes, found there, were a notable event in the recognition of the great antiquity of Man. But Moir, who was a good bespoke tailor in Ipswich, was rash enough to claim that he had flint implements of human manufacture from below the Red Crag formation in East Anglia, a claim that reputable geologists were bound to contest. Of course the society contained much more careful amateur workers in this field, like S. Hazzledine Warren, but Moir was irrepressible. He had a strangely magnetic personality, and in spite of the fierce controversies that his various claims raised in the Society, he managed to impress himself so much on the scientist, Lord Rayleigh, that he was elected to the Royal Society's Fellowship. As may be imagined, this did little to reduce his belligerence and self confidence.

The Hon. Secretary of the Society was Mr Guy Maynard, Director of the Ipswich Museum. He was not a strong personality and, as Reid Moir was the chairman of the Museum Committee, he was in no position to oppose him. The membership of the Society had been originally almost exclusively from East Anglia and meetings had been held alternately in Ipswich and Norwich, but after 1930 the number of members from outside the area had risen to a point where it became necessary to hold meetings in London on Wednesday afternoons when the Great Eastern Railway offered cheap day tickets.

Among the 'foreign' members there were now a number of the rising generation of new enthusiasts who wanted to see the Society widened and its affairs no longer held up to ridicule by some of the barren controversies about the antiquity of Man which disfigured its proceedings. Professor Gordon Childe was President in 1935 and, in the Council of eight, three – W.F. Grimes, Stuart Piggott and Dr. J.F.S. Stone – were leading advocates of change, with C.F.C. Hawkes of the British Museum, and Grahame Clark and myself active among the rank and file. Even in 1934 the general opinion had already been in favour of giving the Society full coverage of prehistory and aiming at national rather than local status.

When the matter was brought forward again in 1933 there was a surprising, but typically wrongheaded estimate of the situation by Gordon Childe, who prophesied the collapse of the Society because of the hurt feelings of typical 'old East Anglians'. These were figments of the Professor's imagination and a general meeting at Norwich on February 23, 1935 decided that the matter should be put to a postal vote.

When this poll was declared it was overwhelmingly in favour of change and the number of resignations was negligible. Grahame Clark was at once voted into the Editorship of the *Proceedings*. In 1936 the reform movement went further, given confidence by the fact that 156 new members had joined. A clean sweep was made of the Hon. Secretary and the Hon. Treasurer, both officials of Ipswich Museum, and I became Hon. Secretary, with E.M.M. Alexander of the British Museum as Hon. Treasurer. It was not long before it became obvious that the printers employed by the old Society would not be equal to the requirements of the new *Proceedings* and the work was transferred to Messrs. Bellows of Gloucester, the printers of *Antiquity*. At the last Annual General Meeting held before the outbreak of war in 1939 the number of members stood at 756, a 100 per cent increase on what it had been in 1935, a sufficient justification, if any was required, for the action which had been taken.

1935 was a momentous year for the archaeology of East Anglia, because in the August and September of that year Grahame Clark and I were able to confirm by excavation the existence of the first 'henge' monument to be found in that part of England. The growth of interest in these monuments had been stimulated when Wing Commander Insall V.C. observed and photographed from the air the first 'Woodhenge' a few miles north-east of Stonehenge. This was later excavated by Mr and Mrs B.H. Cunnington and shown to have an oval setting of wooden posts. In 1929 Insall had another success when he observed and photographed what appeared to be a smaller wooden monument of this type at Arminghall, on the southern outskirts of Norwich. It proved to be a setting of nine full-sized oak trunks in a ring whose butts had been carefully charred to inhibit decay in the ground and they were of a size and weight which necessitated their having been chosen and prepared on the adjacent slope to the south before being brought down to the site and introduced to the holes which had been sloped out on one side to receive them. In their turn they were surrounded by a low bank with an internal ditch. The only material found was Beaker pottery from fragments belonging to the Early Bronze Age and the site was more or less contemporaneous with the larger and more complex 'Woodhenge' in Wiltshire.

I have already said that once we entered the 1930s our generation of young aspirants to success in archaeology began to make some contacts outside Great Britain. My first foreign contact was with Professor A. van Giffen of the University of Groningen in the thick of the 'terp' country of North Holland, where Iron Age and later pastoral folk were living on marginal lands close to the sea where high tides could create temporary inundations. These early Batavian folk improved this situation as cattle-keepers by throwing up an initial low mound on which to live and constantly raising the height of this by the accumulated stable litter and manure of their animals. Many of the existing modern villages, sometimes quite large ones, were standing on the results of enormous accumulations over centuries, and there were many lesser, unoccupied sites scattered about which modern farmers dug into for the concentrated manure they contained. The Dutch State was also removing many terps for application to enrich the meagre sandy soils inland. Many farmers had small museums of objects, chiefly of bone, which they had found in the terps on their land and the study of the whole phenomenon was centred on Groningen.

I went over there at van Giffen's invitation to see if there was any analogy between our Fenland sites and the terps, but although they were contemporary and much concerned with cattle-raising the likeness ended there.

In 1932 the series of International Conferences on Prehistoric and Proto-historic studies which had formerly been held every four years and had been disrupted by the war was resumed at London from 1–10 August, with study tours to various regions, including Wessex and East Anglia. On the whole it was favoured with very good weather and the main meetings were held at King's College in the Strand. There was a large contingent of foreign archaeologists, and T.D. Kendrick of the British Museum distinguished himself in his conduct of the proceedings.

It was here that we also had a fine example of how the conduct of British archaeology was not invariably in reliable hands. The post-1920 rise of a much stricter form of professionalism in the British field left some of the older practitioners behind. A notable figure of this kind was A. Leslie Armstrong, a surveyor in the Land Registry, who had built up a reputation for himself in various cave excavations, notably at Cresswell Crags in Nottinghamshire. He claimed to have found some examples of a crude cave art, but an unpleasant rumour of falsification attached to this and other of his activities.

At the 1932 Conference he offered a paper on certain flint points of a novel type which he had found on a sandy site at Sheffield's Hill near Scunthorpe. He suggested that these were Upper Palaeolithic in date. At question time after he had ended his paper Grahame Clark got up to discuss them. He was now well on his way to publishing his first book on the Mesolithic period in Britain and in preparing it he had widened his researches into Europe and became aware of a range of larger blade products of Mesolithic industry which, having first been recognised at Kunda in

Esthonia, were known as Kunda points. He mentioned these and gave it as his opinion that Armstrong's points from Sheffield's Hill were identical.

The session ended and we moved out into the lobby to stretch our legs and Clark and I stood talking a little apart from the main throng. Suddenly Armstrong, livid with rage, moved over towards us. Clark certainly did not have the look of a senior in 1932 but this did not justify Armstrong coming over and addressing him as 'You impudent puppy!'. We were taken aback and could only look at him in silence. He was a troublesome man and finally withdrew to South Africa, where he had a married daughter, and died there.

The Conference was generally voted to be a great success. I took an active part in helping to guide the East Anglian study tour after the Conference was finished in London, and was able to demonstrate such important sites as the Devil's Dyke on Newmarket Heath and the prehistoric flint mines at Grimes Graves in the Breckland. The only trouble was the wretched lunch served at the Great White Horse Hotel in Ipswich.

The Wessex study tour also had its minor tribulations. The congressists did not hesitate to sit themselves down on the turf during visits to such sites as Stonehenge. Unfortunately, this was in the latter half of August, not a prudent time at which to sit on downland sward on the chalk. Those who had done so soon began to feel uneasy because of an unaccountable skin irritation which set in on their legs and around their middles. Complaints were made that the hotels at which they were put up for the night must be bug-infested. The party were infested indeed, but it was by the notorious harvest-bug, a minute red creature which has its short life on the chalk at this time of the year.

Four years passed away and the next of these Conferences was held at the same time of the year at Oslo. My own private circumstances had changed for the better now and I travelled by boat to Esbjerg in Denmark and went straight on to Copenhagen, where I spent a few days charmed by the beautiful city and in particular by Tivoli. I then went on by train to Elsinore, crossed over to Halsingborg, and then continued up the west coast of Sweden via Goteborg and the Trollhattan Falls to the Norwegian border at Halden and so past Sarpsborg and the Glomma round the head of the Oslo Fjord to the scene of the Conference.

I put up at a rather expensive hotel in Karl Johan Gatan, the main street of Oslo, and lost no time in going up the Holmenkollen rack-and-pinion line to get the splendid view over the whole of the Oslo Fjord. We had two important visits during the week in Oslo. The first was to the splendid ship museum which contains the famous Viking burial ships from Gokstad and Oseberg. The second was a trip down the west side of the Oslo Fjord to Sandefjord at its mouth, the headquarters of the even then declining whale fishery. More important were visits to the actual site of the ship burial at Gokstad and the barrow graves of the Ynglinger kings. A pleasantly informal occasion was a reception given by King Haakon and Queen Maud, a sister of King George V.

The second part of the Conference was to be centred at Bergen and we went by coach to see the famous stave church at Borgund, a completely preserved and regularly used wooden church from the Middle Ages reproducing accurately the plan and the elevation of the Scandinavian pagan temple. It was here that the church was naturally plastered with pleas to visitors not to smoke or strike matches and one of our fellow congressists, to whom I shall have occasion to refer later, gave mortal offence by categorically refusing either to put out his cigarette or to leave the church till he had finished it.

After Borgund we crossed the upland waste of the Hardanger Vidda and arrived at the head of the Sogne Fjord. We transferred to a steamer here and went across the northern arm of the fjord to land at Urnes and see the beautiful low-relief carving on the outer wooden wall of the church which has given its name to the Urnes style of decoration.

We then went for a trip down the Fjord towards the open sea, far enough to appreciate its almost overwhelming scenic magnificence, with its cliffs over a thousand feet high and the streams coming over the ice verges in force and dissolving into mist long before the water could reach the surface of the Fjord below.

We turned back up the fjord and went up a side arm to Stalheim, where we faced the most nearly vertical hill climb I have ever made in powerful old American cars. One had to shut one's eyes during the climb which took us from the landing stage to the Stalheim hotel some hundreds of feet above and, after restoring nature there, we were driven down a more easy road to the station at Flam on the Oslo-Bergen railway. Here we took the train and ran down to sea level again at Bergen. Three memories besides rain come to mind at Bergen. The first is raw fish sandwiches, the second a visit to the ancient Hanseatic trading depot known as the Tyskebryggen down on the water front, a very smelly warren of wooden passage ways and small claustrophobic rooms in which the Hanseatic staff were compelled to live under conditions of virtual imprisonment. The third was a drive with several others to visit the now aged Haakon Shetelig, the excavator of the Gokstad ship, at his home further down the Bergen fjord. It was a fine day and he received us in his garden where he plied us with whisky while we looked across the fjord to the white mass of the Folgefonn glacier which today, alas, is much diminished, in common with the other snowfields of Scandinavia.

I do not recall that anything memorable was said, but since then I have been unable to avoid reflecting that this was a particularly interesting occasion for me in view of what was to happen in Suffolk only three years later.

It was at Bergen that I made the acquaintance of Professor Gudmund Hatt and his wife. He was Professor of Geography at the University of Copenhagen and was particularly interested in the history of Jutland. The Conference came to its formal end at Bergen and Hatt proposed that we should take the boat for Stavanger, a night run with a stop at Haugesund in the early morning.

We put up at a small hotel near the harbour at Stavanger and Hatt's objective was to inspect a number of the recently excavated Viking farm sites which were fairly frequent in this province of Rogaland. We hired a driver and were taken round to a number of them, which were all longhouses of the same type as the 'blackhouses' which were still used in Highland Scotland and the Islands till about a century ago. We also saw the place where the two sides of a deep glacial valley had fallen in and overwhelmed a village with all its inhabitants in the Middle Ages. This kind of disaster peculiar to Norway is known as an 'urr'. The example we saw was composed of great tumbled blocks, many of which were as large as, and sometimes a good deal larger than, a fair-sized house. In the example that we saw the site had not been abandoned, but the church and various dwellings had been set in at any point where the development of soil and vegetation made a large enough level space. The road made a very tortuous course over this vast obstacle.

I was not entirely sorry to leave Stavanger because, although it had a good museum and a cathedral showing strong medieval English influence, the weather was wet, the whole place reeked of the fish-oil manufactory, and the only resource in the hotel was a complete set of bound copies of the *London Illustrated News*.

I had to catch the boat back to England on a certain day at Esbjerg and it was time for the Hatts to return to their home at Middelfart. We decided to be bold and make our way overland round the rugged coast to Christiansand, whence we would take a boat over to Frederikshavn at the north end of Jutland. From there it would be a direct drive by taxi to our destinations, which were not far apart.

But how to get to Christiansand? There was an inland route but it was bad and involved some very difficult hills. Recently, road work had been carrying the projected coastal route past Egersund, but no one seemed to know how much further. We made a rather typical bargain with a young Stavanger man who had a sound car. He agreed to drive us to Christiansand if we would pay for all petrol and oil out and back to Stavanger. He did not ask for overnight subsistence because he intended to turn straight back and return to Stavanger after he had filled up with petrol in Christiansand. I was told that this type was not in any way unusual locally; they were unemployed, often of good family, did not want to go into the family business and in an earlier age they would certainly have been active among those who went as Viking raiders and settlers in foreign places.

So we set off early and made easy running to Egersund, but after that we found the road only half-made and often not better than bare rock. We got on to Flekkefjord, which would normally have been the limit,for not more than ten miles ahead lay the small but very deep-set Jessing Fjord, which had plenty of water communication out of its narrow mouth with the outer world for its titanium, but none by land.

We pushed on in hope and when, after some painful miles, we came to the lip of the fjord we found that the road construction people had cut a tunnel in the side of the fjord with a steepish slope and an exit to the flat ground at the head of the fjord at the bottom. Its surface was mostly bare rock, just as the tunnelers had left it, and it was lit by a series of apertures cut in the cliff sides. At the head of the fjord there were sheds, a loading stage and the end of a ropeway running up into the hinterland where the valuable titanium mine was situated. What about the other side of the fjord? Would our luck hold? It did, and we found another tunnel like the one we had come down leading up to the other rim.

Within little more than three years this extremely isolated spot made the headlines. After the outbreak of war and the German occupation of Norway a German commerce raider, having sunk two British ships and captured their crews, took refuge in this fjord not thinking that H.M.S. Cossack would dare the feat of navigation involved in following him in. In this he was mistaken and with great skill H.M.S. Cossack was taken in, the two crews were rescued, the raider was sunk, the installations were destroyed and the Cossack backed out again safely.

Having struggled up the second tunnel the worst of our troubles were over; the road was now a tolerable track, which improved as we went on and the appearance of the enormously lofty chimney of the smelter which then disfigured the port of Christian-sand showed that we were nearing our destination. On arrival, we wasted no time but made for the Frederikshavn boat which was due to leave soon. We said goodbye to our driver and thanked him, had some supper and turned in. When I woke next morning we must have been most of the way across the Skagerrak; we were proceeding slowly in a dense fog with our siren sounding and others answering as we crossed the busy sea lane. The fog lifted as we breakfasted with the captain, who interested me in some splendid prawns; we landed at Frederikshavn, made a bargain with a taxi man and were off again down Jutland as fast as we could go, crossing the Lim Fjord at Aalborg and on to Viborg, where we paused to visit the cathedral. From there we turned west to Holstebro and then went directly south through Varde to Esbjerg, where I said goodbye to the Hatts and caught the mid-afternoon boat for Harwich with little time to spare. The Hatts continued along the 30 kilometres home to Middelfart by the Little Belt Bridge.

During the Conference, we English folk were startled to find that Agatha Christie, the thriller writer, her daughter by her first husband, and her second husband, Max Mallowan, a rising Middle East archaeologist, were members of our company. Shortly before we left England for Oslo, Agatha Christie had caused a sensation by disappearing but here she was again, a comfortable-looking lady whose behaviour was impeccable. Quite other was the man who would not put his cigarette out at the wooden stave church at Borgund. This man was the Dutch anthropologist, van-Stein Callenfels. He was a tall, stout, heavily-bearded man who stood out all the more clearly from any assemblage because at this time beards were not in fashion. He was in the employ of the Dutch Government in the East Indies and was one of the most offensively rude men I have ever met. Rumour had it that when he was in the East Indies he ate a rijs-tafel meal every day. In the East Indies I believe that this meal is a weekly rather than a daily event. Having partaken of it more than once when I have been staying in Holland with friends with East Indian experience, I can only say that such a practice would be physically disastrous, if not impossible. During the Oslo Conference he was guilty of such a degree of boorishness and insensitivity to the welfare of others that his sanity seemed to be in doubt. Some years later, after the end of the 1939–45 war, I heard that he had not been seen alive since the Japanese invaded the East Indies.

The Oslo Conference was now over and it had been a very broadening experience. I had got to know Gudmund Hatt and had received a warm invitation to return to Denmark in 1937 to see some of his excavations of Iron Age farmsteads on the heaths of North Jutland, classic ground because a Danish schoolmaster had drawn attention to these at the beginning of the nineteenth century, observations parallel with those of Sir Richard Colt Hoare among the Celtic fields of Wiltshire. Nearly a century had passed before these phenomena received serious attention, and then only with the aid of air-photography.

Crossing the North Sea I had an unexpected experience when I had to share my cabin with an American. There was nothing remarkable in that, but it was when we got into conversation that the surprise came. In searching around for a subject of common interest I referred to some of the impressions I had formed during my recent trip round North America in 1931. Franklin D. Roosevelt was now in the White

House and had applied remedies to the sick society of the United States with admirable effect. My cabin mate was by his own account the owner of a cinema somewhere in New England and he reacted with quite alarming vigour to my remarks, answering that Roosevelt was a national disaster and fast undermining the 'American way of life.' I did not want to start a violent argument and so fell silent, and having had a rather exhausting time since leaving Stavanger, turned in and slept. When I woke up next morning he had already packed up and gone and I did not see him again.

Grahame Clarke had not been at the Oslo Conference and in pursuit of his studies of the early Mesolithic culture he was anxious to make contact with a German worker named Alfred Rust, who was excavating some interesting hunter-fisher sites along the line of small lakes and swamps on the site of the well-known glacial 'tunnel-thal' which stretches north-westwards from the Hamburg region.

I now had a Ford V8 car; Grahame had married Mollie White and the three of us set off for Harwich and crossed with the car to Esbjerg. We arrived too late to get any further than the small cathedral town of Ribe, a little way down the coast, but on the next day we resumed our drive southwards towards Schleswig across the German frontier.

Here I should mention that in the summer of 1933 the Nazi movement had triumphed in Germany and by 1937 Schleswig-Flensburg and the adjacent parts of Denmark were sensitive areas and there was already a movement fostered from Germany to secure the transfer of the Tonder district of Denmark, if not more, to German sovereignty.

While at Schleswig there were three great objectives for us, first the Schleswig Museum under the direction of the amiable old Gustav Schwantes, housing the marvellously preserved fourth century boat from the great votive deposit at Nydam in the island at Als. Second, the remains of the Dannewerk, the great Dark Age and Medieval work of varied construction shutting off Jutland from the European mainland and, thirdly, the excavation then in progress of the fortified terminal of the Dannewerk on the bank of the Schleswig fjord. This work was under the direction of Herbert Jankuhn, a man of our own generation. He was showing that the powerful earthwork with half-moon plan, known as Haithabu or Heddeby, with which the Dannewerk met the fjord was indeed one of the major trading posts of the post-Roman period in Northern Europe on a par with Birka, Novgorod and Birkestad and in the British Isles York, Dublin and possibly Thetford.

We spent three days at this intensely interesting site, amid beautiful autumn sunshine and with all the local hedges filled with the tender pink of the spindle berry. Then Schwantes guided us to Alfred Rust's site among swamps and little lakes, teeming with a large population of frogs, newts, snakes and all kinds of water fowl.

Rust was a remarkable man, also of our own generation, who had come of age not long after the end of the 1914–18 war with a burning desire to become an archaeologist, but with no hope of going to a university because of an almost total lack of resources except determination. Trusting that there would be excavations in the Near East to which he could attach himself and so learn the trade, he made the heroic resolve to ride his bicycle to Palestine if necessary. This he did and, although I do not know the details about how he fared, eventually he came through the whole experience with a Ph.D. to show for it. Now, as a fervent anti-Nazi, a sentiment which he shared with Schwantes, he was hoping but scarcely expecting to avoid trouble. He must have succeeded, for as late as 1981 he was living at Ahrensburg on the north-west side of Hamburg with the title of Professor. Clark had a valuable confabulation with Rust, while I contented myself with observing the life of this unspoiled habitat.

Schwantes went back to Schleswig, but not before he had answered another question about the aspect of this region. Of course, most of it was normal farm land in cultivation but I could not help noticing the discrepancy between the up-to-date farming methods being used and the very decrepit state of the farmhouses. Schwantes told me that there was a smoked sausage greatly esteemed in that part of Germany whose distinctive taste was produced by long suspension under the smoky roofs of these old, heavily-thatched buildings. Various other means had been tried in an attempt to increase the supply, but to no avail. Thus many of the farmers of the Schleswig Holstein area drew a regular revenue from this source.

We next went on to the old Hanseatic city of Lübeck, a very beautiful place with its two great churches, its Hospital of the Holy Ghost, Holstentor and many streets of tall narrow-fronted houses. Besides being famous for its marzipan confectionery, it also contained dairy and cheese shops which I am sure were quite hygenic but which gave forth an appalling stench and I wondered how anyone could be found to work in them or in the shops on either side. During our short stay I was always glad to have got past the Rostocker Butterhandel.

The famous Hospital, seen at a distance, looked like the nave of a great church with no tower but a large crenellated front on the street like a galilee. This contained a chapel on one side of the entrance and on the other a large covered area where the inmates could sit and gossip while watching what was going on in the street. Inside the main building the entire floor of the great barn-like structure was divided down the middle by a wide walk with individual rooms for old men on one side and for old women on the other. There was no immediate roof to the lodgings and there was a great space above up to the roof. Some years later I went over the great medieval hospital more specifically built for the sick at Beaune in Burgundy, an even more splendid establishment. Another example, much smaller but similar in detail, survives nearer home at St. Mary's Hospital, Chichester.

It did not seem that the Nazi cult had caught on very strongly yet in Lübeck. When at the railway station there I inspected the book stall, where the usual Ludendorff ravings were on offer without a visible buyer but, more surprisingly, there was also a great heap of copies of *Der Streicher* emanating from the villainous Bavarian of that name. This copy was full of the most scurrilous matter and, in particular, a vicious attack on President Roosevelt. I decided to purchase one to show to my colleagues at Selwyn. I got a queer look from the book stallkeeper as I did so. Back in Cambridge I later left it on the Combination Room table where, so far as I could judge, it was no alarm bell ringing in the night.

We had now to return to Denmark to see Hatt's work in Jutland and we made our way across through Plon to Kiel to spend one night there. During the afternoon Clark and I hired a boat and rowed round the harbour. Kiel was once more a naval base and we saw a new battleship which looked interesting. We proceeded to row round it and found that it was the *Scharnhorst*. We continued in a leisurely manner, while ratings leaning over the rail idly watched us. This was rather extraordinary, for one would have expected that such a proceeding would be instantly stopped, but we completed our circuit and went back to our hotel. In only four years' time both of us would be in the R.A.F. and at the Central Air-photographic Unit at Medmenham, where every move of this ship was followed with the greatest care and particularly during her long period at Brest, till she was finally sunk in a desperate night action near the North Cape while trying to attack a Murmansk convoy in December, 1943.

We went through Eckernforde to Schleswig and then north to Flensburg where we crossed the frontier into Denmark at Kupfermuhle. There the German frontier officials were the least civil that we had met with and the office was dominated by a huge glaring portrait of the Führer. We continued directly north to Kolding and then turned east the short distance to Middelfart, close by the Fyn end of the Little Belt Bridge. Here the Hatts had their country retreat. They were an odd couple. He was a bluff and downright person sprung from peasant stock. In his early days he had spent some time excavating Carib sites in the Danish West Indies; he was reckoned to be a good geographer with a special interest in ecology.

Fru Hatt was a marked contrast to her spouse. She enjoyed quite a reputation in Denmark as an artist and illustrator with an Arthur Rackhamish style, sometimes quite macabre and sinister in her effects. Some credited her with occult powers. Whatever the truth might be, I found her an interesting companion. The Hatts had no children but they seemed to be an united and well-matched couple. They shared a love of living things and here again I could share their taste for the humbler forms. In their garden there was a pond well stocked with frogs, newts, water snails and other aquatic creatures. When excavating out on the heaths they also had a tender spot for a small type of toad peculiar to that terrain. Much of the work consisted of finding and emptying postholes, evidence of the former farm buildings. At night the toads had a habit of invading the sites and falling into the holes, so that one of the first duties of the day was to remove them on compassionate grounds.

Hatt's interest in ecology had stimulated an intensive study of what proved to be Iron Age agriculture on the heaths of North Jutland, the area known as Himmerland. He had come to the conclusion that various climatic changes and other similar factors had compelled these folk to abandon their land as unprofitable and move off southwards in search of more favourable territory, thus setting in motion that great chain reaction which caused the massive Gallic intrusion into North Italy and as far as Asia Minor, a movement which threatened the existence of the rising Roman Republic and was stemmed only by the crushing victories of Marius.

These Himmerland features were the same signs of ancient agriculture that had attracted the attention of the early nineteenth century schoolmaster, but no one gave them any more thought until Hatt took the matter up. We examined a number of sites, some under excavation, and in the course of this we drove freely about on the heath and I was not sufficiently aware of the occasional small boulder lurking in the heather. One of these damaged our brake controls and I rashly thought that I had got them repaired efficiently.

Before we went off on our own we also paid a visit to the Lim Fjord, the long stretch of water between the Baltic and the North Sea, which cuts off Vendyssel, the northernmost part of Jutland, from the mainland. We wanted to see one of the surviving kitchen middens, vast accumulations of *Littorina* shells, the remains of meals of strand-dwelling folk which provide an index for the differing relations between land and sea as the last great ice sheet melted. They were once a common feature of the Danish coastal areas, but in the nineteenth century it was realised that they had commercial value, when crushed as a manure and so were removed wholesale.

We said goodbye to the Hatts and made our way up the east side of Jutland. At Horsens we visited the home of an aspiring young archaeologist who had visited us at Cambridge. His father was a veterinary surgeon and had served with the Boers as a volunteer in the South African War. Later, young Christiansen was to make a name for himself as an expert on the archaeology of the Eskimos. We also visited the valley of the Gudenaa river which falls into the Baltic near Randers, walking the fields to look for fine specimens of flint work. It was at Randers that our luck deserted us.

We decided to make a run up to the Skaw and back, but when we were only a couple of miles out of Randers we had a heavy collision with a large farm lorry which pulled out suddenly from a farm entrance without taking the obligatory legal precaution of having someone to signal it out. Incredibly I was only shaken, but there were no seat belts in those days and both Clark and his wife were slightly concussed and a small bone in one of Grahame's feet was broken. An ambulance was quickly on the scene and fortunately there was more than one witness to the accident, but the car was badly damaged and I suspect that the brake which had been damaged recently had not been adequately repaired. The Clarks were both in hospital for three weeks and when I knew they were on the mend, I went home, followed by the damaged car which was set to rights by the Ford depot at Ipswich. I had all the necessary assurance and when the case came up before the court at Randers I was fined £2 for having exceeded the speed limit, then 20 miles per hour in Denmark and generally ignored, and the lorry driver had to pay rather more. It was an unfortunate end to an otherwise rewarding journey.

We never saw Hatt or his wife again and I am sorry to say that his career had a sad ending. While I got on with him well, I had noticed more than once in conversation that he had some peculiar geo-political notions not entirely hostile to the idea that Denmark ought really to be part of Germany. I heard about a political group at Randers which seemed to be tainted with this sort of notion, though I never heard that he had any connection with it. When Denmark was taken over by the Nazis in 1940 it seems that Hatt was not entirely unprepared to co-operate with them and gave some lectures which gravely offended Danish patriots. I have never been able to get an entirely clear picture of what happened, but he certainly lost his Chair of Geography in 1945, although I do not think his pension was withdrawn. All I do know is that he did not live long after the war and I have heard no more about Fru Hatt.

Chapter 6

In the mid-1930s the Victoria County History of England began the preparation of Volume I of the Cambridgeshire series. This was an organisation comparable in many respects, not least in the slowness of its progress, with that of the three Royal Commissions on Ancient and Historic Monuments in England, Wales, and Scotland.

They were already having to contemplate the drastic revision and supplementing of many of their earlier volumes because of the progress of knowledge over the years, but such is the fate of large enterprises of this kind. In each county Volume I was concerned about the basic facts relating to the tract of country involved which included sections on various aspects of its archaeology. I was now asked to contribute a section on the ancient earthworks of Cambridgeshire. This would involve prehistoric defensive works, linear earthworks and medieval sites, including the earthworks of castles, and also the many homestead motes common in East Anglia.

Among the hill forts only three were readily recognisable: Wandlebury and Arbury Banks along the general line of the East Anglian Heights, and Ring Hill in the upper valley of the Cam near Saffron Walden. Air photography and chalk digging have revealed several other minor examples, one of which, Cherry Hinton Hill, showed plain signs that it had been destroyed by an enemy before it had been completed, a situation found in other parts of England. A small multi-vallate site had been ploughed out at Hoy's Farm just north-west of Royston and has not been further examined. On Limlow Hill, about a mile south-west of Hoy's Farm, an air photograph showed what looked like a minor circumvallation of the summit which Grahame Clark and I proved by excavation to be no more than the first marking-out ditch of a large work which was not proceeded with.

An important feature of this area which had to be carefully examined and assessed was the system of great linear defences successively barring the Icknield Way on its route into Suffolk. Four of these lie within the limits of the county. The first, the Heydon Ditch, runs in a straight line three miles long from Heydon on the crest of the East Anglian Heights down to rest its lower end on the swampy ground near Fowlmere. Moving eastwards over the line of the river Cam there is then the much degraded mile and a half of the Brent Ditch between Abington Park and the present site of Pampisford Hall. Continuing another three and a half miles brings us to the formidable and well-preserved Fleam Dyke which has two sections, the first from near Balsham up in the hills down to the edge of Fulbourn Fen and the second, shorter and less well preserved, from the other side of the Fen to meet the Cam at Fen Ditton. Finally, there is the powerfully impressive Devil's Ditch covering the western edge of Newmarket Heath in a straight line of some nine miles from Wood Ditton up in the hills to the edge of the main Fenland at Reach.

The date of the Brent Ditch is uncertain but, while much work remains to be done on the other three, given their siting and the positive archaeological facts which have been established about each one, they must be parts of a fluctuating frontier of the East Anglian kingdom in its long and unsuccessful struggle with Mercia.

The county had its share of the motte-and-bailey castles which followed on the Norman Conquest, but none have left impressive remains – in the case of Cambridge and Ely because of early incorporation with more complex structures. At Castle Camps its development was more normal as a castle out in the country controlling the route between the Cam valley and the upper valley of the Stour leading down to Colchester and the sea.

There is also an enigmatic earthwork which may have its origin in William the Conqueror's assault on the Isle of Ely to suppress the revolt of Hereward the Wake. This is the slight ring-work known as Belsar's Hill in the parish of Willingham by the side of the ancient Aldreth causeway, once the original line of entry into the Isle of Ely from the south.

The anarchy of Stephen's reign, when Geoffrey de Mandeville terrorised much of the country north-east of London, produced a big reaction in the Cambridge region with the digging of a defensive ditch round the east and south of Cambridge town and the more or less complete building of several small defensive works of unusual design to keep him away from the country north and north-east of the town. Geoffrey's main stronghold locally seems to have been at Fordham between Ely and Newmarket though there is no sign of it today, and to oppose this another stronghold was begun at Burwell. Today the site is under grass and consists of a large rectangular excavation of some depth in the chalk with two fair-sized square islands left standing in the middle. It was designed to be flooded, and the islands built up, but before the chalk had been excavated down to the required depth and barrowed up slopes to be dumped and be distributed later, Geoffrey decided to come over from Fordham and put an end to the work. In this he was successful, but the chronicler tells us that a workman took a shot at him with a bow and hit him in the eye. He was taken back to Fordham to die and the castle was never completed, as an excavation by T.C. Lethbridge demonstrated.

Small versions of Burwell are the 'Giants' Hills' at Rampton on the verge of Willingham Fen and at Caxton in the west of the county and close enough to the Old North Road, Ermine Street, to control traffic along that very important route.

The survey was completed by an examination of all moated sites. In two cases only were these obviously defensive, at Kirtling Tower and Cheveley, both on the south side of Newmarket, and the result of licences to crenellate. Among the others, round or oval examples were rare, Flambard's Manor at Meldreth and Yen Hall at West Wratting being the only instances, the latter certainly pre-Conquest.

The main purpose of moats seems to have been to prevent the depredations of animals, deter the casual thief and drain the actual dwelling site. When a moated site contains more than one moated area, the one which usually enclosed the buildings was built up into a platform, while the other at the general level was garden or orchard ground. There may, of course, be more than two moated areas, but two are the norm. There is a considerable complex at Bassingbourn which is believed to have been a country residence of John of Gaunt and there are a number in various parts of the county which are pointed out as having been sacked in the Peasants' Revolt.

When I first met O.G.S. Crawford in the late 1920s it was the practical topographical part of his work which most attracted me, and to forward this I was prepared to spend my time up to the limit imposed by my situation at Cambridge. This position became more stable as we advanced into the 1930s and by that time I had served my voluntary apprenticeship in the revision of the Lincolnshire maps. One of Crawford's biggest contributions to date had been the introduction of the period map in the form of the map of Roman Britain which, in its second edition, was to hold the field for many years.

In 1930 he produced his first essay into the field of historical mapping when the map of England in the seventeenth century was published. I made a large contribution to this in all the Civil War information, the principal drainage achievements in the Fenland and some odds and ends like Winstanley's Eddystone lighthouse, but it would have been a more sensible map had it been confined to one major aspect of the century, say the Civil War. In the years just before the 1939–45 war he also entrusted Mr Neville Hadcock, a noted authority, with the compilation of a map showing the position of monasticism in Britain between the Norman Conquest and the Dissolution of 1536–9. The production of this was held up by the war but it fell to my lot to see it through publication when I was Archaeology Officer later.

Another much wider scheme occupied his mind, a series of regional maps called, in the cases of those which actually appeared, Neolithic Wessex, Neolithic South Wales and a map of the Trent Basin in Neolithic times. These maps showed the distribution of megalithic monuments, 'henges', long barrows, stone circles, cairns – a regular mish-mash of features about which our knowledge at the time was all too imprecise and only now, as we move towards the end of the century, capable of sound classification and treatment. I did my best with the Trent Basin map, which was a wretched affair appearing in 1933, and was toiling with another covering north-eastern England when the 1939–45 war put an end to it and the others by the destruction of all the reproduction material relating to them when the Office was bombed at Southampton in 1940. No attempt has ever been made to revive them.

It was in the later 1930s that the disastrous effects of the economies in men and resources applied to the Ordnance Survey after the 1914–18 war became very apparent. War clouds were once more darkening the horizon. A committee was set up under Lord Davidson to make a report on the situation. The Ordnance Survey was in no condition to meet its wartime duties. An immediate large recruitment of new staff was recommended and put in hand without delay. The Committee reported favourably on Crawford's activities and he was at last allowed to have an assistant. I had been in and out of the Office a great deal in recent years, but I did not need the job, beside the fact that the pay offered was modest, was no attraction, and I did not want to leave Cambridge. But I did know that W.F. Grimes, an assistant curator at the National Museum of Wales, badly wanted to change his job because he was finding it increasingly difficult to work under the Director, Sir Cyril Fox. All this I had learned when I went over to lunch with Grimes at Cardiff. I therefore stood down and suggested Grimes, to whom the offer was made and who lost no time in accepting it.

Meanwhile, there had been developments on the side of the Prehistoric Society, of which I was now Hon. Secretary. The old Prehistoric Society of East Anglia having shut up shop and the Prehistoric Society having taken its place, Gordon Childe automatically ceased to be President at the end of 1936. The records of the old Society were transferred from Ipswich to Cambridge, where the headquarters of the Society were now to be located, with its Hon. Secretary and Hon. Editor, Grahame Clark, both resident there. As a rapid increase in the membership began at once, it was recognised that the Society's meetings should take place in London in the Society of Antiquaries' Rooms at Burlington House. Crawford was anxious to have time to mature his plan for a rigidly scientific excavation under the aegis of the Society, to throw light upon some aspect of Iron Age life in Southern Britain. The Council also agreed that Adolf Mahr, director of the National Museum of Ireland in Dublin, should be approached to be our President for the time being, his only positive duty being to give us a Presidential Address in London, which would later be published in our Proceedings.

The last year before the outbreak of World War II was now approaching, and the new German Führer, Adolf Hitler, had finally eased the Weimar Republic out of the way in favour of the Nazi-dominated State. He was making no secret of his expansionist policy and every time he gave a major speech, which was often, the whole world listened anxiously and worried over what it portended.

Ireland was settling down after the convulsions which accompanied the creation of the Free State, shortly to be declared an outright Republic, and when the main museum post in Dublin had fallen vacant there was no native Irishman with enough museum experience to fill the post, and painful memories were too recent to bring in an Englishman.

The choice fell upon an Austrian from the museum at Vienna and he moved in, but almost at once fell ill with and died of a cattle disease which rarely attacks humans. Adolf Mahr was then appointed, another man from Vienna, who was vociferously anti-semitic and probably already a Nazi sympathiser. Mahr was quite an able archaeologist and did well at Dublin but it is ironic that at the time when Crawford was negotiating for the services of a distinguished archaeologist victim of Nazidom, Gerhard Bersu, to direct the Society's first planned excavation, the Society should also be seeking the aid of a Nazi sympathizer to give it a Presidential Address.

Bersu was a very able German archaeologist with special skills in excavation who, until 1935, had been director of the German Archaeological Institute's branch at Frankfurt-am-Main but had been removed back to the Berlin headquarters, the suspected motives for this being professional jealousy and, the Nazi menace being on the upgrade, an accusation that he had some taint of Jewish blood. He was living under a considerable mental strain and the arrangement would provide an opportunity for him to introduce his own methods into Britain and to live in a more friendly atmosphere for a period.

Mahr came over to London in the autumn of 1938 at the time of the Munich crisis, when our Prime Minister signed away the freedom of Czechoslovakia and proclaimed on returning that he had brought back 'peace in our time'. Mahr must have laughed up his sleeve. He proceeded to give us a good Presidential Address on an Irish topic and afterwards the Officers of the Society and some of the more senior and influential members entertained him to dinner at the Imperial Hotel in Russell Square. All went well during the dinner and we adjourned for drinks and conversation.

I was rather uneasy over this part and drank very little because alcohol always makes me feel ill, but Mahr proved to be a heroic drinker, downing an incredible quantity of Drambuie liqueur whisky which we had procured at his request. The drink made him increasingly loquacious so that before long he abandoned discretion and the truth began to come out. He praised the Nazi system to the skies, gloried in Hitler's recent triumph and when someone mentioned Menghin, one of his former colleagues at Vienna, he vilified him as a Jew.

We left the hotel in a state of shock. It was the last we ever saw of Adolf Mahr. We received the text of his Address and it was published, but we heard later that about a month before the declaration of war in 1939 he placed his wife, children and all his personal belongings on to a German boat that was lying in the Liffey. He boarded it at the last minute before it sailed and that was the end of him in Ireland. I do not know if the Irish authorities made any surprising discoveries after he had gone, ostensibly to attend a conference in Germany.

After the war in the summer of 1945 a number of us, including myself, received letters from Mahr which were written from a detention camp set up by the invading Allies somewhere near Hamburg. In this he begged intervention on his behalf and recounted his sorrows, including the loss of a son. I do not know if anyone replied; I could have done so in scathing terms, but soon the news filtered down to me that he was dead and that was the end.

The site chosen for the Society's planned excavation was on the brow of the hill overlooking the river Avon from the south-west at Britford on the southern outskirts of Salisbury. A little further across the flat hill-top westwards was a minor hill fort called Woodbury, and so it has become a convention to call the site to be excavated 'Little Woodbury'. The site lay in arable land with a very thin covering of soil over the underlying chalk and had long been levelled, though it showed up extremely well on air photographs.[1]

Bersu's wife Maria accompanied him, all their expenses were defrayed by the Society and they received much hospitality from members of the Society and friends living in the district. Prominent among the latter were Stuart Piggott and his wife Peggy, who were living at Rockbourne only a few miles to the south. At about the same time, Mortimer Wheeler was probing the secrets of the gigantic multi-vallate fortress of Maiden Castle, forty-five miles to the south-west outside Dorchester.

Our site was roughly circular with an entrance to the north-west towards the river, prolonged on either side by long 'antennae' designed to assist the driving in of cattle which, no doubt, pastured on the meadows below by the river. The enclosed area, with little more than a defining bank and ditch, contained a large number of black dots which showed the presence of pits. There were also spaces where presumably the dwellings had been and one or two large dark areas which awaited explanation.

I acted as guardian of the interests of the Society, quarter-master, general provider and often pit excavator. We had the co-operation of the Salisbury and South Wiltshire Museum, where we stored and sorted finds and members of the Society came and went with others as voluntary workers. Most of the party were accommodated at the Mill Race Hotel on the bank of the Avon's tributary, the Nadder.

1 Proceedings of the Prehistoric Society, New Series, Vol.VI, 1940. pp. 30–111.

The summer of 1938 was an uneasy time with constant doses of ominous news from Germany, where Hitler, now firmly in the saddle and having absorbed Austria, was raising the question of the Sudeten Germans in the republic of Czechoslovakia, and the Maginot line was being built, or so we thought, in France to be countered by the Siegfried Line in Germany.

In the middle of all this the Prehistoric Society was carrying out an excavation at a spot which entirely overlooked the city of Salisbury, the headquarters of Southern Command, and placing its direction in the hands of an unknown German! In our innocence we had not given this a thought, but it is quite possible that the fact had been noted by the police and also by the brass-hats in the big building on the road to Wilton.

Bersu was a great note-taker and had also soon accumulated a big roll of plans. No one stayed at the site at night and it was one of my jobs to combine, as far as possible, the purchases needed for the day with the transport of the Bersus to the site. Every night Bersu brought home his site archive, which was soon a very unwieldy bundle, and this was a part of our cargo next morning. One day we set off from the hotel and made a number of purchases at shops as we went. I remained in the driver's seat but the three others got out variously, leaving their gear and Bersu's belongings on the back seat. It was the morning for collecting waste from the shops and various bundles were standing here and there in the gutter for removal. It was only when we were half way up the hill to the site that Bersu noticed with shock that his documents were missing. We at once returned, contacted the police and also the city's waste disposal unit. The van which had been collecting from the street where the loss occurred had not yet got back to the yard but when it arrived its contents were carefully examined under the eye of one of our volunteers who could have recognised the plans, but they were not in the load. The police were polite but not actively helpful. We could only conclude that we were under some form of surveillance and that the plans had been abstracted so that they could be examined and the genuineness of our activities established. We never saw them again, but fortunately the work was not too advanced and Bersu was able to reconstitute them. Such were the times in which we were living in 1938.

In the 1938 season there was only time to work through half of the site but we established the fact that there was one large circular timber farmhouse, and that only a small part of the enclosed area was occupied by large grain store pits in any one season. They soon became infected, new ones were dug, and the old ones filled up with the resulting rubble and any casual rubbish. In this way much of the enclosed area was successively involved. The pits were up to nine feet deep, cut in the solid chalk and belling out below the neck. Having emptied many of them I can testify that each was of a convenient size to have been cut by one man. The large dark areas of indeterminate form proved to be shallow excavations which ended their lives as dumps for rubbish and chalk rubble, and we interpreted them as open-air working places where the inhabitants could work together at various jobs out of the wind, which can be very sharp on this hilltop. There were also sets of postholes at the corners of a square which were regarded as being the supports for seed corn granaries which required protection from rodents and the damp. The site was much visited by archaeologists, including Mortimer Wheeler and Christopher Hawkes and his wife

Jacquetta, who were themselves working not far away on the unfinished hill fort site on Quarley Hill.

The first season at Little Woodbury lasted for three months and closed with a full, and in the event justified, expectation that it would be resumed and completed if possible in 1939. But although it had been a technical success, very valuable to a number of the voluntary workers who were themselves to become important figures in British archaeology in later years, it had not been a very comfortable experience for me. While our experience of Bersu in action entirely confirmed his brilliance as an excavator, he also had that type of dominating personality seen in some small round men.

He was lively and stimulating, an incessant pipe smoker and a great meat eater. It was something to see him tackle a whole tin of bully beef. His position and that of his wife as guests in a foreign country was one of great delicacy, particularly in 1938, but they were also often singularly lacking in tact. Maria Bersu was no help to her husband. She was a pale pasty-faced creature, lacking the charm that Gerhard certainly possessed and she was always complaining. It was hardly a time to keep telling us how much better things were done in Germany. Each news bulletin made this claim a nonsense and one really began to wonder whether Bersu's demotion from the Frankfurt directorship was entirely unjustified.

They had brought comparatively little from Germany and it was startling to see the way in which they would indicate to some of our friends that they required certain expensive objects and when duly presented with them did not return a word of thanks. After one or two misfires, we found them rooms in a good house but this soon became the centre of a storm. The inmates of the house had small children and one day one of them had a mild attack of some infectious childish ailment. At once the Bersus demanded to be rehoused and wanted to know why an official notice of the presence of infection had not been posted outside the house as a matter of course. In the previous summer the Bersus had been working in Bulgaria under rather primitive conditions and this had been the obligatory practice there and I had great difficulty in assuring them, and particularly Maria, that they were in no danger at Salisbury.

Bersu had one unique distinction: he was the first German to fly in a heavier-than-air machine. As a conscript doing his military service he had been a member of a squad standing by to be generally useful while the Wright brothers demonstrated their machine to the German army High Command at Potsdam. After a successful demonstration the Wrights were asked if the machine could carry a passenger. They looked over the fatigue squad and picked out Bersu as the smallest of them; there was no proper accommodation on the machine but he was strapped to the undercarriage and was successfully carried through the air for several flights up and down the parade ground. He had put on weight since then.

Inside Maiden Castle, Wheeler had already found and cleared out some grain store pits. By this time at Little Woodbury we had already excavated a large number of these pits and had clearly demonstrated their association with a large type of dwelling hut above ground. That they were grain store pits was incontestable, no one would be able to live in such cramped quarters. Although we did not find any grain in the Little Woodbury pits, I have myself seen pits of this type which have been sectioned vertically in a shallow modern quarry which was being worked in the small hill fort called Little Solsbury in 1929 near Bath. One of these pits was still filled with carbonised ears of emmer wheat which were identified as such by the famous wheat specialist, Professor Percival of Reading University. It was spilling out of the pit down the face of the shallow quarry and at the time I took several full biscuit tins of samples. In this case, only the ears had been reaped and the carbonisation which had taken place in the pit had perfectly preserved the glumes of the ears so that the type of grain could be precisely recognised.

In emptying some of these pits I have found distinct traces of fire on their floors. This could only be casual fire rubbish, thrown in as part of the filling when the pit was abandoned, although it is conceivable that it may have been possible to prolong the useful life of a pit for grain storage by making a quick hot fire on the floor to destroy moulds and fungi.

Shortly after the 1938 season was over I was back at Bristol, where my mother had now sold her business and retired to a flat in Pembroke Road. My sister-in-law wanted to make the trip to Glasgow to see the launching of the new liner Queen Elizabeth and I drove her with my brother Jack to and from this affair at the height of the Munich crisis when the question of the future of the Sudeten Germans threatened the early outbreak of war with Germany. As we drove northwards, slit trenches as temporary air raid shelters were being dug in many of the places we passed through and it was rumoured that anti-aircraft batteries had been moved into position on Clydeside to ward off a possible surprise attack on the launching. I did not attend this myself but, having deposited them at Glasgow, I made my way into the nearer Highlands and drove round in an agony of mind in very gloomy weather. We met up again at Carlisle, where there was an anxious quest for news, and then drove all the way south to Bristol all day. It was only when we got to Gloucester that evening that we heard the news of Mr Chamberlain's return with the shameful Munich agreement.

So we came to 1939 and I began training as an A.R.P. warden. In archaeology, all our hopes were focussed on the completion of the Little Woodbury enterprise. In due course the Bersus arrived. This time they were not to see their native land again for six years.

Before I went down to Salisbury to make all the necessary preparations, I had an unexpectedly interesting visit to Suffolk. I had already heard a casual rumour that someone was making enquiries in the Isle of Man about one or two minor Viking ship burials and apparently this enquiry had come from Ipswich Museum. We shall see the surprising outcome of this in the next chapter.

Chapter 7

Now that I was the Hon. Secretary of the Prehistoric Society I still could not get the papers of the older Society from Guy Maynard, my predecessor, and also from Cullum, the former Hon. Treasurer so I drove down to Ipswich to collect them. I decided to ask Maynard about this enquiry in the Isle of Man and he told me that he was at his wits' end how to proceed with something which the Museum had become involved with over at Woodbridge. He had just come back from one of his annual jaunts with Colonel O. Pearce-Serocold to dig sites in the Lizard Peninsula to find himself confronted with this awkward problem.

In passing, I may say that Maynard, who was a very worthy fellow, spent much of his time at the beck and call of the chairman of his Museum Committee, the overbearing J. Reid Moir, whose influence had been badly shaken when we changed the old Prehistoric Society of East Anglia into a national concern. As I had my car at the door, I suggested that we should go the eight miles to Woodbridge and see the cause of the trouble. We passed through the long street of the little town and turned eastwards across the river Deben and the railway line and went up on to the road across the Sandlings to Sutton and Bawdsey. Almost at once, we turned into the grounds of the large house known as Sutton Hoo, the home of a local magnate, Mrs E.M. Pretty, widow of Colonel Pretty, a well-known Ipswich business man and a very rich lady in her own right as an Elder Dempster Line heiress.

Maynard introduced me to Mrs Pretty and it was proposed that we should take a short walk over the heath to the edge of the woodland which spreads up from the valley of the Deben more than 100 feet below. As we proceeded I could see that there was a sizeable group of bracken-covered mounds at the edge of the heath and I learned that Mrs Pretty, a convinced Spiritualist, had become interested in this group of what were almost certainly burial mounds on her property and had applied to Ipswich Museum for advice and help in examining them further. The museum had suggested that she should employ Mr Basil Brown to excavate some of the smaller ones experimentally in the summer of 1938, under the general supervision of Mr Maynard. It was clearly understood that Mr Brown would be Mrs Pretty's paid employee and that he had some help from her garden staff.

Brown was an unusual man who lived at Rickinghall, a place some 25 miles to the north-west near Botesdale. He was someone with whom I had a lot to do in the coming years. I have been told that he was the last survivor of an old and once well-established farming family in the district, most of whom had emigrated. He was a pure piece of rustic Suffolk with a wide knowledge of his locality without much formal education, but surprisingly, if not accurately, informed all the same. I would hazard a guess that he may have had a severe illness in his youth, but in 1938 he was nobody's fool and a keen and able observer. For much of his life he and his wife had a newspaper and general convenience shop in Rickinghall and he was correspondent for the local press. He took a sharp interest in old things and was responsible for drawing attention by field walking to a variety of sites. Rickinghall has had potteries for centuries, there are extensive old clay diggings and some of these may be as old as the Bronze Age. For some years before the Sutton Hoo affair Brown was employed by Ipswich Museum at various times, but he always insisted that correctly he was in Mrs Pretty's employ in 1938 and 1939.

In 1938 he had excavated two of the smaller barrows and a larger one with a flattish profile. The two smaller ones proved to cover rich cremations and the larger one contained a boat about 18 feet long from which the burial deposit had been robbed. This barrow was very important to Brown because it showed him how a clinker-built boat nailed with iron rivets would appear after it had been buried in the almost pure sand of the site and decayed in position. No wood could be expected to remain but there was no reason why the iron fastenings, though almost nothing but rust, should not remain in their relative positions. What remained of the cremation deposits was carefully collected from the smaller barrows and it was clear that costly and exotic objects had been destroyed in the funeral fire.

Mrs Pretty was satisfied with the results in 1938 and she resolved to have the largest of the mounds opened in 1939, that nearest to the edge of the slope down through the wood, incidentally known as Top Hat, to the bank of the Deben. This barrow was oval, and longer on its east-west axis, but it was known that a good deal of material had been carted away from the west end of the mound. Brown began by making a cautious exploration into the east end of the mound and it was not long before he began to meet with ship nails. It was here that his decision not to go blindly on digging into the mound made a major contribution to the success of the whole 1939 excavation. He recognised that he must be meeting either the bow or the stern of a boat (it was the bow) and so he began, with the aid of two of Mrs Pretty's gardeners, to remove the upper part of the mound and slowly adumbrate the form of the boat which he had good reason to suspect had been buried. They had to remove a great deal of barrow material, decayed sandy turf, down to the old ground surface and a little lower before the signs of the boat's gunwales began to appear. No attempt was made to expose them further.

I do not wonder that Maynard was worried by what was going on at Sutton Hoo. Enough had already been revealed of the site's great potential in 1938. The cremations, though not fully studied at the time, implied a high social level for those cremated and the finding of the rifled boat burial should have brought the 1861 excavation of the Snape boat, only a few miles away on the north bank of the river Alde to mind. Seeing before him the clear indications of a buried boat, possibly most of 100 feet long, Maynard must have been conscience-stricken at having been pottering about with his crony examining hut sites in the Lizard Peninsula while great developments were taking place almost at his museum's back door.

Reid Moir certainly wished to claim all possible credit for the museum of which he was the chairman. I suspect he felt that Maynard should have kept the new development secret a little longer, and that he had committed a further gaffe by letting in one of those pernicious Cambridge characters (namely me) who had already ruined the Prehistoric Society of East Anglia, and at Sutton Hoo could be relied upon to manoeuvre this affair away from Ipswich also. If he really had these fears they were to be fully justified.

While full of admiration for the way in which Brown had proceeded so far, I knew that a great responsibility rested on anyone who knew of the current Sutton Hoo situation but failed to inform both the British Museum and the Office of Works about it with the absolute minimum of delay. Therefore we returned to the house where, with Mrs Pretty's consent, I went to the telephone and told my story to both these authorities. The ball was now placed firmly in their court, Maynard was relieved of further responsibility and, while commending Brown's work, it was agreed that it should be suspended for the time being.

The news must have caused some embarrassment in London, where all government agencies were already examining their responsibilities in view of the growing threat of war, but they reacted quite quickly and within a week I was asked to attend a consultation at Sutton Hoo. I drove down to Woodbridge on the appointed day and found Christopher Hawkes, well known to me, representing the British Museum and R.S. Simms, a rather ineffective member of the Office of Works staff, who would have been more at home with a monastic ruin. Maynard was there and, of course, Brown, but I do not recall Reid Moir putting in an appearance. The Sutton Hoo burial group was not a scheduled monument at the time and though surveyed and appearing on Ordnance Survey maps, it had never been indicated as an antiquity, a surprising omission.

The party had a thorough look at the position on the ground and went back to London to make their report. Full notice had now been given in all the right quarters. My own immediate business was the second season's work at Little Woodbury and in less than a week I was at Salisbury. We had scarcely begun work again up on the hill when I received an urgent message from the Office of Works asking me to undertake the direction of the rest of the work at Sutton Hoo in 1939. I made my decision very quickly; Little Woodbury was not likely to produce many problems which we had not met with in 1938. Bersu was a highly skilled director and this year's work was a clearing up operation. As for the excavation of ship burials, there was no expert on them in England and time was of the essence. I had seen something of ship burials in Norway and Denmark and I could only do my best.

I telephoned my acceptance and returned to Cambridge at once and, gathering what I thought I should require, I went on to Woodbridge where I took a room at the Bull Hotel. One of the great problems at Sutton Hoo was anxiety about the weather. The only shelter available on the site in 1939 was a shepherd's hut on wheels which was parked conveniently close to the barrow and in the upper edge of Top Hat Wood. There were also the interiors of cars which might be present, but all this compared very unfavourably with the temporary hutments which would accompany a major excavation today. The site was at the edge of the stretch between the Deben and the sea which is known as the Sandlings, in 1939 often no better than a bracken-covered desert, but soon under the pressure of war time, in large measure to be brought under the plough.

Thus a visit today is made along tracks which come through cultivations right up to its eastern boundary. The site is on sand with a very slight admixture of gravel and containing haphazard thin rafts of clay. This means that it cannot be muddy, but that rain will channel and bring down the sides of any excavation and strong winds will also cause troublesome erosion. The only solution is the erection of a complete translucent cover over the whole operation, something very expensive, difficult to erect and liable to damage by high wind.

We had none of these things and so could only thank the good Lord for a very fine July and August in which both wind and rain were very rare. The weather bordered on the miraculous. The threat of war worked both for and against us: it gave the official archaeological world so many other preoccupations that it was compelled to let us get on as best we could and this probably saved us a lot of time; only the most startling discovery could bring officialdom down from London.

It was an advantage to have Top Hat Wood, conifers planted in 1881, so close to the excavation. Conditions on the site were often torrid and the wood provided a cool retreat for refreshment breaks. Water which seeped out of the slope among these trees fostered a lavish growth of moss in this well-established woodland. Later, when we had to pack highly perishable and fragile material and objects from the burial deposit it proved to be ideal damp packing material, available in unlimited quantity. The fir cones were also useful for tea-making fires. This woodland has been stripped since 1939 and something like the original appearance of the spot at the time the ship-burial was made must have been restored. The placing of this great barrow – arguably that of Raedwald, the one East Anglian king to achieve the title of Bretwalda, would probably have been set at the point most visible to those passing up and down the river Deben below.

I arrived at Woodbridge on July 3. There was no time to be lost and while Basil Brown and I continued to remove the barrow material from where we judged the burial area to be, Mrs Pretty's two gardeners cut back the main mass of the barrow on either side of the developing excavation trench, in order to lessen the chances of those caving in, and to provide a sufficiently wide walkway along the outside of the gunwales of the boat which were now appearing.

It was necessary to move the excavated sand as far away from the excavation as possible and I found that a very useful tool for this was a stout fire shovel. The amount which could be thrown up and out at one time was small but the implement, which was light, being fitted with a long ash handle, could be handled easily and had a vastly longer distance to its throw than the conventional shovel.

In taking out the central mass of the barrow we noticed that there had been an effort to rob it since its construction. This we were able to date because at the bottom of the incompletely filled-up hole that had been made we found the remains of a fire, beef bones and a broken piece from a tiger-ware jug, presumably of the Bellarmine type. It was significant that this late sixteenth century (?) attempt had been abandoned when the old ground level had been reached and nothing had been found. The robbers had no idea that the treasure they were seeking was intact some five feet below them on the floor of a boat which had contained a wooden burial chamber long since collapsed and filled with barrow material. It has been suggested that the 'lunch of the disappointed' was a result of the activities of the notorious Elizabethan alchemist Dr John Dee, who is believed to have had a licence to open barrows in this neighbourhood.

We worked steadily and it was not long before we saw vague forms of objects veiled in sand which showed that we were coming to the burial deposit. Knowing my Gokstad and Oseberg ship burials of the Viking Age four hundred years later in Norway, I knew of the use of burial chambers in this kind of grave and I was on the lookout for 'verticalities' in the barrow material we were removing which would indicate the surviving traces of the ends of the burial chamber at Sutton Hoo also. These duly appeared and we knew that the delicate task of revealing, recording and removing the burial deposit must begin.

Noting the way that the work was already developing I had already called up Crawford and his very skilled assistant, W.F. Grimes, from the Ordnance Survey for Crawford's special skill as a photographer and Grimes' proven capacity as a dissector of complex archaeological deposits. I also called up Stuart Piggott and his wife Peggy because they were exceptionally well informed, and Peggy was also an excellent photographer. John Brailsford came with the Piggotts and at various stages we had on-the-spot advice and their support as witnesses from T.D. Kendrick of the British Museum, the Grahame Clarks from Cambridge and J.B. Ward-Perkins, the Director of the British School at Rome, who fortunately looked in just as the most splendid part of the treasure was being found. It was a matter of regret that none of the Ipswich Museum people came to see the work, though they would have had a cordial reception. The Office of Works Ancient Monuments people also never put in an appearance. Half a dozen scaffold poles were sent over by them from Framlingham Castle where some repairs were in progress.

The general sense of imminent crisis was now so oppressive as July moved into August that it affected everyone, though few yet showed it openly, and soon it would be affecting everything. Several times it came into my mind that there is a vague belief in East Anglia that the fate of England depends on the unbroken sleep of some ancient king buried near the shores of the North Sea and we seemed to be in a fair way to committing this offence. Perhaps there may be some truth in it, for 1939 was a very crucial point in English history.

So much has been written about Sutton Hoo in the past forty years and the British Museum has at last completed the great three-volume study of the contents of the grave that it would be tedious for the reader for me to say more about it in detail here. The nature of the soil and the forbearance of the weather permitted an unusually sharp demonstration of the shape and construction of the boat as it had rested in the ground. The unfortunate indisposition of Lieutenant Commander F.K.D. Hutchinson R.N., the ship expert sent by the Science Museum, along with the outbreak of war on September 3 prevented an official account by him as he was recalled to the Admiralty almost at once and was dead from kidney disease before Christmas. However, the place of this 85 foot-long rowing boat in the history of North Sea navigation seems clear.

The events at Woodbridge were sensational, even though their impact on the public mind was muted by the apprehension of the prospect of impending war. Fortunately the site was not close to any major holiday resort, but every precaution had to be taken against invasion by unwanted onlookers. As soon as it was plain that a big discovery might soon be made at the site I made an agreement with Mr Fairweather, the editor of the *Woodbridge Observer*, who was also the local correspondent of the London dailies. At an appropriate moment I would supply him with an accurate account of what was going on at Sutton Hoo, which he could publish in his own paper and release simultaneously in London. I was also keeping Reid Moir generally informed about what was going on at the site and got a promise from him that he would not reveal the story to the leading East Anglian paper, the *East Anglian Times* until Mr Fairweather had published. He broke this promise so that Fairweather, who had been very helpful to me in many ways, lost his scoop. It was a mistake to trust Moir in any matter in which his personal prestige and dignity as chairman of the Ipswich Museum Committee was concerned.

He was soon to increase his offence. It was already plain that the Sutton Hoo find was of national importance and that its destination must be the British Museum. A treasure trove inquest had yet to settle the question of who owned it but, without waiting to see what would happen, Moir started up a scheme for the creation of a special museum to house the finds at Woodbridge and approached Lord Churchman, the Ipswich tobacco magnate, for support; in this he was unsuccessful.

We had already found and exposed objects of inestimable value, including gold jewellery, on the site and we could not take it up and remove it to a safe place as it was found; it had to remain out under the night sky during the inevitably slow process of dis-engagement. We applied for the site to have police protection at night and this was arranged. We were now constantly exposed to the attempts of press men to get interviews and they even penetrated into our lodgings. In one case, two press photographers took us in the rear by crossing the Deben in a rowboat at high tide and coming up through the wood. Flights over the site were organised for trippers from Felixstowe and even further afield.

Mrs Pretty's desire to know more about some of her property had started the whole Sutton Hoo operation which was to end in such a remarkable manner. What sort of person was she? I never knew her precise age but I judged that she was approaching sixty in 1939 and she plainly was not in a robust state of health. I do not know when Colonel Pretty died but I understand that theirs was a very happy marriage and only unusual in one respect – that a son, Robert, was born to them when Mrs Pretty was upwards of fifty years of age. The little boy visited the excavation a number of times with his nanny and I should judge that he was about seven years old. I have been told that in her younger days Mrs Pretty was notably healthy and active and that her present frail appearance was due to the belated birth of Robert.

She was a Justice of the Peace and was esteemed locally as a person of public spirit. She lived quietly, although a very wealthy woman; the death of her husband had turned her to Spiritualism for consolation and on Thursday in each week she kept an appointment in London with a Spiritualist mentor who put her in touch with her husband, with whom she was thus able to commune about her affairs. Unless the man was absolutely honest, this was a dangerous practice but I have no reason to think that he was anything less than that. She is said to have believed that she saw shadowy figures in the dusk moving round the barrow group which is just visible from Sutton Hoo House. This might have had a very mundane explanation and I do not know whether the decision to open three of the barrows in 1938 came from the London source, but she was encouraged by the results and decided to proceed further in 1939.

This background to the events at Sutton Hoo shows that much diplomacy was required in keeping the work on proper lines, particularly when it became clear that a ship burial was involved. Mrs Pretty and her luncheon guests who visited the site in the afternoon thought that Vikings were involved. Someone had lent her a copy of the report of the Oseberg ship-burial in Norway, which had certainly been that of a Queen, but she did not realise that this was nearly four hundred years younger than what we had before us. Nothing would convince her that this was not a woman's grave until the starkly masculine character of our dead man's weapons and accoutrements became obvious. At this stage one could not hazard a guess at his identity, but at least he belonged somewhere in the first half of the seventh century A.D.

The splendid gold, garnet and millefiori jewellery and important silver objects were temporarily secured in Mrs Pretty's house and then removed to the British Museum under police escort. The legal ownership of this could only be determined by the verdict of a Treasure-trove inquest and this was held on Monday, August 18 in a hall in Sutton parish before the Coroner for West Suffolk, Mr L.H. Vulliamy. The East Suffolk Coroner, who would normally have acted, stood down because, being a solicitor member of the Pretty family, he could not officially be recognised as being impartial where such an enormously valuable treasure was concerned.

Mrs Pretty's ownership of the site was not in question. The gold and silver treasure, jewels, brooches, belt fittings, bowls, dishes, spoons, Merovingian gold coins and some small billets of gold had been brought back from the British Museum and displayed for the jury's inspection. These were all within the jurisdiction of the court as gold and silver, while a number of other objects of the greatest value and importance which had been found were safely in London.

Several of us gave evidence. The crucial question was whether the persons who carried out this elaborate burial had any intention of divesting themselves deliberately of any property in the objects buried with the dead man. Stuart Piggott described this burial and made it abundantly clear that this was no casual hiding of gold and silver with the intention of recovering it later. The whole thing took place publicly and it was clear that there had been no serious attempt to disturb the grave until nearly a thousand years later.

So the Crown failed to establish a claim to the treasure and it was declared to be the property of the capital landlord, Mrs Pretty. I have never heard any figure quoted as the probable value of the Sutton Hoo treasure, but it would be certainly in seven figures. If it was to find its proper resting place in the British Museum the Treasury would have to foot the bill and this it was not prepared to do.

I have no idea of what may have been going on behind the scenes but apparently this was a moment of great embarrassment. I had myself heard another member of the Pretty family (not the Coroner) say when she visited the site that the treasure must not be allowed to go out of the family and that Robert's interests must be safeguarded.

Mrs Pretty's spiritualist adviser had come to Woodbridge and was staying at the house on the evening after the inquest. He came out to look at the excavation and I went for a stroll with him on the heath. We discussed the events of the day and I found him a pleasant person. He asked for my opinion on what should happen now, and I told him plainly that I thought the time had come for his client to make a very generous gesture. The next day brought the news that this had been done and I do not think she required any prompting to make this great gift, the largest ever made to the British Museum in the lifetime of the donor. She was later offered the honour of Dame of the British Empire, but declined it and died in 1943.

Once the burial chamber had been studied, recorded and emptied it was time to consider the boat. It was some 80 feet long as traced in the ground and its widest beam amidships was 14 feet. Its prow must have risen at least 12½ feet above the level of the keel plank; the boat was five feet deep and drew two feet of water unladen. It was clinker-built of oak, with nine strakes to a side including a reinforced gunwale strake. The hull was stiffened by 26 ribs, the third of which from the stern was broadened out on the starboard side, where it was attached to the gunwale by a quincunx setting of five bolts. At that point outside the boat there must have been attached the loop in which the steering oar played. This accounts for the reinforcement. Evident repairs showed that the boat was not new at the time of burial. No wood which was certainly part of the boat survived.

I think it may be assumed that it was some decades old and certainly not a quite recent example of shipping contemporary with the burial. The boat would have to be hauled up from the bank of the Deben, which would mean a rise of about 100 feet. There are two combes which lead down to the river and the easier, though longer, combe has a gradient of 1 in 22, easing a good deal as it rises to the level of the heath.

The great trench which was dug to receive the boat was still sharply defined round its sides and it cannot have stood open very long before the boat was moved into place. One of the most striking things about this trench was that the strokes of the tools used in cutting it could still be seen on its sides when the filling fell away, and both ends of the trench were vertical, making no provision to slide the boat down into position. This means that it would have to be lowered into the trench off cables, as a modern coffin is off stout tapes today. This had been managed with great skill, leaving the boat in place with only a slight list to starboard. The bow end was directed eastward across the heath towards the sea.

Presumably a large force of men, with the possible help of horses or oxen, must have been employed in getting the boat up the combe on wooden rollers. A team of carpenters was employed to erect the burial chamber on a level platform put in amidships with the eaves of its roof resting on the gunwales, stout vertical ends and a two-ply plank roof, a few utterly rotten traces of which would be seen still showing this feature on the floor of the burial chamber. Some of the discarded offcuts arising from the carpenters' work were still scattered about.

No estimate can be given of how long this chamber stood before it collapsed and part of the main mass of the overlying barrow slumped in, but when it came the fall was disastrous and all kinds of objects already far gone in decay were smashed flat. Only a stout metal object like the great silver dish could preserve its general shape and here the dish was pounded down on to its heavy foot ring, which in its turn was driven into the miscellaneous objects piled below.

I cannot in this account discuss whether this whole monument was a cenotaph, i.e. the commemoration of a man whose body could not be recovered for burial. My own view at the time was that it was one. No trace of any human or animal body was found, not surprising in the general dampness of the level of the burial chamber, caused by the subsoil water of the heath making its way to appear in the seepages in Top Hat Wood on the slope down to the Deben.

Since 1939, the analysis of soils to detect abnormal phosphate content arising from the decay of bodies has been introduced and this technique has been applied at

Sutton Hoo with no result decisively in favour of the former presence of a body. A close study of the relative positions of the various magnificent parade objects which have survived any trace of a body have shown that they by themselves could support the view that the body was once present, but if it is so it is curious that the fine finger ring, breast pendant and various metal fastening tags belonging to clothes are absent. Both situations are possible.

Apart from the question of the presence or absence of a body, it would seem to be reasonable to expect that a period of several weeks must have elapsed between the actual death of a man of this rank and the completion of all the funeral arrangements with the final placing of the body in the grave. The time of year at which the death occurred could thus be an important factor. If it occurred during a spell of hot weather the condition of the body at the time of committal to the grave could have been very poor. Conversely, in the depths of winter the preparations for the burial might take longer and the end result be about the same.

To me, one of my most satisfying experiences in 1939 was to be able to show the completely emptied hull of the boat with all her clench nails in position, the details of her gunwale strakes strengthened to resist the strain of forty rowers, the faintly visible ghosts of the tholes against which their oars laboured, and the specially strengthened point in the stern where the steersman managed his great steering oar.

I had no secretarial help at this time and one of the most troublesome of my chores when away from the excavation was contacting by letter or telephone those who ought to visit the site. Chief among these was T. D. Kendrick, then Keeper of British and Medieval Antiquities at the British Museum, and he was particularly important because of his interest in the Anglo-Saxon period. I kept him regularly informed of our progress but he was himself so much engaged in all the arrangements which were being made to safeguard the collections in the event of war that he was only able to make one or two visits, the most important being shortly after the major find of jewellery. I knew that he would be almost unable to believe his eyes when he saw what we had and I tried to minimise the shock. When I met him at the station at Woodbridge I brought with me one of the best of the simpler buckles from the belt set carefully wrapped in cotton wool in a tobacco tin. Before we drove to Sutton Hoo I asked him to step into the waiting room for a moment because I had something to show him; when he saw the buckle he was both astonished and elated, astonished because of its beauty and perfection and elated because I was able to tell him that it was part of a much larger collection of pieces in the same style. Some years before, on the strength of a small number of kindred pieces in England and abroad, he had postulated another major school of Anglo-Saxon jewellery, possibly in Eastern England, and here was the confirmation.

The man to whom I particularly wanted to show this was the elderly Professor Hector Munro Chadwick, doyen of Anglo-Saxon studies at Cambridge. He was eccentric in some matters, preferring the life of a recluse with his wife when he was not actually teaching. All I knew in 1939 was that he had retired to a secret address somewhere on the borders of the counties of Hereford and Monmouth. Time was running short and the only thing I could do was to telephone to the Head Porter at Clare College, who should have a forwarding address, and tell him of my predicament. I duly got the address and the Chadwicks set off for Woodbridge. Mrs Chadwick drove, but was not allowed by her husband to exceed 20 miles an hour, so that they took a whole day to get to Cambridge, but on the next afternoon I had the satisfaction of showing him the reality of an Anglo-Saxon royal barge almost of the migration period.

I had another curious encounter. The artist, W.P. Robins, was conducting a summer field class based on the Bull Hotel at Woodbridge and was interested in what we were doing. He took the opportunity to make an etching and a number of detailed sketches of the excavated boat, pleasant souvenirs of the event. Duncan Grant, the eminent artist, was with Robins and the latter made a special request to me to take Grant with me to the site every day and do my best to see that he did not get away until after midday. At this time Grant was in a fair way to becoming a confirmed alcoholic and so by this device, making sure that he took no liquor with him to the heath, Robins knew that for a number of the daylight hours Grant was not drinking. The fact that Grant had many years before him and did famous work shows that he won through.

We also had one Royal visitor before the work closed. News of the events at Woodbridge came to Princess Marie Louise, who was living at the time with the Dowager Queen Mary at Sandringham. She was a guest of Mrs Pretty and a refreshing experience after some of our less exalted visitors. The Princess proved to be a very knowledgeable and intelligent person, interested in all aspects of the work. When she left she said that she would certainly bring Queen Mary to see the site but in the event the war threat was so great that she never came.

Before we closed down, the lines of the ship were surveyed by staff from the Science Museum under the direction of Lieutenant Commander J.K.D. Hutchinson. In all the stages of the final removal of all sand from the interior of the boat, two volunteer amateur photographers of great skill, friends of Stuart Piggott, the Misses B. Wagstaff and M.K. Lack, took a series of record photographs of the same quality as those which Crawford and Peggy Piggott had taken earlier to illustrate the removal of the burial deposit.

It was sad to leave the boat open to the sky and I took a large sample of clench-nails and spikes from different significant parts of the ship. With any luck the clench-nails still retained, fused on by corrosion, the diamond-shaped rove against which the clenching of the red hot nail had been done. The grain of the wood of the two strakes being clenched together could still be seen on the shank of the nail because iron rust had taken the shape of its grain. But no metallic iron ever remained, all was rust more or less retaining the shape of the original iron.

I did not see the site again until some years after the war. By that time the heath had been used as a tank training ground. Rain and wind had made the trench slowly cave in and quite a lot of the spoil on the north side which had not been moved back very far had also come in. There was therefore some excuse for a Polish tank regiment having used it as an obstacle to be surmounted in practice. The remarkable fact is that after the war quite a large number of the boat's clench-nails were found to be still in position.

I went back without delay from Woodbridge to Cambridge, for I should not have fully discharged my responsibilities to the Sutton Hoo excavation until I had written as full an account of it as possible while my memory was still fresh and, for that matter, while I was still alive, for we were on the verge of war. The latest Nazi aggression had been the seizure of the Polish port of Gdansk (Danzig); a blitzkrieg on Poland began and the inevitable consequence was the declaration of war which came at 11 a.m. on September 3, a Sunday morning and just as many people were going to church.

I had already qualified as an Air-raid Warden in the winter of 1938–39 after the Munich crisis and now I was to waste a lot of time in A.R.P. posts in the western part of Cambridge, for this was the period of the 'phony' war in which virtually nothing happened. I had a large photographic archive of the excavation with me as well as my diary, which the fullness and stress of the days compelled me to the necessity of making up in the small hours of the night when I should have been asleep. It contains errors due to fatigue but not, I think, any of real consequence.

Crawford, who if he had not taken up archaeology, might have been an ace journalist on Fleet Street, had extracted the promise of an article on the excavation from me for the next issue of *Antiquity* and this he got before Christmas, but I was billed to lecture on the subject before the Society of Antiquaries in the spring of 1940 and on the basis of this I wrote the first formal account, which was published by the Society.[1]

Before I leave the subject of these early publications I must mention a further bizarre incident which occurred in my relations with Reid Moir in this context. He lived in a house on the Henley road on the western outskirts of Ipswich and, shortly after the outbreak of war, there were one or two forays by single enemy aircraft over the Ipswich area and the only one which dropped a bomb let a small one fall at the end of Reid Moir's garden, causing very little damage but giving him a shock which did not improve his already-deteriorating state of health. I was sorry to hear about this, for I bore him no ill-will, although he had not been helpful when we were at work. Not long afterwards, I had a letter from him asking if I could help him out of a difficulty. An idea that something had been happening in Suffolk had reached the editors of the National Geographic Magazine in America and, finding, I suppose, in the reference books that Reid Moir was the chairman of the Ipswich Museum Committee, they had applied to him for a publishable account. He said that he was neither sufficiently informed nor well enough to undertake this. I replied that I was prepared to send a suitable article but that it must appear over my name. I had already had private advices that his affairs had been in trouble since he had sold out of his business to a multiple tailor in Ipswich and so I offered to divide any fee which arose with him. He agreed, and later I was able to send him quite a useful sum of money. This was the last contact I had with him, and before long he left Ipswich to live at Flatford Mill on the Stour. He died before the end of the war.

The war which broke out in Europe in September 1939, was one in which archaeologists as such often possessed skills valuable in the contest, much of which was fought with the aid of aerial photography, and although little could be done on the ground till the war was over, the amount of damage done to historic centres by aerial bombardment and fires was to provide great opportunities to examine the early phases of communities during the process of restoration in the years of peace.

It was also fortunate that the last decade before the war in Britain had been one in

1   *Antiquaries' Journal*, Vol. 22, (April, 1940) pp. 149–200.

which Sir Mortimer Wheeler had turned mere archaeology into news by applying his able, if flamboyant, personality to major enterprises like his demonstration of the drama of the Roman capture of the vast native fortress of Maiden Castle in Dorset. Important and well-publicised work had also taken place at Roman centres like Colchester, St. Albans and Wroxeter. The number of reasonably competent amateurs and field walkers had increased and the public at large were not entirely unprepared for the great upsurge in activity which was to follow the end of the war. The most intensely exciting of all the pre-war excavations, that at Sutton Hoo, only escaped the onset of war by a margin of days, but publicity would only have been very embarrassing, and the demonstration of the Anglo-Saxon king's full splendour had also to wait till the end of the war.

In this war we quickly lost any foothold in Europe and the only scraps we still held on to were Gibraltar and Malta – useful perches although Malta was subject to constant aerial bombardment from Sicily. At the tail end of the 1914 war those who took part in the campaigns in Mesopotamia, Syria and Palestine on either side could not fail to notice the startling way in which the ancient civilizations of those parts showed up on air photographs as clearly as did the details of modern life.

It had been noted at the time by various persons and particularly informative photographs of Mesopotamian sites were later brought back to Britain by Crawford from R.A.F. custody in Iraq and made available for examination. A Frenchman, Père Poidebard, working for the French and Germans in the Turkish service, had similar experiences in Syria and Palestine. It was fortunate that Crawford, who survived a number of risky employments on the Western Front, took to flying as an observer in the Royal Flying Corps and noticed the conditions under which archaeological features showed up under the damper conditions of France and Belgium. Oddly enough, Bersu did this on the opposite side with the same results. It was the flair of Crawford as a publicist and a fortunate collaboration which brought the breakthrough.

Shortly after the war he drew attention to the Celtic field systems visible in the country north of Winchester and it was after he had given a lecture to the Royal Geographical Society on the subject, which was also attended by the wealthy and enthusiastic Alexander Keiller, that the latter offered to supply the flying and resources for an extensive exploration of the chalk lands. The result was the publication by the Oxford University Press in 1928 of *Wessex from the Air* and the subject was fairly launched, as least as far as England was concerned. From this time, Crawford continually used the pages of *Antiquity* to publicise each of any successful observations, such as that of 'Woodhenge' which constantly disclosed widening vistas over the palimpsest which is Britain from the air.

Before the war had burst out of its 'phony' phase in May 1940, some beginnings of an R.A.F. surveillance unit to keep track of enemy activities was forming and when I joined it at its principal station at Medmenham, on the north bank of the Thames between Henley and Marlow, a regular task was photographing and counting the assemblage of barges which the Germans had gathered from all the canals in Western Europe, awaiting a chance to flood south-east England with German troops when the German forces could dominate the Straits of Dover and establish a bridgehead. This they signally failed to do owing to defeat in the air by the Royal Air Force in the Battle of Britain, and when air photographs began to show a notable decline in their numbers, we were assured that the scheme was being abandoned. With the fall of France we were able to observe the construction of new airfields in Normandy and Brittany as well as, still later, the building of submarine pens at Brest, Lorient and St. Nazaire. I say 'we' and by the middle of 1941 this meant the strongest concentration possible of practical archaeologists on this side of the Channel and soon, through Japanese treachery, to be increased by an able contingent from the United States.

There was one particular occasion when I was asked to give my opinion as an archaeologist with experience of Denmark about the appearance on air photographs of an unusual feature taken over the big German experimental station at Peenemunde on the coast of the Baltic, where in due course the flying bombs and rockets of the last stage of the war were evolved. The coast at Peenemunde has ample sand dunes and in a short time between two photographic sorties a circular flat area of at least fifty yards across had appeared, surrounded by an embankment about five or six feet high. In the precise centre was a dark object to which two closely parallel straight lines which could be pipes leading something to and from the central feature were directed. Not a great distance away in Denmark, similar embanked circular enclosures had long been known at Trelleborg and proved by excavation to be training camps for Viking warriors in the tenth century A.D. and, as is often the case, this recognition had been followed by that of others variously preserved and sometimes differing somewhat in detail elsewhere in Denmark. Some brass-hat seems to have had a vague idea about these and had suggested that the apparition at Peenemunde was another. I was called into a conference and was asked my opinion as an archaeologist. I replied that it was altogether smaller and bore no more than a superficial resemblance to a genuine antiquity of this class, and in any case, a look through the photographs taken over Peenemunde in the past year would show that it was a new development.

This was the first premonition of the rockets of 1944–45; the propellant of these was hydrogen peroxide and at a certain stage in its manufacture it is liable to be unstable and explode. This enclosure housed the sensitive point in the chain of manufacture, the stuff being brought to the central point, treated automatically and then sent away in the other pipe in a stable condition. The explosions would be severe and they were taking no risks.

My life at Medmenham was varied and though I did not rise above the rank of Flight-Lieutenant, I was soon Security Officer to the station which, in view of the extremely sensitive nature of some of its lesser known activities such as the construction of amazingly life-like models of the objectives of coming operations, some to be used and some to veil our real intentions, carried a heavy responsibility. I had to note the occasional leaks of information occurring in the neighbourhood and secure the removal of persons found guilty of careless talk. Incoming personnel had to be briefed on the station security and my position was not made any easier by the fact that the commanding officer of the station was not of the first quality.

When after Pearl Harbour the Americans began to send air-photographic interpretation staff, I had to lecture these intakes on the history and geography of Europe to the extent of their requirement. Although these Americans were of excellent quality for the most part, their education had not always included much information about the Old World in which they now found themselves. As far as the British personnel were concerned, they were normally highly-educated people.

Brian Hope-Taylor, one of the professional artists working in the model-making section, was also interested in archaeology and I was able to give some encouragement which in later years, led to his being one of our most brilliant if rather erratic excavators. One has only to mention his work at the Northumbrian royal centre at Yeavering and kindred sites to know what I mean.

My part in the war was entirely as a non-combatant in the active sense, but I had not been at Medmenham long before I saw a weak point in the system there which wasted a great deal of time when speed could be very important. We received an incredible number of reports from agents and those who wished to injure the common enemy. I have no knowledge of how these reports reached us and it was not my business to know, but they were sent to Medmenham for our attention. We first looked to see if we had any photographic cover of the place or thing referred to by the informant. In all this, maps and the most up-to-date possible ones were of the first importance. The cry was always going up 'Where is this place?" when agents named them in their reports. Much time was wasted searching for them without any success and the obvious requirement was good gazetteers of all the maps that we possessed.

I resolved to supply these locally at Medmenham, even if the Geographical Section of the General Staff had not done so as a matter of course. I began in a small way by making a gazetteer of Northern France involving only places at or above a given size. This at once so increased the speed of compiling reports that I extended it to include every commune, however small. We had most of the map series for the countries of Europe and I steadily plodded through them, one after the other, and copies were cyclostyled for general use in the Unit. As the theatre of war extended, so the list of gazetteers followed suit, with the inclusion of Tunisia, Libya, Lower Egypt, Algeria and Morocco.

Finally, in the spring of 1944 I was transferred from the rural peace of Medmenham to the western outer suburbs of London to be with the Directorate of Military Survey at Eastcote, near Harrow and this body was tantamount to the Ordnance Survey in uniform all the year round. I went on with the compilation of some belated gazetteers, but G.S.G.S. were busily turning the old cyclostyled efforts of Medmenham into properly printed handbooks. It was now a case of much proof reading.

The commanding officer was Brigadier Hotine, in peace time a brilliant member of the Ordnance Survey staff and a man who had done much to resolve the crisis resulting from the insufficient stocks of maps when the country was threatened with invasion in 1940. Here at Eastcote I lived through the V1 and V2 attacks on south-east England after D-Day but my war was virtually over.

It was always a matter of astonishment to me during the war years that the enemy did not at any time make a deliberate attempt to disrupt the aerial photographic intelligence side of our war effort at its source. He must have known our location, placed in a light-coloured building perched on a prominent bluff overlooking the Thames. The river follows a sinuous course as it makes its way towards London through the Chilterns and it should have been an easily-discoverable target on a bright night and no great distance from the enemy bomber bases in occupied France. Instead, the attacks fell heavily on our cities, which suffered severely.

I do not know if we ever attacked our opposite number, wherever that may have been, but we were prepared to pay a high price in losses of crews and aircraft to make devastating raids on the distant Peenemunde experimental station, in which it is known that many important German scientists were killed and development of the V1 and V2 missiles was seriously delayed.

It was these missiles which were the only serious threat to my life as it happened in my war. When, immediately after our landing in France in June 1944, these flying bombs began to fall at all hours of the day and night and at random over most of south-east England and London in particular, the sound of their passage became familiar at Eastcote and some fell close by, causing damage and casualties. But at least you could hear these things coming and know that you were in no danger as long as the steady sound of the motor continued, but as soon as it spluttered and cut out it was a matter of seconds before it plunged to the ground from no great height and exploded with a powerful blast effect.

But the V2 rockets were quite another proposition. They could be discharged from any good firm surface and they took about five minutes to arrive over the London district, where they tilted downwards and fell at a greater speed than that of sound, making a great crater and causing severe devastation and casualties in built-up areas. Here again, they might come at any time by day or night and those who were its still-living victims on the outskirts of each blast heard the explosion only after it had actually taken place.

Several V2s fell in the district round Eastcote and we were mercifully preserved from one of them. They had an occasional habit of exploding on re-entering the earth's atmosphere, resulting in less serious damage from the fall of their disintegrating parts. One very fine day I was at lunch in my billet near the Eastcote office when there was a loud explosion. We went out into the garden to see what had happened, but there was nothing obvious. Then I looked up into the sky. Far up in the blue there was a large white puff of smoke being carried away by some upper wind current. After a short while, a number of sheets of light metal came sliding down into the neighbouring gardens and I realised that a rocket had been about to fall not far from us when it had been destroyed by one of these premature explosions which we had heard. All this had taken place at a great height above us and it had taken time for parts of the metal casing to float down. News soon came of the heavy part, the rocket engine, which had already fallen on to an old disused air-raid shelter near Ruislip station and had done no harm.

Between them, these two menaces seriously affected the morale of the public for a while and there was some exodus to remoter parts of the country, but the progress of the armies in France eventually overran the territories from which they were being fired and they ceased. I cannot refrain from recounting an experience I had at the height of the threat. I was returning by an early morning train from Cambridge to King's Cross and in the last part of the journey it filled up with the usual morning quota of commuters all reading their newspapers. The last stop before King's Cross was at Finchley Road, where tickets were taken. No sooner had we stopped than the sirens sounded and the distant roar of an approaching flying bomb was also heard. This steadily came nearer but did not falter, nor did the commuters in the carriage, who continued to read their newspapers. It passed by, still with a steady note and then the spluttering came and after a few seconds of silence there was the crash of the explosion. The Angel of Death had passed by, the public was becoming imperturbable; Hitler could not prevail. Not long after this we saw models of V1s in toy shops.

During these momentous years I had changed from bachelor to married man: I married Miss Margaret Mann, the director of Modern Languages at Newnham College on July 3 1940 and by October, 1943 was the father of a son.

Chapter 8

During the war years, most of us who were archaeologists were entirely unemployed as such. An exception to this was W.F. Grimes, the Assistant Archaeology Officer at the Ordnance Survey who, after the heavy German raid on Southampton which severely damaged the Ordnance Survey Headquarters in London Road, had no office left in which to work. His Number One, Crawford, had foreseen disaster and had already arranged for the removal of all the Archaeology Branch's record material to a place of safety in Pembrokeshire. Most of the reproduction material belonging to the period maps which had been published before 1939 was destroyed, but this was not a great loss because all but two of them were failures, except those of Roman Britain and Britain in the Dark Ages (North and South sheets); no attempt would be made to publish them until quieter times, if at all.

Crawford was due to retire in 1945 and in the meantime he was seconded to the National Buildings Record for the period of the war, where his skill as a photographer was of great value. Before his quite recent appointment to the Ordnance Survey staff, Grimes had established a reputation as a skilled excavator while he was still with the National Museum of Wales. A notable feature of the war effort was the great programme of airfield construction undertaken by the Air Ministry. The Ancient Monuments side of the Office of Works was concerned that, as far as possible, any antiquities plainly visible, or discovered during construction work, should receive as much examinination and recording as possible before disappearing under the concrete and Grimes was seconded to direct this work, in which he was helped by other archaeologists. As a result, by 1945 they had a long list of excavations of various kinds to their credit.

Many of those archaeologists who worked at Medmenham and elsewhere during the war were professionals in civil life and could live on their salaries. The few of us who were still technically amateurs in 1939 and had lived on our service pay during the war had to look to ourselves when that pay ended with the war. I was one of these; it was true that I had some private means by this time, but I was now a married man with a son and the possibility of more children. My wife had good academic qualifications and could make important contributions to our exchequer, but the wisest course would be to take a professional post if a congenial one should offer.

Meanwhile, we lived at 9, Madingley Road, Cambridge, a house which my wife had been able to secure on very favourable terms before I was finally demobilised in September 1945.

The Cambridge archaeology scene was much changed. Shortly before the outbreak of war Minns had retired from the Disney Chair to be succeeded as I have said earlier by Miss Dorothy Garrod, the first woman to hold a Cambridge chair. She was the daughter of Sir Humphrey Garrod, lately Regius Professor of Medicine at Oxford. She had pursued an independent career mainly in Palaeolithic studies and excavations in the Mediterranean area of Gibraltar, Bulgaria and lately in Palestine at Mount Carmel, where she had made notable discoveries in connection with Neanderthal man and his successors. When the war broke out she joined us at Medmenham in the womens' R.A.F. and was one of the two people on the station entitled to wear the General Service Medal of the 1914–18 war. In the last two years of that war she had been an ambulance driver in France and had met the famous Abbé Breuil, whose apt disciple she became both in science and religion. But the war ruined her life in one respect, for she lost both her brothers in the general holocaust and the rest of her life was deeply tinged with melancholy.

The coming and going of the war years, the night duties, the frequent alarms and anxieties all combined to lower my own state of health at the time of my demobilisation. I had an attack of shingles and was only too ready to spend the rest of 1945 and much of 1946 in utter laziness. As I was still a Fellow of Selwyn, I dined in Hall occasionally and admired the improvements which were being made under the stimulus of the Reverend George Chase as Master.

I undertook no archaeological enterprise of my own, but was more or less involved as a witness or a helper in three events. There was now a major airfield at Mildenhall in Suffolk and during the war, planes often made the direct flight back and forth between this and the various seats of war in the Mediterranean area. It was notorious that some quite valuable objects of flint and bronze were often found during the course of activities round wartime airfields and Mildenhall was no exception. There was a regular trade with dealers in the pubs of the district and a certain doctor was prominent in this. One day he had called without warning on one of his cronies, a local ploughing contractor named Ford, and had noticed an astonishingly large silver dish and other antique silver objects on Ford's sideboard. The pieces were Roman, and of exceptional quality, and Ford claimed that he had ploughed them out of a field in the neighbourhood which was his own property. But the soil in this field, like much in this area, was very shallow and had been ploughed many times. It was inconceivable that such large objects could have remained in the field after ploughing unless they were deposited in a hole dug in the underlying chalk to receive them.

When this matter came to a treasure-trove inquest, it was demonstrated by excavation in which I took part, that such a pit had never been dug in Ford's field. As a ploughing contractor he turned over other people's ground and not far off there was the site of the major Roman villa at Icklingham, whose owner might well have possessed such silver but buried it when barbarians overran the area and then was unable to recover it.

Equally, there was the possibility that this might have been found during military activity in North Africa, smuggled back in a plane and temporarily hidden on the edge of the airfield, accidentally found by Ford, and removed by him before those who had imported it had been able to take any action.

Plainly someone was not telling the truth, and the silver was declared to be treasure trove and so went to the British Museum, where it makes a fine show. Ford was awarded a useful sum of money, but not the great sum for which the Government would have had to buy the dish if his story could have been shown to be true.

The second affair was a disaster which was caused by the policy of ploughing up waste ground to get the ploughing subsidy, without regard to whether it had any value as cultivable land. This occurred on Cavenham Heath, a sandy waste just west of the point where the Icknield Way crosses the river Lark. The heavy plough threw out a great number of Anglo-Saxon cinerary urns which had been buried in four tiers, one above the other. The damage to many of them was great but we got out a good many of them intact and I was able to help T.C. Lethbridge with this. They were of importance since many of them bore impressed designs made by sharply characterised stamps. This find started up much closer study of these impressed decorations and the possible existence of travelling potters was borne out through pots having closely identical stamped impressions being found in widely scattered locations.

The third new enterprise was far from Cambridge on the bank of the Humber at North Ferriby. In the last years before the outbreak of war in 1939, two bright young brothers named Wright, later to hold important executive positions with Messrs Reckitts of Hull and in the War Office, had been keeping observation on the foreshore of the Humber close to their home at North Ferriby, where from time to time they had noticed some mud-covered bulky objects revealed by low tides. These they suspected to be old boats of some kind but had been unable to look further into the matter until 1946. Knowing that I had some knowledge of early boats they asked me to come to North Ferriby and advise them. I accepted the invitation.

The estuary of the Humber is the most formidable obstacle to movement by land up the east of Britain between the Wash and the Firth of Forth, and interrupts contact between the ancient trackway known as the High Street along the western escarpment of the Lincolnshire Wolds and the old routes across the East Yorkshire Wolds and so by the Howardian Hills to the western escarpment of the North York moors and to the lower Tees Valley and points north. It is therefore not surprising to find two villages with the suggestive names of North and South Ferriby facing each other across the tidal waters of the Humber at the point where the estuary interrupts the natural line of movement by land.

The Wrights had begun to examine the elongated and bulky objects they had seen earlier. They appeared to be dug-out canoes but their great length and wide beam made it difficult to believe that they were simple dug-outs, although a 48 feet long example had been found at Brigg in 1886 in the bank of the river Ancholme, not far from its outfall into the Humber over on the Lincolnshire side. Unfortunately, this had been destroyed in Hull Museum by an air-raid in the recent war.

The boats found by the Wrights were in fact not monoxylons but they consisted of three elements, a great keel plank adzed out of the solid trunk with a marked lift to bow and stern both of which were square. Across this plank at right angles lines of cleats were left standing proud from the plank with holes through them so that a succession of ribs could be pushed through. The sides of the boat were two single planks cut on the curve with their lower edges grooved to make a male and female continuous joint with a similar groove cut along the edge of the keel plank. These two long junctions were secured by a series of large countersunk stitches secured by ties of rough roots and both tightly caulked with moss to prevent leakage. The ends of the pliant ribs thrust through the cleats left standing on the keel plank were turned up and secured to the side planks. The general effect was to produce a long parallel-sided, bluff-ended barge-like vessel big enough to carry considerable loads and cattle, and strong enough to stand rough water.

No doubt the crossing has changed in detail since these boats were in use, but it can never have been less than three miles. The propulsion must have been by paddle and full advantage was taken of the set of the tides. All the construction work on these boats was beautifully carried out and was clearly the result of long experience.

The sad part was that although a careful removal of the mud allowed all the details above to be established, the wood had the consistency of butter. The boats were enormously heavy and, if they could not be got well up on the foreshore and over the low flood bank, their only hope (and that a faint one) of receiving preservative treatment that would turn at least one of them into an object fit for a museum display, was to be taken to the National Maritime Museum at Greenwich, more than two hundred miles away by road.

The Wrights had asked me to come up to North Ferriby thinking that my Sutton Hoo experience might be useful. This was a vain hope, but I went there and joined them in a fearsome bout of mudlarking at the end of which one boat was got off to Greenwich with the help of a tank transporter. I do not think that anything exhibitable beyond plans and models came from this but it was a remarkable discovery in maritime archaeology. In 1946 the general idea was that they probably belonged to the Iron Age and did not long pre-date the later Roman ferry between Wintringham at the Lincolnshire end of Ermine Street and the Roman site of *Petuaria* (Brough-on-Humber) on the Yorkshire side, from which the Roman road continued on to York via Stamford Bridge. But the whole matter of the Humber ferries will be pursued further and it now appears that the Ferriby boats may have belonged to the Bronze Age at the latest. There is much more to be learned here.

We must now return to the affairs of the Prehistoric Society, which came through the 1939–45 war successfully, largely as a result of the fact that Clark and I were both part of the large group of archaeologists who staffed R.A.F. Medmenham. I as Hon. Secretary and he as Hon. Editor were able to have almost daily personal contact between May 1941 and the spring of 1944, when I was posted to Eastcote and he left for London to work on materials for an official history of the R.A.F. during the war. Before its outbreak we had already made another breach with the practice of our East Anglian predecessors, as I mentioned earlier, when we had great difficulty with their printers, over the proof reading of an important contribution to the new Society's *Proceedings* from the Abbé Breuil which he insisted must appear in the French in which he wrote it. We could not dispute this with him but although a very carefully typed and accented copy was sent to the printers, they proved to be quite incapable of producing a version which was not full of errors. We had to give them up and for the next number and many years to come we were better served by John Bellows of Gloucester, who were also the printers of *Antiquity*.

The second season of the Society's excavation at Little Woodbury was ended by the outbreak of war; the Bersus received various hospitality in England and Scotland and made no attempt to go back to Germany. The immediate problem of their future was solved for them by the general internment of those who were enemy aliens in the Isle of Man in May 1940. Between then and the end of the war Bersu's enforced leisure was put to use by the authorities of the Manx Museum in carrying out some important work on Viking and Dark Age sites in the island.

I have already dealt with Mahr's abnormal tenancy of the Presidency in 1937–38 and how Crawford succeeded him in 1938–39. With the outbreak of war Miss G. Caton-Thompson, the excavator of Zimbabwe, was elected and although meetings continued and *Proceedings* were published at a reduced size, the life of the Society was at a low ebb. The meetings between 1937 and the early months of 1940 were very well attended and each was preceded by the reading by the Hon. Secretary of a long list of applications for membership. This held up better than might have been expected through the war and in 1943, after the landing of our troops in Sicily, we received a piece of news both sad and gratifying. One of the fairly recent accessions to the membership had been Lt. Col. Sir Gray Hill, a doctor descendant of Sir Rowland Hill. He had been on the staff of the Children's Hospital at Carshalton and was now serving in the R.A.M.C. The plane in which he was accompanying a number of wounded from Sicily to a hospital in North Africa crashed, killing all the occupants and we learned that in his will he had left the Society £20,000 to be used as it wished. This was a most welcome addition to our resources, though naturally we deplored the way it had come to us. Our possession of it was to cause some dissension in the councils of the Society when peace returned after 1945.

The Society owed Miss G. Caton-Thompson a great debt for bridging the five years before normality returned in 1946 and she was succeeded as President by Sir Lindsay Scott, a leading civil servant who had been knighted for important services at the Air Ministry during the war. He was a man used to having his own way and his Presidency was to be stormy. He had established a reputation as an excavator of sites of the broch and wheel-house type in the western islands of his native Scotland and for some time past, in such weekends as he could snatch from war work, he had been excavating what appeared to be an oval barrow with a wooden chamber on the edge of the Chiltern escarpment by Princes Risborough, where he had a weekend cottage. It appears that this barrow was of Neolithic date but I am not sure that the excavation was ever completed. He had formed a friendship with Professor Gordon Childe, probably during his earlier work in Scotland.

At the early council meetings after the war the Society gave consideration to the Hill bequest. No strings of any kind had been attached to this legacy and when Scott came out with a proposition (in which he had probably been prompted by Gordon Childe) that the Society should use the capital to finance field work dealing with Central Italian problems of the Iron Age, there was a shock. The other officers and a large majority of members of the Council believed that the sum should be treated as capital in this early stage of the Society's history and that, at the most, only the income from it should be available at need, though even here it was generally hoped that it would be allowed to accumulate. Scott soon noted that his idea was unpopular and he was moved to open anger when the Hon. Treasurer, L.V. Grinsell, who was an official of the Westminster Bank, said that he must offer his resignation if the idea was accepted.

Grinsell was a well-known and respected amateur, who had devoted his weekends for years past to visiting and making a complete record of all the prehistoric barrows in the south-east of England and had published the results in a book. His warning made Scott lose his temper and he told the astonished Council that his project should not be thwarted by a 'mere bank clerk'.

This outburst killed Scott's idea stone dead and we heard no more of it or of any other way of using the money at this stage except to allow it to accumulate as a reserve. We had no repetition of this kind of scene, but Scott made no apology to Grinsell that I ever heard of. However, this drama was not yet played out. I was myself obliged to resign the Hon. Secretaryship on taking up my appointment as Archaeology Officer to the Ordnance Survey in 1947 and T.G.E. Powell took my place. Scott's Presidency ended in 1950 and we expected to hear that he would go back to Scotland and resume his valuable work in the islands, but he died of cancer of the liver after a very short illness. He never said anything to me about this condition but he might already have been in its grip when he retired from the Air Ministry, consequently we had no idea of the strain under which he might have been living.

Before I turn to deal with the really major development in my professional life, I must record that while Dorothy Garrod was still occupying the Disney Chair and I had not yet left Cambridge for good, a Newnham candidate for the Ph.D. was sent to me by Garrod for advice on an archaeological subject to pursue. The lady was Mrs Sylvia Hallam, who was now the wife of a Jesus graduate and expecting soon to go and live at Spalding where her husband was going to teach History at the Grammar School. I made and she accepted my suggestion that as Spalding was well situated on the river Welland and close to large areas of Romano-British settlement on the two types of fen area, silt and peat, she might give these the close ground exploration that most of them had not received and report her findings. Much of this work would have to be done under uncomfortable conditions and in the winter when the ground would be generally free from crops. She carried this out with great thoroughness, as I shall report much further below and her husband, who was an able historian and later to occupy a Chair, took up the study of some aspects of the exploitation of the Fenland in the Middle Ages before the drainage.

In 1946 the whole episode of the Romano-British exploitation of the Fenland, which had lasted for almost four hundred years, was far from being completely understood and the Research Committee showed no signs of revival. Gordon Fowler had retired with a well-merited M.A. *honoris causa* from the University of Cambridge for his pioneer work on the ancient drainage system and was settling in his native Isle of Wight, where he was soon to die of lung cancer. Sir Albert Seward had also retired from the Chair of Botany and the Mastership of Downing to live in London, where he was also soon to die. Harold Godwin had succeeded him in the Chair of Botany, but he had many projects on hand. Professor Steers, the geographer, was studying coastal problems all round Britain for the government and had a special concern of his own with the north coast of Norfolk; and this sad account could be prolonged further. But in fact, Fen studies were not destined to decline for long, since new workers like the Potters of March, as yet quite unknown to us Cambridge folk, would eventually give the whole subject a lift into a higher dimension in the early 1980s, but the prospect did not look very bright for some while after the 1939–45 war.

As far as I was concerned, by 1947 I was totally immersed in the problems of setting up, and running an effective Archaeology Branch in the Ordnance Survey. To give a proper idea of what this involved there must now be a long digression into the history of archaeology in the affairs of our national survey and cartographical service.

The Ordnance Survey has always regarded the eighteenth century cartographer and geodesist, William Roy, as its real founder. During his work in carrying out a proper survey of parts of north-east, central and southern Scotland for the preparation of a reliable map after the suppression of the Jacobite rebellion of 1745, he became interested in finding and plotting the still-visible traces of the progress of Agricola's Roman army into those parts in A.D. 81–4. In 1755 he went further and surveyed the whole line of the Antonine Wall from the Firth of Clyde to the Firth of Forth. At that time a great many more traces of Roman activity were visible on the ground before the improvements in Scottish agriculture at the end of the century. The plough has now obliterated them and many have only been rediscovered by aerial photography today.

With the outbreak of the Seven Years War in 1757 Roy received a commission, distinguished himself, and duly rose to the rank of Major-General. He was a fellow of the Royal Society when he died in 1791. Before his death he prepared a major work on the antiquities of the Romans in Scotland, which contains plans of many sites and a map of the whole country in Roman times which is little inferior to the first attempts of the Ordnance Survey in the early editions of its maps of Roman Britain. The Royal Society undertook the publication of this work in his memory.

Roy had strongly advocated a national cartographic survey and this, as far as the south-east, south and south-western part of the country, was made essential because of the danger of invasion from France with the onset of the Revolutionary and Napoleonic wars. Without good maps of common scale and style an effective defence would be difficult if control of the sea was lost.

The scale was 1 inch to a mile and the first sheet covering the south-eastern corner and much of the Thames estuary was published on January 1 1801. On this no attention was paid to antiquities as such, unless they were large and surveyable features. The invasion danger came to its head in 1805, when Napoleon's preparations at Boulogne were nullified by Nelson's defeat of the combined fleets of France and Spain at Trafalgar.

There were precedents for including antiquities on the various commercial county maps which had been printed and sold in the eighteenth century. The customers for these maps were mainly among the classes with whom some acquaintance with local antiquities was a polite accomplishment. Products like Isaac Taylor's six-sheet map of Dorset (1765 and 1795–6) are a good example of this type of map at its best.

Roy had no known proselyte among those who directed the Survey in its early years, but the Royal Society, which in those days was liable to contain the most competent archaeologists of the day, certainly gave it advice. The general climate of a period dominated by a figure like Sir Walter Scott was favourable to an increasing supply of archaeological and historical features on the maps, for this was the time of the Romantic Revival.

The only surviving instructions to the 1 inch surveyors are dated in 1816 and give a very limited and arbitrary category of the ancient features which they should supply and this when some sheets had already appeared which were almost modern in the extent of their content in this field. It is clear that the inclusion of antiquities depended on the interest of the surveyor or the desire of a local antiquarian to have features included on them.

When these two factors came together in the production of one sheet, as in number XIV covering south Wiltshire and some parts of Hampshire, the result was remarkable. It was achieved through the application of the field work of the famous antiquary, Sir Richard Colt-Hoare of Stourhead, and his friend and fellow-worker, William Cunnington, to the sheet by Philip and Edmund Crocker, civilian surveyors working for the Ordnance Survey. They had already worked in parts of West Sussex and East Hampshire and were now in Wiltshire. They belonged to a family of surveyors at Frome and Philip had worked for Sir Richard before he joined the Survey staff; he was to end his career as Sir Richard's estate agent. The effectiveness of this collaboration may be judged by the fact that sheet XIV and some of its neighbours did not require serious improvement in the portrayal of antiquities until after 1920.

Sheet XIV of the original 1 inch survey was the great example for antiquity supply in the early decades but good work was also done on their own initiative by surveyors in Cornwall and Dorset although they were less successful in Devon.

By 1911 the work had moved into Wales and over the whole of this country the standard was quite high. It was here also that the use of the Gothic type in printing antiquities and Egyptian type to distinguish those that were Roman was introduced. In several places in Devon, Flintshire and Worcestershire the later practice of showing the sites of famous finds and lost antiquities was used for the first time.

In 1824, when Thomas Colby had succeeded William Mudge as Superintendent, the main effort of the Survey had quite suddenly to be removed to Ireland by a political decision, owing to the discovery that the absence of a standard map system there in connection with the collection of the 'cess' (rates) caused much difficulty. The small size of the many parcels of cultivated ground also made the larger scale of 6 inches to the mile desirable.

Ireland teems with antiquities and they are often an important element in any Irish scene. Although Colby was in overall control, the man in the executive position on the spot was Lieutenant T. A. Larcom at the Survey's Headquarters at Mountjoy House in Phoenix Park in Dublin. He was soon in trouble with the establishment of the place names, some 200,000 in number, many of them pure Irish, others anglicised, in their correct forms. He solved this problem by employing the most noted Erse scholar of the day, John O'Donovan, who also had a deep knowledge of Irish history and lore. He was a sympathetic and tactful man, a Roman Catholic and able to mingle on equal terms with all grades of society, something which made him very valuable in the interrogation of an often hostile Irish-speaking peasantry.

A great deal of local archaeology and tradition was observed and collected, and to organise this a topographical survey was set up in 1830 with Charles Petrie, an eminent Irish archaeologist, at its head. It had a maximum staff of eleven, including Eugene O'Curry, another noted Irish scholar and O'Donovan's brother-in-law.

In 1837 a 37-page *Heads of Inquiry* was issued on the authority of Colby and almost certainly drawn up by Larcom. These contained a most comprehensive list of the different types of antiquity likely to be found in Ireland. Officers in the field were instructed to enquire into these and verify if possible the researches of Petrie's staff, but as their normal work only took them on to cultivated land great areas of waste went unvisited. Religious bigotry could also be an obstacle. As many of the officers were Presbyterians from Northern Ireland and often the ancient features they were instructed to report on were ecclesiastical, they could not bring themselves to search for relics of what they regarded as Papist superstition.

Much more could be said on the subject of this Inquiry. It had a brighter side, in that an immense amount of material dealing with the older Irish culture was collected, even if imperfect, and was safely deposited with the Royal Irish Academy before the famine disaster struck in 1846 and many of the informants were to die or go away as exiles.

When O'Donovan's appointment to the Survey ended in 1842 he became Professor in the Queen's University at Belfast. O'Curry took the chair of Irish History at the Catholic University of Ireland in 1855. There was much that was disappointing in the archaeological side of the Irish 6 inch survey but for the first time the business had been placed in professional hands and O'Donovan was, in effect, the nearest approach to an Archaeology Officer for the Ordnance Survey till 1920.

The Irish potato famine began its terrifying course in 1846 as the 6 inch survey was brought to its conclusion and the officers of the Survey were to distinguish themselves by the part they played in helping to organise relief. Larcom, in particular, was to earn a knighthood and become a leading official in the Irish administration.

In Great Britain during the 1840s and 50s many of the less savoury aspects of the Industrial Revolution were demanding attention. Great cities had grown up without the provision of pure water supplies and adequate sanitation. In London the Thames was an open sewer and there were severe outbreaks of cholera in many places.

Meanwhile, the 'Battle of the Scales' was being fought in official circles as the need for early progress with large scale survey of the country and particularly the urban areas was urgent. Some survey at 6 inch scale had already been started in the north of England but it was clear to Sir Henry James, who became director in 1854, that the 25 inch scale must be adopted for the complete survey of Great Britain which was only to finish in 1894. The few exceptions to this would be barren and uninhabited moorland areas, mainly in the north-west of Scotland, for which the 6 inch scale would suffice.

As a young officer, James had been well exposed to archaeology in Ireland. He had published papers on the subject, had views about the Pilgrim's Way between Winchester and Canterbury, and took a benevolent interest in the antiquities of the Holy Land. In an Order of 1865, he exhorted his field officers to read the history of the area they were surveying and to visit all the items of antiquarian interest in them 'in order that all such objects shall be properly represented on the plans and fully described in the Name Books'. So that the officers might have access to this reading, a very notable collection of county histories and other relevant literature was progressively added to the Survey library as the need arose and the total loss of this library by fire in the Southampton blitz of November 1940, was not the least disaster resulting from that attack.

Another factor which began to help the placing of antiquities on the new maps was the rise by the middle of the century of a large number of county and local archaeological societies. These varied a good deal in their capacity to help the Survey but collectively they were important. However, the flaw which spoiled many of these efforts was in the Survey itself. Here there was no truly professional archaeologist endowed with the best knowledge available at the time who could accept or reject all the submissions from the field, and so prevent some of the new large-scale plans being disfigured for many years to come by such grotesque features as 'The Hanging Walls of Mark Antony', a few old cultivation terraces on the lower slopes of Cross Fell with which some local wag had pulled the leg of an innocent surveyor taking up names.

It was no fault of the surveyors that follies of this kind appeared upon the published plans. They should have been subject to informed inspection at headquarters before the plan went to print. This particular oddity remained on the plans for many years until the day of revision came and I had to remove it, almost with reluctance, for it was by then an old friend. Here again, the interest in archaeology of a particular officer in charge of a surveying party could be very important. A certain Captain Crawford R.E. was in charge of much of the large scale survey of the Yorkshire Wolds and he was very interested in the large group of deserted village sites in that area. He secured their survey in fully comprehensible detail. We now know that in other areas, for example, some of the Midland counties, the number of deserted village sites is great and, until the ploughing-up campaigns of two world wars, they were mostly under grass and in an excellent state of preservation. However, few of them have made much of a showing on the large scale plans until recent times. The average late nineteenth century officer and those working under him were usually content to record them and the frequent traces of early agriculture on the chalk downs as 'natural slopes', which exempted them from the tedious task of surveying their detail.

Another difficulty which affected the whole system of Roman town sites then recognised in Britain was the persistence on the plans of a long set of town names taken from an ingenious eighteenth century forged itinerary by an imaginary 'Richard of Cirencester'. It deceived the learned for a long time but when the forgery was proved the damage was done. A number of the forged names continued to infest maps of various scales for years for want of a professional to draw attention to the gaffe. When the penny dropped at last, one again regretted the passing of some old friends.

The completion of the 25 inch scale survey in 1894 was followed by a lull in revision which was to consecrate the errors which had been made since the time of Sir Henry James. The Survey rested and the Directors were no more than worthy caretakers.

Meanwhile, archaeology had made great progress. The state was making a start with the scheduling of ancient monuments of various kinds and the first inspector, the formidable General Pitt-Rivers, was appointed. He was making archaeological history on his Cranborne Chase estates in Dorset and was developing a modern technique of excavation on sites of various periods, which were promptly followed in each case by exhaustive model reports which he circulated widely. He had also founded the pioneer country museum at Farnham, also in Dorset.

Professor Haverfield had begun to make Romano-British archaeology scientific and W. and R.G. Collingwood were also beginning the study of Roman defensive frontiers in Britain. In December 1905, Haverfield gave a lecture at the Royal Geographical Society at which two directors-general were present: Colonel R.C. Hellard, who had just taken office, and his latest predecessor Colonel E.A. Johnston. In it he lambasted the Survey for its ignorant treatment of Hadrian's Wall on the large-scale plans, though all the required information to correct it was available, and also for its continued use of the forged 'Richard of Cirencester' itinerary as its correct authority for the names of Roman towns in Britain. But in spite of these strictures, and more from other directions, no remedy was to be forthcoming for the next fifteen years.

The only period in which archaeology has been able to make any significant progress in the Ordnance Survey has been when a great archaeological personality like Sir Richard Colt-Hoare has been temporarily in charge of one of its operations, as in the creation of Sheet XIV of the original 1 inch survey, or when one of the leading officials of the Survey is entirely sympathetic to the subject for technical reasons connected with the work in hand. Larcom was in local control in Dublin during the Irish 6 inch survey and his promotion of the Topographical Department of that survey is a case in point, and perhaps it would only be charitable to the memory of Sir Henry James to say that he just fell short of being another.

But Sir Charles Close, who became Director-General in 1911, had a real enthusiasm for archaeology. Even so, it was only by a lucky chance that he met O.G.S. Crawford when the latter was temporarily back from the Western Front in 1915 where, after a period in the trenches, he was engaged in map distribution and in command of a small field unit for printing them. Their meeting was at Southampton and their business was soon dispatched, after which, finding that they shared an interest in archaeology, they had a long chat on the subject.

In 1919 a new bond was forged between them. Close believed that his duty as Director-General justified him in issuing maps free of charge to competent people who would make the necessary corrections and additions to them for use at the next revision – they were to be honorary correspondents. On these terms Crawford received a large batch of 6 inch maps of Berkshire, Wiltshire, Hampshire, Somerset and Dorset, making frequent visits to the Survey at Southampton in 1919 to hand in completed sheets. Many errors and omissions were found and rectified, and Sir Charles saw that the Survey should have a permanent member of its staff capable of doing this work to the best standards of the time. The suggestion that he should join was put to Crawford, who accepted with alacrity, and Close used an approach that he promoted himself through the British Association in making a request to the controlling Ministry of Agriculture and Fisheries that the post should be established. The request was granted and the salary was modest, but the work was ideally to Crawford's taste and by October 1920 he was at Southampton as the first Archaeology Officer.

C.W.P. on Knap Hill, 1937

Mollie and Grahame Clark

Sutton Hoo, 1939: C.W.P. (front left); T.D. Kendrick; Basil Brown (back left); W.F. Grimes (front right); Stuart Piggott; Sir John Fosdyke (back right)

Sutton Hoo, 1939. The excavated ship

Sutton Hoo, 1939

Sutton Hoo, 1939: uncovering the great silver dish. W.F. Grimes (standing right), O.G.S. Crawford (foreground)

C.W.P. in 1940

Flight Lieutenant C.W. Phillips
at Medmenham, 1942

Charles, Margaret and John, 1944

O.G.S. Crawford in his retirement, reproduced by permission of Weidenfeld & Nicolson Ltd.

Officers of the Ordnance Survey October 1949. C. W. P. is ninth from the left in the second row

Chapter 9

Before 1920, and certainly before 1894 when the 25 inch survey of Great Britain was completed, it was a matter of chance whether an antiquity which appeared on one of the printed maps was correctly presented in all its aspects. If it was a thoroughly surveyable object its detail might not be correctly shown, either through ignorance of what this detail implied, or mere failure to take trouble. If it had a proper name, such as Figsbury Rings, that would no doubt be correct but if it were just an earthwork fortress with no proper name it might often be called *Roman Camp* in the appropriate type. An archaeologist, skilled in the field side of his trade, would see the impossibility of this at once.

Surveyable banks, terraces and ditches showing where various forms of land use had once been practised might be shown without description or not shown at all, simply absorbed into the category of the surveyor's 'natural slopes'. As we have also seen completely bogus names could continue on the maps and remain there for years until some future informed revision, and meanwhile holding the Survey up to ridicule in this particular matter.

Close gave Crawford the opportunity to show what could and ought to be done with the antiquity information when he supplied him with the contemporary map cover of a number of Wessex counties in 1919–20 and was shocked at the defects revealed. This honorary correspondent scheme was clearly the way in which a complete cleaning up of this side of the maps could be effectively prepared in advance of revision. Thus when he was appointed to the new post of Archaeology Officer in 1920, Crawford at once set about recruiting a widespread body of honorary correspondents, including myself for Lincolnshire, wherever he could find amateurs who were gaining practical experience with interpreting field features, or at least had a good general knowledge of their own locality and its history.

It was well that he got busy at once, for the Director Generalship of Close, so favourable to this development, ended in 1922 leaving Crawford to do his best with his successor, Brigadier Jack who, though not unfriendly, was obliged to reprimand Crawford for having spent official time on the planning of the first version of his map of Roman Britain without official permission. However, the work having been done, Jack permitted it to go forward with a caution. The Survey was startled by the enthusiastic public reception of this first edition of that map and it paved the way to an early and better second edition and the whole series of period maps which was to appear over the next half century.

By the time of his effective retirement from the Survey in 1940, Crawford had collected a vast amount of material for the next revision at the basic scale but the fierce economy drive which set in after 1922, known as the 'Geddes axe', reduced this sort of revision by the Survey to a trickle, a situation made more serious because of the many topographical changes brought about by the 1914–18 war. The total staff of the Survey was reduced to around 1000 when it should have been increased to make up for the fearful backlog which was now compelling many local authorities to bring the detail on the maps covering their area up to date.

Crawford was able to clear up some of the archaeological detail on some of the maps of smaller scale which were revised, and it is not surprising that he was also able to do excellent work in other enterprises such as period maps and the international 1/1,000,000 scale map of the Roman Empire which arose from a lecture he gave to an international congress of geographers at Cambridge. His convincing demonstration of the use of aerial photography in archaeological discovery, the success of his private venture, *Antiquity*, and his personal field work in most parts of Great Britain which gave great encouragement to the amateurs who were added to his team of honorary correspondents who, in their turn, stimulated interest in others in their localities – all of these were factors in intensifying the explosion of public interest in archaeology which followed on the war of 1939–45.

The great expansion of the Survey staff (in the mid-1930s), resulting from the recommendation of a committee under the chairmanship of Lord Davidson, came too late for much to be done about archaeology before the outbreak of war in 1939 brought it to a halt for the duration of hostilities. However, the committee had approved Crawford's work in general and W.F. Grimes was brought in and appointed Assistant Archaeology Officer in 1938, though little time remained in which he could be effective.

It is significant that Crawford had a clear idea of the most valuable result of his period as Archaeology Officer when the item which he took absolute care to have removed to a place of safety was the large collection of record 6 inch maps and his own field notes. The maps contained the observations of himself and his honorary correspondents over most of Great Britain. If these had been destroyed at the London Road Office in Southampton on the night of November 30 1940, when his office was gutted by fire, it would have been a loss indeed. The core of the archaeological work of the Survey had been saved and it fell to my lot as his effective successor to apply all the matter contained in it to the post-war general revision of the whole country.

Crawford's official retirement came in 1946. He was awarded a C.B.E. in 1950 and I am quite sure that this was a recognition of his general services to archaeology, rather than specifically for his work in the Ordnance Survey. I think that in their eyes his stormy career among them would only have merited a more modest rank in this Order, but his essential contribution was also recognised by institutions like Cambridge and Southampton Universities which honoured it with doctorates. He had always had close relations with the Royal Geographical Society and here again his services to learning and cartography were signalised by the award of the Society's Gold Medal for the year 1940.

He continued to live in his old lair, Hope Villa, at Nursling on the Romsey Road out of Southampton and although before the 1939–45 war he had built himself a bungalow by the seashore in Cyprus and as a sun-lover had often announced that this was to be his retirement home, he sold it, probably because he saw that it would be impossible for him to edit *Antiquity* from that island. So he settled down at Nursling and became an active member of a group known as the Friends of Old Southampton, which was trying to prevent the rebuilding of that badly bombed town from destroying its character as a fine example of a medieval walled seaport town. In this he had some success and his services were much appreciated. He went to Germany from time to time and spent Christmas at Frankfurt, where Gerhard Bersu and his wife had returned from their internment in the Isle of Man. Bersu was reinstated in his post as Director of the Roman-German Commission's Institute in the Palmengartenstrasse. The original building had been wrecked in an air-raid and Bersu had been able to design and supervise the erection of an ultra-modern institute.

As Archaeology Officer I operated from the temporary war-time headquarters at Chessington in Surrey and was thus unable to see much of Crawford, but I was sadly rebuffed when I tried to discuss the new arrangements I was making and he blankly refused to discuss the Ordnance Survey or any of its affairs. My relations with him had always been excellent and I had done him many services since 1929, so this was an index of how thoroughly the iron had entered into his soul. He had some justification, but I was saddened by the thought of how much a little readiness to compromise might have eased his career. The Royal Engineers of his time may have been stiff in some of their attitudes, but they were not fools.

As the 1950s drew on I became uneasy about his isolated situation at Nursling, as the old lady who had looked after him for so long at Hope Villa was now in her eighties. This menage was near its end and if Crawford had any surviving relatives, they were very remote. His old friend, Roland Austin, had retired from helping in the management of *Antiquity* in 1948 and his place was taken by a bookseller friend, H.W. Edwards, and for the last nine years of his life *Antiquity* was run as a private company with Edwards and his wife as directors and Crawford as chairman.

Mercifully, all the problems which might have arisen for his friends as he grew older were solved by an easy and unexpected death. On 28 November 1957, Crawford spent the day in Southampton supporting the cause of the Friends of Southampton. He returned to Nursling, spent the evening as usual and went to bed without complaining of any indisposition. When he was called the next morning there was no answer, and it was found that he had died peacefully in his sleep. He was 71 years of age.

A few days afterwards, in December fog, a small group of his friends, including W.F. Grimes, myself and some of the Friends of Old Southampton gathered at Nursling's little church, where we buried him. I regret to say that the headstone which marks his grave carries on it only his name, dates and 'Founder and Editor of *Antiquity*', presumably at his own request – independent to the last!'

It was abundantly clear that the Edwardses wished to rid themselves of any responsibility for the continuance of *Antiquity*, which was now thirty years old and of international reputation, so a committee of archaeologists was formed, financial guarantees were given, and Glyn Daniel was appointed with his wife Ruth as an able assistant, an arrangement which has proved very successful and would have been entirely satisfactory to the founder.

When I became Archaeology Officer in my turn in the New Year of 1947, I had to start from scratch. At least six years had passed since the Survey had any contact with Crawford, because of his wartime secondment to the National Buildings Record for photographic work. There he had been able to put his great skill as a photographer to good use. Grimes, his natural successor as Archaeology Officer, had also been seconded in 1940 to the Ancient Monuments side of the Office of Works, and was employed till 1946 doing rescue excavations in advance of aerodrome and other forms of wartime construction. Leaving this shortly after Crawford retired, he succeeded him automatically, but almost at once applied for and got the vacant Keepership of the London Museum, something for which he was well fitted by his earlier long experience on the staff of the National Museum of Wales.

I knew Grimes well and he urged me to apply for the vacant Archaeology Officer post when it was advertised and this I did. Ever since I had that fateful meeting with Crawford in Burrington Combe in 1929, my own activities had become progressively more enmeshed with those of the archaeological side of the Survey. Although I was in no official sense a member of the staff, it was not very long before it was considered that I ought to be issued with an official pass of the kind used by all field staff who had to enter private property in the course of their work. I think the only time I had to use it was in 1931, when the weekend invasion of the Peak District by walkers from the Manchester area had led to serious collisions between keepers and walkers on the Derbyshire moors. At the time, I was wanting to examine some features on the moors above Chatsworth House and I took the precaution of visiting the Estate Office first, to show my pass and explain my business. Of course, no objection was raised but when, later on that day, I was moving through the heather I heard angry shouts coming nearer and was soon confronted by three Scots keepers who converged on me from different directions. They were disgusted when I showed them my pass and I was thankful I had taken precautions.

The fact that I had stood down in favour of Grimes when Crawford was given a graduate assistant in 1938 paid off providentially when I was a demobilised ex-service man with family responsibilities in 1945. No doubt there would be other applicants now that the post was advertised, but my pre-war record with the Survey should secure my success. However, before this could be put to the test the Treasury suddenly decided that the candidature of a woman would be in order. This was premature at the time, although today it would be a perfectly normal thing. The number of women who have achieved high distinction since 1945 would now make the chances about equal for both sexes. But this action held up progress in filling the post while the Treasury worked out the special conditions for a woman, should she be chosen. When the interviews took place there was a long list to work through and among those who were obviously unsuitable was a Greek lady who had married a British soldier during the war, had only recently come to this country, and knew little English.

Since Grimes had already moved to the London Museum, and he was the only member of the old archaeology branch who remained in it even for a short time after the war, it was imperative that it should be mobilised again as soon as possible and this delay in appointing a new Archaeology Officer was no help at all. As I have said before, I had to begin absolutely from scratch.

The temporary quarters of the Survey at Chessington were built on green belt land which lay alongside the road from Kingston to Leatherhead. Under wartime emergency conditions no objection could be raised to that. It was regarded as being essentially temporary, even though the site was not evacuated until 1966 and is still in use as a trading estate. After the disaster of November 1940, which severely damaged the old headquarters, it had spent 1942 partly in what could be made usable of the old London Road site, in various requisitioned houses, and also in huts on the Crabwood site.

The new site at Chessington was on a very sticky London clay; it became a sea of mud in the wet winter of 1942 and its opening was delayed till April 1943. The main feature was a straight corridor almost a quarter of a mile long, from which a series of nineteen opposite sets of bays set off at regular intervals. There were other necessary ancillary buildings and a concrete ringroad, large garages and parking spaces. I had two very small rooms to start with, my own which had little more than a table, two chairs and some bookshelves but no carpet. The plain wooden furniture bore the branded mark 'Ed. VII' and was far past its prime. The other room, slightly larger, accommodated my superintendent, A.C. Bickers, a legacy from Grimes' short period, and two minor clerical types, one with a serious nervous affliction – a very odd team.

There was no doubt about the versatility of Bickers. Publicly he was a skilled photo-writer and privately a conjurer of professional status with a boundless self-confidence and a good general knowledge of the working of the Survey. He knew nothing about archaeology but had a great capacity for getting things done. He had a far from immaculate reputation. In the recent war he had been engaged in various parts of the Mediterranean theatre, working with map-printing units in the field. Brigadier Papworth, my immediate chief, experienced him during that period and it seems that the rumours which were current about the surreptitious sale of precious printing paper to local villains were probably true. The proceeds of such sales were believed to be salted down in various places awaiting collection by him when the opportunity arose after the war. Algiers was probably one of these, for there he still had a French lady friend.

It was my bad luck that the first months of my time at Chessington coincided with one of the most severe and unbroken cold spells to date in the twentieth century. It was not possible for me to think of moving my family to the Chessington area until I knew a great deal more about my situation and meanwhile they were comfortable at 9, Madingley Road.

My mother was living in the bungalow at Woodley outside Reading, where she had been through most of the late war, but she was now alone since the death of her sister Emma in June 1943. The distance between Woodley and Chessington was not more than twenty-five miles by the shortest route, and I resolved to spend the nights at Woodley and go home to Cambridge for the weekends. My reason for this rather Quixotic conduct which the dreadful weather conditions made very fatiguing, was to keep up my mother's morale till we could all be housed near my work.

The daily journeys in this severe weather were very hard going over roads which had not been cleared of snow and now were sheets of ice. After each journey to Woodley I often had to spend some of the evening trying to increase the warmth of the bungalow by cladding the upper side of the ceiling with layers of newspaper and sealing up all cracks. Fuel was also in short supply over the whole country and I scavenged any loose wood I could see along the road. But in these three months, with the aid of Bickers, I recruited the beginning of a staff in J. Fox, W.G. Stanhope-Lovell and D.C. Ball. Although in the course of my eighteen years at the Ordnance Survey the Archaeology Division came to contain among its final staff of fifty-seven a number of very able people, several of whom left to better themselves in other departments of the state's care for its ancient heritage, it was these three men who were its main pillars.

Fox was a man of determined character and appearance and belonged to an old Survey family. He was a native of Hawick in the Border country and had been brought up as a Roman Catholic; at one time he was destined for the priesthood. In the war he had attained the rank of major in the Royal Engineers and took part in the difficult action at Keren in the reconquest of Abyssinia. He was feared rather than loved in the Division but he supported me loyally in the various tussles I had with the administrative side of the Survey. When we had settled down, the Assistant Archaeology Officer's post was filled by two graduates in succession and when the second man resigned to take up a University post, Fox became his successor, the degree requirement being waived because by that time he had been elected to the Society of Antiquaries. After my time, when my successor had also retired, he succeeded to the Archaeology Officer post and should have done so when I retired, for after eighteen years in the business his practical knowledge for the post was perfect. My advice was not taken in this case, with disastrous results.

W.G. Stanhope-Lovell was a different type, this time from a clerical home with a more scholarly background. At one time his father had been archivist to the Marquess of Salisbury at Hatfield House. He was in the Royal Artillery in the war and was in many ways the antithesis of Fox. He played a major part in organising our recording systems and worked very well with Fox. He had a notable determination to carry out all that he began to a successful conclusion.

D.C. Ball provided the final link between the field activity of the division in securing and checking the accurate transfer of its results to the printed map. He insisted on meticulous accuracy in his part of the staff, without which our service to the public would be in vain, and had a thorough knowledge of the drawing and reproduction side of the Survey. After retirement, he was successful in other forms of public life and was Mayor of Winchester.

It was a mercy that three such able people had been added to my staff when, early in March, with the frost still holding, I decided to have a short break and go down to Bristol to see how my brother Jack was settling in again at Clifton. I drove over the Cotswolds and from Stow-in-the-Wold went down to Andoversford and so on to Cheltenham and Gloucester from where on to Bristol conditions were easier. From Stow to the top of the hill above Andoversford the drifts of snow were enormous. A one-track way with occasional passing places had been cleared along this section and it was an unusual experience to drive several miles through snow banked higher than the car on both sides.

It snowed again at Bristol that night and I decided not to prolong my visit but to make for Woodley, where I would sleep and then go on to Cambridge the next day. I made my way over slippery roads through Bath as far as Box, where I decided to take the Devizes rather than the Chippenham branch of the road on to Reading. Conditions under wheel were very bad but I got as far as Devizes and then turned up the easy slopes to Beckhampton where I should rejoin the road to Reading. But when I got on to the level stretch beyond the passage through the Wansdyke and within half a mile of Beckhampton, the road had disappeared below a level and unbroken drift of snow which had not yet been cleared. Before long I was joined by others until a

R.A.F. lorry appeared from the direction of Devizes with a large crew of diggers. It still took some time to get through to Beckhampton, but at last we were free and I reached Reading and Woodley without any further trouble. I drove on to Cambridge the next day and although road conditions were not good across the higher ground between Stevenage and Baldock I pushed along Therfield Heath to Royston and so was home before dark.

It was a cheerful homecoming, but almost my last. Next morning I sat down to my breakfast in comfort but before the meal was finished I was seized by severe abdominal pain. Soon I was only semi-conscious; our doctor came and diagnosed an internal stoppage and in the afternoon I was removed to the Evelyn Nursing Home where I was operated on by Mr Pennell. The trouble was caused by a congenital intussusception of the bowel and it was a mercy that the attack did not take place while I was on the road, for my chances of survival might have been small. As it was, I withstood the operation well and was home, weak but convalescent, in three weeks time. While I was in the nursing home, a general thaw set in and large areas of Fenland were flooded.

My period of convalescence, which lasted till May 27, would have been easier had I not known that there was a big task awaiting me at Chessington, as I was reminded by Bickers, who came down to Cambridge to see me and to report how Fox and his colleagues were shaping. There is no doubt that I should have prolonged my absence till at least midsummer, but I was anxious to make a beginning.

When I got back to Chessington I found that there had been an important achievement during my absence for which Bickers must get full credit. While examining the materials available for our work, I found that the original drawings made between 1796 and 1844 during the surveys for the first 1 inch series were still present in the office, but in a bad state of neglect. No-one seems to have realised their importance as documents showing the precise state of the country over much of England and Wales at the various times of their creation. They had been lucky to escape the holocaust of November 1940.

To safeguard this information it was obviously necessary to have at least one photographic copy made to increase its chance of survival, but at the same time it seemed unlikely that the photographic side would undertake the duplication of this mass of some four hundred sheets of various shapes and sizes, to say nothing of their filthy condition. I was therefore delighted to find that Bickers had privately managed to get this done in my absence. His combination of almost impudent persistence where his interest was engaged, together with his readiness to by-pass all the proper channels, had somehow achieved this, and he can never have done a more useful piece of work. I did not enquire how it had been done but gladly accepted the result.

Some years later, when Brigadier M. Collins was Director of Map Production I drew his attention to this important record material. He was another unconventional type of great intelligence and he at once set about having the originals transferred to the Map Room of the British Museum, where R.A. Skelton had them all cleaned and restored. Thus an invaluable record was preserved and made available for public consultation instead of continuing to moulder at the Survey. At the same time, all the original hill drawings for this first edition went to the same place. Shortly after my return to Chessington Bickers handed in his resignation, to no-one's surprise, and retired to Algiers, where he was united with his wartime lady friend, leaving his wife and adolescent daughter behind him. To the best of my knowledge he was never seen again in this country. So much for Bickers.

It is now necessary to describe the post-war programme of the Survey in revision, a process which followed the recommendations of the pre-war Davidson Committee. First priority was given to an entirely new 50 inch to the mile survey of all cities, towns and built-up areas. Parallel with this a general revision of the whole 25 inch map cover of Great Britain was to be carried out, with its completion expected in the mid-1980s. From this would be derived a 2½ inch series. Great Britain was to be divided into six regions, of which Scotland would be one, and in these regions a new system of continuous revision would be established.

Before Davidson, the revision procedure of the Survey had been that of the travelling circus. The decision having been made to revise an area, advance notice of this would be given by posters announcing the fact, and warning all occupiers of premises and land of the penalties attaching to refusal to permit entry of Ordnance staff to do their work under the terms laid down by the Ordnance Survey Act of 1840. The revision completed – and probably a very necessary one – the surveyors would depart and perhaps not to be seen again in that area for twenty years, during which period the maps would again become progressively more out of date. This was called cyclical revision. There was also the human factor involving the position of the surveyors themselves. Under the cyclical system the surveyors doing the work, Royal Engineers of the rank and file of the Ordnance Survey to a man, were absent for long periods from their wives and families, who had to remain in the barrack accommodation at Southampton. So much for cyclical revision.

The new scheme brought in by the Davidson Report provided that the field staff in the six new regions would be progressively settled in town and country groups. In each of the six regions the first areas to be revised would be the most populous ones and as each was completed, staff would be left permanently living there to keep the area under constant supervision as members of the local community. They would note all topographical changes, keep in touch with the local authorities, survey changes and enter them upon the documents of the local map cover kept in their local group offices. The same arrangements would be made later for other groups permanently settled in the more thinly populated areas of the region, Staff would be able to live with their families and the whole field staff of the Survey would be progressively deployed in this way as the post-war revision proceeded. Once all the town and country groups were in place at the end of the revision, an up-to-date map of any area could be published without delay.

Of course, a map of an inhabited country is out of date in some degree almost from the day it is printed, but the old scandal of Ordnance Maps being grossly out-of-date over large areas was ended and the whole of the field staff were now able to live normal lives with their wives and families.

In developing an organisation to match up to the requirements of continuous revision we began with the handicap of a late start. We could do very little until the early summer of 1947, when I had returned from my operation, whereas the Field Division had already begun its work with the 50 and 25 inch series nearly two years earlier. However, there was not too much to worry us in this because all the early work was being done in built-up or intensely urban areas on the two scales. Almost all the antiquity information that we could ever hope to show was already on the maps of these areas, usually in the form of ancient buildings or their sites. Many of the country's older towns had suffered from attack in the late war and much of their earlier history would no doubt be revealed during the rebuilding process or by deliberate excavation in the coming years, but the area in which we should find much to concern us would be the countryside. We should require six field groups, each with a competent leader, who would have a good working knowledge of archaeology and be capable of increasing it by field experience. These groups would also require briefs provided from Headquarters of what they might expect in the particular area in which they were working.

When Crawford began back in 1920 he had to remind even Sir Charles Close, who was not ignorant of what field archaeology involved, that he must actually go and verify the character of antiquities in the field. This verification he later did in a very big way during his career but there is reason to believe that his superiors in the Survey became quite willing that he should be absent for long periods in the field because life was quieter for them at the office when he was not at Southampton. But things should have moved on by the later 1940s when I asked permission for some of my earliest field staff go into Sussex in order to verify the character of some antiquities on maps under revision there. My action was challenged by the administrators, but my immediate senior, Brigadier Papworth, had to remind them that this could not be done while remaining seated in the office.

On my return to Chessington in May 1947, there could be no question of my resuming my daily journey between the office and Woodley. This, and the freakish weather in which it had been carried out, had probably been contributory factors to my illness and now compelled me to live near the office in the week, and I was well looked after by Mr and Mrs Rodwell in their house at Prince's Avenue, Tolworth, only a couple of miles away.

We now set about the recruitment of a staff for the Archaeology Branch which would be capable of taking advantage of the new interest of the public at large in archaeology which had been growing quietly before 1940, greatly due to Crawford's influence and which exploded in a remarkable way after 1945 when the B.B.C. put on its *Animal, Vegetable or Mineral* programme, wonderfully compered by Dr Glyn Daniel and with its most striking participant the flamboyant personality of Sir Mortimer Wheeler. This brought archaeology into the British home as an entertainment and it was exemplified in a practical way by the many excavations which began in war-damaged cities and towns in advance of rebuilding. Working as a volunteer in these occupations became a fashionable and instructive form of activity for thousands of people, young and old.

The discovery of new sites by aerial photography was constantly extending the boundaries of the subject. The aerial photography of Professor St. Joseph from Cambridge University was the best and most dramatic example of this. In the case of specific fields like the archaeology of the Anglo-Saxon and medieval periods, instead of a limited range like pagan cemeteries, some great linear earthworks and a few famous early churches and crosses, there was added a much wider range which included a number of royal residences, fortified sites and a great increase in the number of pre-Conquest churches. After the Conquest there was the development of the castle, moated sites and deserted villages. In all but the earliest periods much had been learned about the various systems of agriculture. Today, far on in the Industrial Revolution as we are, there is much belonging to the earlier stages of this which may require the notice of the Survey.

We now met with one of the most persistent encumbrances arising out of our position in the Survey. No one could be recruited from outside the Survey staff on the sole grounds of archaeological competence. If anyone wanted to join our staff they would have to enter the Survey as an ordinary entrant and take the basic training. If they were then posted to one of the divisions, they would be open to apply to join us when we invited applications though, of course, their superiors in their division could always refuse to release them, and in any case we might not choose them. We simply looked among the applicants who had passed through these preliminary stages for a reasonable amount of intelligence, readiness to take on the work when its general character had been explained to them, and a genuine willingness to learn. Occasionally, I think, the B.B.C. feature mentioned above attracted people to us who had found their present employment in the Survey dull and monotonous, and saw a much more varied and interesting prospect in archaeology. During my time we collected quite a number of these 'refugees' and most of them became informed and useful after a short time.

The fact that we drew most of our recruits from the Field Division did not always make us very popular in that quarter and the more so when we had secured someone who they thought might be really useful among them. I need hardly say that James Fox, Stanhope-Lovell and Ball were all products of Field. When I joined the Survey staff, archaeology was under the directorate of Map Production, but before I retired we had found our logical place as part of the Field Directorate.

Since none of my staff had any practical knowledge of archaeology, except of the most superficial kind, I now had to decide who were most fit to head the six teams we were creating to match up to the pattern of the general revision. I therefore took them out personally for a road tour through most of southern England south of the Thames, excluding Devon and Cornwall west of Exeter. We visited as many and as varied a list of sites as possible and I did my best to demonstrate and explain each one, pointing out the problems, if any, which would arise in representing it with the correct conventions on an Ordnance Survey map.

Several of these men proved to be 'naturals' for this kind of work and within a year or two were already wide-awake to the various clues which would lead them to their quarry on more than one type of geological background. At this stage we were not yet able to do much about the moorish and mountainous country which is so frequent in parts of the south-west, Wales, and the whole of the Highland zone from the Peak of Derbyshire right up north to the Shetlands, but in 1947 and 1948 the general revision was still almost entirely engaged in urban and densely built-up areas. The upland country could wait.

Meanwhile, as a whole, the staff was recommended some basic reading and this raised the whole question of books. The disaster of 1940 had consumed Crawford's private library in his office, as well as all the books available in the old Survey library, which was another casualty. I found nothing but empty shelves waiting for me at Chessington and I had to bring my own collection of books up from Cambridge for use till we could get our own. We required either access to, or possession of, as much of the literature relating to antiquities in Great Britain as possible. This deficiency at Southampton and the need to go to Oxford, Cambridge or London to consult books had been a great tax on Crawford's time, and expensive to the Survey in railway fares.

Whenever a party went into an area to check up the accuracy and detail representation of a map that was to be revised, a group permanently in the office under the supervision of Stanhope-Lovell would have examined every book bearing on the archaeology of the area concerned, and the same search would be made in the periodical publications of local and national archaeological societies. Any available photographic cover of the area from the air would be examined and here a most valuable liaison was made with Dr St. Joseph, who was in charge of the newly-created Cambridge Committee for Aerial Photography, and increasingly able to provide us with new features observed from the air during the exploratory flights that he was making, mainly in the earlier part of the year, when the differential growth of crops could be very revealing.

Our contribution to this arrangement was the free supply of his map requirements, which could be considerable, but it was a good bargain for it enabled us to get a mass of information direct 'from the horse's mouth' without waiting until the information came through, often much later, in formal reports to the archaeological journals. This serves to remind me that the Division was also required to become a regular subscriber to these journals, as well as to the proceedings of the local archaeological societies. Most of these were on a county basis but they were thin on the ground in Wales and Scotland.

For a while there was an idea that the Archaeology Branch might be sited in the Cambridge Town Group Office – there was a large regional complex of Civil Service and other Government offices in Brooklands Avenue at Cambridge – and permission might be got to make use of the very large resources of the University Library. Additionally, we would be within a walk of Dr St. Joseph's office. This idea was the more attractive because a post-war plan was being considered to end the Survey's hundred-year old association with Southampton, which was not very convenient in relation to the country as a whole, and to build a new headquarters on a site between the east midland towns of Wellingborough and Kettering, not more than thirty-six miles from Cambridge.

All this came to nothing because the University objected to the accommodation it required for post-war students, many of them married men, being pre-empted by civil servants, and at the same time the people of Southampton petitioned for the restoration of the Survey to their town. It had housed the office since that body had been forced to quit the Tower of London owing to another fire in 1840 and it had become an important part of the local community, which would be impoverished by its loss.

Forced back on Chessington, we were able to make arrangements by which we could send staff regularly to make use of the required books at both the British Museum library and also at that of the Society of Antiquaries at Burlington House. The administrative staff agreed to this and the work went on quite efficiently, but it also had grave weaknesses, which I had to point out would be overcome by our possessing the books ourselves and continuing to build up the collection.

The view which I pressed upon the administrators was that, if this work was to be done at all, and this was not disputed, we should proceed at once to buy all the books required and that this would be an expansion of the Survey's own library, but housed for convenience with our division. The second-hand price of books was rising steadily and the cost of sending a number of people to London every day and supervising the performance of their work when they got there, would be solved by making it possible to do the work at Chessington. The cost of buying all the books would be heavy, but set against this, the travel expenses would cease and the cash value of good archaeological books was always increasing. If properly cared for they would not be a wasting asset and the same thing applied to the subscriptions to periodicals which we required. This view was accepted, very much to our advantage.

Chapter 10

In all my eighteen years as Archaeology Officer I had my eyes on larger issues than those solely concerned with the work of the Survey. The rate of destruction of antiquities which had taken place since the outbreak of the 1914–18 war had been alarming. The ploughing-up campaign, made necessary to provide more food when the life of the country had been threatened by the German U-boat campaign, had broken up the great tracts of downland country which were covered with the clear evidence of ancient agriculture, but had long reverted to the grazing of sheep. There had been much construction work which had not been watched for what it might reveal of archaeological interest. But the recent war of 1939–45 had been far more destructive. There had been further ploughing-up for the same reason and the damage done to marginal lands in this way by people wanting to qualify for a subsidy, and by the Forestry Commission breaking up ground to plant conifers, ravaged areas where there were more than the usual quota of antiquities which had survived hitherto because of the poverty of their background. The extent of land which had disappeared under concrete in the construction of aerodromes and other wartime works was very large. In the coal-mining areas a wave of open-cast mining to remedy fuel shortages contributed its quota of destruction and, particularly in the second war, the development of earth-moving machinery accelerated all these disturbances of the surface. In early days the hummocky areas marking the sites of deserted villages had often been left as pasture because of the labour of levelling the area, but a bulldozer could do the job in a couple of hours. New towns, new suburbs and new roads all made their contribution.

Of course, these developments were inevitable but in 1947 they meant that unless something was done quickly to obtain some record of surviving traces of antiquity, all effective knowledge of them must be lost, and this when air-photography had vastly increased the power to recognise them. The protection afforded by scheduling under the Ancient Monuments Acts was still liable to be ineffective in practice, save in exceptional cases.

In 1947 the archaeological services of the state did not have the resources to meet the needs of the time. Their work was admirable in quality but its production was geared to the more leisurely age in which they were created. As matters stood in 1947 the completion of the Royal Commissions' work over the whole of Great Britain could not be expected within a reasonable time without massive reinforcements. Since then there had been a marked improvement through an increase in staff and its redeployment, but at the time completion could not be expected before much of the matter of their enquiry had been either damaged or destroyed.

The need was for a speedy reconnaissance and non-intensive record of everything in field archaeology which could be recognised while it still existed, to be completed before the end of the twentieth century. Such a record would be invaluable and would act as a preliminary briefing course for the Commissions as they took up new areas in their work. Much time and duplication of effort would be saved in this way.

The only body which was scheduled to make a complete investigatory passage through all parts of the country in a matter of decades after 1945 was the Ordnance Survey. It was therefore a duty to attempt the expansion of its archaeological work to meet this requirement, while also serving the purposes of the Survey. It was not only a question of doing what was necessary to give an adequate treatment of archaeological topography on the published maps. This should be backed by a recording system which would give, in relatively simple form, an accurate view of the archaeological content of all the areas covered by the general revision. It would provide a source from which period maps could be compiled and revised, as well as being a basic public record.

Once we had got our books and material began to come in from the field parties working in the six regions, Stanhope-Lovell and his office staff could get to work setting up this record, and here at once we faced the problem of recruiting a staff for this specialised work. After a phase of trial and error which led to one or two false starts the record was launched.

It took the form of an index on specially ruled and compartmented cards measuring eight inches by five inches. The National Grid was adopted as a means of pinpointing locations with speed and accuracy. At first the index was based on parishes grouped by counties but later this was re-ordered into the series of 100 kilometre squares of the National Grid. Each monument, site and find received its own card ranged in a National Grid numbering sequence within its 100 kilometre. The National Grid reference and parish were given along with an account of its state at the time of the field section's visit. Where appropriate, a field sketch was provided and also photographs of sufficient quality to aid identification if this should be needed. Literary references were given and the names of any local informants were included along with the initial of the member of the staff responsible for the card and also the date of its creation.

The contents of cards varied much in importance but it was customary to collect all valid information arising from books, informants or direct field observation, even when the subject might not be of sufficient importance to put on a published map. The purpose of this was twofold: to make a record of items which might otherwise escape notice elsewhere, and to provide a source for period map work. It was unwise to ignore items without much apparent importance; they might be clues to important discoveries later. As an instance of this, casual finds of human remains may be the first hint of the presence of an Anglo-Saxon cemetery.

In the same way, records were made of material relating to historic sites. The Division only dealt with buildings when they were either ancient ruins or structures of historical or antiquarian importance which should be noticed on maps. No attempt was made to survey them as buildings except for ground plan, but care was taken to describe them accurately. The abandonment of the old rule which confined the Survey's interest to antiquities older than 1688 now permitted the recording of industrial archaeology and other relevant features down to 1850.

Parallel with the card record a visual record was also maintained on the 1/50,000 maps covering each 100 kilometre square. On these each feature was noted in its place as it became the subject of a card in the main record; in this way it was possible to make a quick inspection of the known content of any area before consulting the fuller information provided by the cards. Some areas where features occurred in large numbers or had unusually complex plans were also recorded on the 25 inch maps when those at the smaller scale were inadequate to carry all the various notations.

On the whole the record worked well. It was appreciated by its users, including other official bodies, and was accorded recognition as the non-intensive record of British archaeological topography. It supplied all that was basically necessary but, as part of the apparatus of a national cartographic survey, its value was primarily topographical. In an ideal world there would also be a subject index of archaeology. The creation of this would be an enormous and highly complex business requiring a fully qualified staff and no part of the business of the Ordnance Survey.

Finally, it must be confessed that the maintenance of a good standard in this record was a subject of continual anxiety. The division's limited field of recruitment, which has already been mentioned as a troublesome factor in the membership of the field parties, made it difficult to procure staff fully competent to do this kind of work. But at the time of its inception it had the merit of being part of an organisation which must of necessity be continuous in its action and completely nation-wide in scope. It did not encroach on the sphere of action of the other organs of state archaeology and could provide a continuing record of developments in archaeological topography guaranteed by full survey accuracy and nationwide field experience on which anyone could call at need.

I have already described my illness of March 1947, and the complications it introduced into the beginning of my period as Archaeology Officer. I returned to duty in May, Bickers withdrew permanently to North Africa, and during the summer and early autumn of the year I was busy procuring all that was necessary towards getting together the elements of the six field parties we should now need to match the six regions of the general revision now under way. These men were all trained surveyors but they knew very little, if anything, about archaeology and the various guises under which it appears in town and country, some of them very obvious but grading down to features which require genuine detective work to recognise and understand. I had to lecture to them on all this with illustrations from the maps we were going to revise. This was all in the office but it had to be demonstrated by actual experience in the field.

I have mentioned this above, but will now deal with it in more detail. We made a long trip in warm weather, which covered at least one example of practically every kind of antiquity to be met with in the south and south-east of England. We visited sites like Portchester and Pevensey where Roman coast defence forts had later been used as the baileys of medieval castles, had sheltered monastic buildings, and been used in quite recent times as prisoner-of-war camps. Inevitably we visited Maiden Castle in Dorset, where a Neolithic causewayed camp had been incorporated into a gigantic Iron Age contour fortress with multiple defences and death-trap entrances, the whole site to house nothing more than a small Romano-British temple and the home of its priest.

Further north in Dorset we examined the site at Hod Hill where the Roman invaders, having stormed a more or less rectangular native fortress whose shape was determined by the sloping hill top it occupied, used the highest corner as the site for a small cavalry detachment. In West Sussex we visited the Trundle where I held forth about the excavations I had taken part in under Curwen, which had revealed another case of a Neolithic causewayed camp being later made the site of an Iron Age hill fort whose entrances, built of heavy timbers, had been deliberately removed when the Romans of the Claudian conquest created a new centre for Cogidubnus the local 'Quisling' prince's realm on the plain below at *Noviomagus Regnensium*, now known to us as Chichester. The last stage at the Trundle was the building in the Middle Ages of a chapel for St. Roche on the very summit of the hill that bears his name.

We saw many examples of the still numerous traces of prehistoric and pre-enclosure agriculture and I explained with field and map illustrations how the actual or former course of a Roman road may be identified. At Chute Causeway, in the hilly country north-west of Andover, I showed how the Roman road builders were prepared to deviate from the straight course in the face of a really serious obstacle.

This rapid and exhausting tour went off without any mishap but I remember one curious encounter that we had during its course. We were in the central area of Salisbury Plain between Chitterne and Shrewton and at lunch time we halted by the roadside to eat. Although the weather was very warm there was a strong hot wind blowing and as the deep dry ditch which carries a 'winterbourne' stream was right by the side of the road I suggested that we should get down into the ditch to eat our meal. We had been eating for a few minutes when there was a startled cry. I went down to see the cause and it was because someone had spotted a morell as large as a moderate-sized pumpkin growing on the floor of the ditch. I had to explain that it was only a fungus, a rarity, and a very odd looking one, but that it would not bite and was even edible if treated in the right way. We left it undisturbed in the hope that it would beget others. Before many of these men had finished their service with the Survey their wide-ranging travel within Great Britain was to give them a complete view of most of the country's fauna and flora.

All this activity took us on into the autumn and I was looking forward to a real beginning of work with the opening of 1948, when I was incapacitated once more and had to take to my bed at Cambridge. I was at home about a week before Christmas for the usual weekend and was sawing up some logs when I suddenly felt too weak to continue. This was the penalty of too short a convalescence after my operation in March and our doctor packed me off to bed at once because I had developed a pleural effusion. The only way to deal with this was to remain in bed and hope that it would disperse without having to be tapped. In bed I stayed until the liquid dispersed.

This was a distressing time, for I could not help worrying about what was happening in the office, though in fact Fox rose nobly to the occasion. But I was able to do one useful job in bed. My friend, Harry Godwin, had now succeeded Sir Albert Seward as Professor of Botany and was laying the foundations of his famous *Flora of the British Isles*. This had a great index as its base and I was able to be useful to him by punching a great many cards for this. But I was now in a serious position with regard to the Survey. My two illnesses had kept me from the office for more than six months and I was now on half pay; I think that the authorities at Chessington were expecting to receive my resignation.

Whatever the expectations at Chessington I did not resign. By March I had settled in again and had resumed my lodgings with the Rodwells at Tolworth in Prince's Avenue. In fact, from this point on until my retirement at the end of March 1965, I lost almost no time at all through sickness. Not even a privately recognised touch of coronary thrombosis brought on by my being overweight and cycling back and forth twice each day between the office and the home I eventually set up in Surbiton involved me in any more than some advice from my doctor, a course of dieting and less cycling uphill.

Any hope of the branch being sited at Cambridge had now ended with the effective abandonment of the Wellingborough re-siting project and the ban placed by the University on any further basing of groups of civil servants at Cambridge. Chessington was to be the site of the headquarters, while the Field Directorate and the Drawing and Reproduction sides were to be carried out at the two Southampton sites, the old London Road Office restored from its ashes, and a set of temporary offices occupying the Crabwood House site, on which the whole Survey would be accommodated in one large purpose-built building, a dream only to be realised in 1968. Contact between Chessington and Southampton was maintained by a daily road shuttle.

By midsummer in 1949 it was clear that we must leave Cambridge and find a house near the office at Chessington. The housing situation in Surrey was still very difficult and my family was now increased by the birth of a daughter in 1947 and their education had to be considered. Our search ranged round the pleasant country south of Chessington – Effingham, Great Bookham, Leatherhead, and Epsom, but all these would have meant varying degrees of road travel every day and in October we decided on a largish semi-detached house: No. 103, Ditton Road, in the upper part of Surbiton and about a mile and a half from the Office.

I shall make no attempt to describe this house, except to say that it had been built circa 1878–80 and was now in need of thorough modernisation, which I fear we never gave it. However, its long-term value depended largely on its area of land, which was a source of much labour to keep in good condition but did provide us with a generous amount of fruit and vegetables over a period of thirty years and was its principal attraction to developers when we came to move in 1979.

There were also good schools close by for both our children and Surbiton was within fifteen miles of London with a very frequent train service which was of great value to my wife when she began to resume her former life as a scholar and teacher in the University of London. But life in the one-time 'Queen of the Suburbs' was not unclouded, for it was an unfriendly community which kept itself to itself; however, this did not outweigh its advantages. I was away a good deal of my time visiting regional offices, and going into the field to see how our regional sections were faring. I had also to visit our honorary correspondents, assess their value (not always very great) and lecture to local societies to publicise our work and recruit more helpers.

While I had been struggling up out of my pleurisy my superintendent Fox had not been idle. Before I went sick we had recruited enough Grade IIIs and Grade IVs to man the six field units and Stanhope-Lovell, with the help of D.C. Ball, now also had lower-grade staff learning the business of making cards of reference to antiquities in books, interpreting air-photographs supplied by St. Joseph at Cambridge and, in the light of discoveries from this source, drawing up briefs for our survey parties to use in the field. Ball was also training others in seeing the results sent back from the field properly presented for drawing and reproduction on, or removal from, the new edition. The field parties visited local museums and any other reasonably well-provenanced collections in private hands. They also sought out and made contact with local antiquaries and any other knowledgeable folk. Their concern was always with the precise location of find-spots.

Of course they had to be critical of much of this information for the mere fact that pottery, coins or other moveables have been found on a certain spot does not mean that *ipso facto* there was a site of the indicated age there. It may be a sign that their original site is not far away. Circumstances alter cases, and mistakes in identification could be relied on to decrease and vanish with experience.

It was no part of the Survey's duty to deal with the Isle of Man and the Channel Islands. This was a matter of history but in practice, surveys of these islands were carried out by the Ordnance Survey on repayment. During my period of duty we revised the 6 inch maps of Man once and also did work in both Jersey and Guernsey.

The Channel Islands had been in enemy occupation through almost the whole of the 1939–45 war and the occupying forces had made many topographical changes in them in the course of incorporating them into the defensive system against Allied attempts to invade Europe, the so-called Atlantic Wall. Perhaps the chief sufferer in the course of this defensive work was Alderney. It is the smallest of the significantly inhabited islands in the group and only two miles long. It was the object of the special attention of the Germans, who removed its population and brought in 'slave labour' from eastern Europe to build a section of the wall at Longy Bay, the only stretch of flat coastline. They also built a small airfield with a runway along the lofty spine of the island. This spine carried the only cultivated land in the island, divided into small fields by boundary walls, and all of these had been swept away in the process. The Ordnance Survey had put a small party on to the island to re-establish all boundaries and rights of way in their old positions on the pre-war map and I had to check up on the state of the antiquities. There were a few minor megalithic tombs, mostly still buried in heather, which might have suffered, and an interesting Roman site.

I flew out from the newly-opened airfield at Gatwick on a very hot summer day in 1950 in a little Rapide aircraft and after a very bumpy flight, in which I passed almost directly over my old home at Arundel, I landed safely on the airfield which was the cause of most of the trouble. I put up at the Harbour Lights Hotel and soon found that many of the pre-war deported population had not returned and had been replaced by a curious collection of drunks and ne'er-do-wells, some of whom were based at my hotel and were taking advantage of the low price of drinks and tobacco and the fact that only one policeman from Guernsey came over each month, and that he was generally indifferent to closing hours. It was often difficult to sleep through the noise downstairs which often went on into the small hours.

The antiquities in Alderney were few in number and minor, with one important exception, and they had not been disturbed. This exception, the so-called 'Nunnery', was interesting, a small Roman coast defence fort tucked into the corner of Longy Bay and commanding a view over the Race of Alderney and the north-west corner of the Cherbourg peninsula. It played a part in the defence of the coast of Gaul similar to the British system from Brancaster in Norfolk round to Portchester and Carisbrooke in Hampshire and the Isle of Wight. It was in a remarkable state of preservation, rectangular, and with most of its defensive walls still standing to the height of crenellation and rampart walk. But the seaward side had been undermined and had collapsed forward on to the beach. It was still complete enough in the eighteenth century to shelter the hutments of the local garrison, which kept an eye upon the French over the Race. The name 'Nunnery' is a slighting reference to the morals of this garrison. Having completed my check of the antiquities of Alderney I flew back to Gatwick via Southampton airport and resumed my normal work at the office.

Now to continue my account of my relations with my colleagues at Chessington. In many ways the Ordnance Survey was a very anomalous institution. Like Topsy, it had 'growed'. When it began in 1791 it was unquestionably a military body under the control of the Board of Ordnance and, ultimately, of the War Office. From its earliest days there had always been civilians on the staff in some numbers both as surveyors, draughtsmen and printers. After the 6 inch survey of Ireland was completed and the 'Battle of the Scales' had been settled in favour of 25 inches to the mile, control of the Survey was taken from the War Office and given to the Board of Agriculture, continuing in this relationship through the various changes which this body had undergone, ending up at the time of the second World War as the Ministry of Agriculture, Fisheries and Food, a typically British process. As it had been since 1791, the Survey was still the source of training for the Royal Engineers as the survey and cartographic side of the Army. In 1920 Sir Charles Close had secured the appointment of the first civilian officer to deal with archaeology and another civilian officer was introduced when Crawford secured Grimes as his assistant shortly before 1939. There were various reasons why the Royal Engineer officers resented Crawford's appointment and some of them may have been farsighted enough to see that he was the first breach in their monopoly, which was to be lost after the next sixty years when the Survey was completely civilianised.

In the early twentieth century a great preponderance of the staff was civilian but the best jobs available for civilians were seldom attained by them because when the sappers of the Royal Engineers Battalion became time-expired they were liable to move into the higher-grade civilian jobs and so skim off the cream of the able civilian's reasonable expectation. This grievance ended when the Ordnance Battalion was permanently disbanded in the 1939–45 war.

The Davidson Committee, which considered the run-down state of the Survey in the mid-1930s, did nothing to remove the anomalous situation under which the Director-General's post and all the Directorates continued to be exclusively in the hands of the military, while the Survey as a whole still remained under the direction of a civilian Ministry and the opportunities for civilians continued to be very limited.

Until this time, the control of Establishment and Finance in the Survey had been in the hands of an Executive Officer (R.E.), but since the Survey was ultimately under a civilian Ministry the Director-General of the time, Major-General McLeod, thought that there would be convenience in substituting a civilian Director of Establishment and Finance for this officer.

This was a further stage in the civilianisation of the Survey and was regarded as a selling of the pass by his fellow officers. But the position of Great Britain in the world had changed by the end of the 1939–45 war and, although the survey and cartographic needs of the country were as great or greater than ever, the needs of the Army were not what they had been before 1939.

McLeod's request was accepted and the first appointee from the Ministry was Mr S.A. Smith, but he was soon gone because he was near retirement. Even before he went he had created a small hierarchy of civilian administrators in the office, much disliked by the military, and his successor, Mr F.G.C. Bentley, was to last most of my time and, as a stern guardian of the purse strings, was involved in many a tussle with me.

One of the clearest revelations of why we tussled is to be found in a question which he once asked me when I was seeking his approval of my estimate of the right number to be printed of the first edition of our period map *Monastic Britain*, which I hoped would go on sale just before Christmas, 1950. Its preparation had been delayed by the war. It was designed to show the exact situation in Britain of all monastic houses founded after 1066, the Order to which each one belonged, whether of men or women, and any changes of location until they were all abolished in the sixteenth century.

We were coming to the Christmas season and I was sure many people would buy them as presents as well as for themselves. I therefore ventured the figure of 5000 as a first printing and I was confident they would find a ready sale. However, Bentley was aghast at my asking for so many; his comment was: 'Only Roman Catholics will buy them.' I disagreed and said that the map was not a cult object but was a work of general interest and educational value. But he imposed the figure of 2000 and I made the mistake of not standing firm and appealing to the Director-General, who would certainly have supported me. But I had as yet had little experience of handling Mr Bentley and I weakly gave way. My advice on a technical matter was not taken. In the event, the 2000 were all snapped up almost on the day of publication and the presses had to be set turning again to produce another 5000 and more before Christmas. I do not recall the precise details now but an order of 10,000 would have been nearer the mark. Before he retired from his directorate, Bentley and I came to a much better understanding; in the last two or three years of my own time his successor from the Ministry, L.F. Lundie, was a less formidable person and easier to handle.

In justice to the Royal Engineers in general, their level of ability and culture was usually of a high order and they were unlikely to be guilty of gaffes of this kind. They understood, as the civilian administrators often failed to do, that archaeology for Ordnance Survey purposes could not be practised by sitting in a room. The duties of those who were building up the record under Stanhope-Lovell involved a great deal of reading, handling of maps, air-photographs and making out briefs for the field parties. However, it was arranged that all the office staff should have turns out of doors where the field work was going on, so that they could fully understand that their own work was just as important to the production of a good new edition as that of the field parties.

I have just been mentioning a period map in describing conflicts which could arise with the civilian ministerial element brought into the Survey after World War II. The preparation and publication of period maps were to be important concerns of mine right through the official and non-official phases of my contact with the Survey. I have already credited Major-General William Roy as the real father of the period map. His map of Roman Scotland, published posthumously in 1793 was not to be succeeded in its accuracy until the second edition of the Ordnance Survey's map of Roman Britain appeared in 1928. Many of the features shown have since disappeared owing to cultivation but air photographs have verified their existence. This second edition, compiled by Crawford, was a great success but the public had to wait till 1956 for a third edition, a delay of twenty-eight years, during which it continued to be a good seller.

When I became Archaeology Officer in 1947 there was already enough information about the topography of Roman Britain to justify a third edition, but all normal work had been disrupted by the 1939–45 war and the business of finding my feet and creating a new archaeological organisation to meet the needs of the general revision was paramount.

As an unofficial helper of Crawford I got some early experience in the period map field with several of his projects, some of them failures because they were premature, and others successes like his *Map of Britain in the Dark Ages* and Neville Hadcock's historical compilation *Monastic Britain*. We were able to launch the latter, a gratuitous work offered to the Survey by Hadcock because it had reached proof stage in 1940, but fortunately its materials were not in the London Road Office when it was bombed in that year. This was doubly fortunate because Hadcock had done further work on its subject and this could be incorporated. I did not consider that there was real evidence for the restoration to the map of the medieval road system which he had attempted in his first draft and, when published in 1950, it was the clearer for its removal. The map was a success and provoked so much interest that it went into a second edition in 1954. Many scholars had sent in additional information and, in particular, Dr Easson made considerable changes in the Scottish part of the map which had always been less easy than that pertaining to England and Wales. This 1954 edition was to last long after my time at the Survey.

Period map compilation and similar business which required informed and scholarly handling was beyond the capacity of the staff, and in any case it was desirable to fill the post of Assistant Archaeology Officer held before 1940 by W.F. Grimes. The vacant post was advertised in October 1948, and the mistake was made of not mentioning that the successful candidate must be a graduate. The result was that there was a list of nearly one hundred applicants most of whom were obviously, and sometimes ludicrously, unqualified. Mr Peter Gouldesbrough, a Scottish graduate, was appointed. He was pleasant and helpful but was not more than interested in archaeology, something which was not enough for our requirements. He was really an archivist and his ambition was to join the staff of the Register House in Edinburgh, to spend his life amid the records of Scotland. Fortunately he achieved this in the summer of 1950. He helped to tide us over a difficult period.

The net was cast again and this time the catch was Mr A.L.F. Rivet, a graduate of Oriel College, Oxford, who had read classics and was a thoroughly scholarly type, lately engaged in bookselling but ready and able to apply himself to period map work. The long-overdue compilation of the third edition of the map of Roman Britain was put in his hands and this appeared with great success in 1956.

The categories of sites and features shown were much increased. New supporting aids were a fifteen-page introduction, which included a chronological table of events in the period and an explanation of the source for the Roman names of places and the native tribes. Two maps showed the British Isles according to Ptolemy and the British section of the Antonine Itinerary. Three other maps at scales ranging from 1¾ inches down to ¾ of an inch to a mile, illustrated specially dense areas of settlement. An eighteen page index was also provided listing all the more important categories of features shown and giving their grid references as well as the number of the 1 inch map on which they were to be found.

In 1962 a return was made to the borderline between history and prehistory by the publication of a single-sheet map of Southern Britain in the Iron Age at the 1/625,000 scale. Its temporal range covered the four centuries preceding the conquest of Britain by Claudius in A.D. 43. This was again the work of Mr Rivet and the introduction contained an essay on the Celtic coinage of Britain by the numismatist, Mr D.F. Allen. This had eight distribution maps and a chronological table, an outstanding work of scholarship in its own right. There was also an imaginative cover design by Mr Brian Hope-Taylor incorporating some of the most famous artefacts of the period.

Chapter 11

I shall not attempt to give a detailed account of how the field parties developed their skills during our early years so that by the close of the 1950s they were not easily surpassed in archaeological field craft in Britain and their leaders were certainly real experts. It was a case of *solvitur ambulando.*

The work could contain a detective element and be quite exciting, as in the case of the Southern Region group's discovery of the quite unknown Roman road from Silchester to Chichester from what looked on an air-photograph like a small Roman fort at Milland in north-west Sussex in the depths of what, in Roman times, must have been a dense part of the forest of the Weald.

Stretches of straight road extending over a long distance are liable to be Roman, as in the case of Stane Street running from London to Chichester, unless certainly known to be of recent construction. Examination of the 6 inch map showed that this Milland site was on a narrow road in modern use which, while frequently wandering from a straight line in this heavily wooded country, still contained some meticulously straight stretches.

Soon after the Milland site had been noted, a bungalow was built on part of it and a lot of the normal rubbish of a Roman site was found. In the event, Milland proved to be a fortified posting station similar to the one at Hardham on Stane Street, both abnormal in having a small garrison because of the special danger from robber bands in dense country like the Weald. In the course of subsequent work on other north-west Sussex and Hampshire sheets this regional group were able to find many more traces of this road for the whole of its nearly forty miles and so make an important addition to the map of Roman Britain. In any case, there must have been a direct road between two important centres such as Silchester and Chichester, but without benefit of air-photography it was difficult to find because almost entirely avoided by modern roads.

I am sure that the Field Division was wary of many of the surveys of antiquities sent in by our field parties for incorporation in the new map when these took a distinctly new view of the precise detail of a number of well-known hill forts which had apparently been shown accurately on the maps of years past, but the truth was that the surveyors of the later nineteenth century often did not understand the features they were surveying or were sometimes casual about what they regarded as minor detail. We, benefiting from the results of large excavations since their time, now had a clear idea of what these forts looked like in their prime, when their gate towers and heavy stockades built of timber were still intact. We also understood the precise original detail and function of cunningly defended entrances and tried to express their surviving detail in carefully considered 'slopes': the same principles held good with other sites whose earthworks alone survived. As far as possible the surveyor had to be able to visualise the object of which the earthwork was the surviving trace. After a while, Field gained confidence in our work and would accept our surveys as a matter of course. This was quite a compliment from them and avoided much duplication of effort.

The region which caused us most trouble was Scotland. It was remote from headquarters at Chessington. As the crow flies the distance from Chessington to Edinburgh Regional office, to Thurso, and to the northern end of the Shetlands was 300, 500 and 630 miles respectively. By road or rail it was very much greater and the heavily indented nature of the east and west coasts did not help. Much of the terrain was rough and inaccessible and there were few local correspondents. Large parts of the more thinly populated parts of the country had never been surveyed at better than the scale of 6 inches to the mile and that in the later nineteenth century. The notorious Highland clearances had taken place in these areas and they had left behind a large number of deserted village sites, rapidly sinking again into the peat.

Many of these 6 inch maps were sub-standard in accuracy and there was a meeting in Edinburgh of representatives of major Scottish interests at which Director-General Willis had to stand in a white sheet and promise early action to set things right. One of the chief complaints was the bad state of the 6 inch maps of the Highlands and Islands. It was decided to re-survey all the 6 inch areas by air methods, a much quicker process.

The Archaeology Division could not possibly hope to play its part in this from Chessington and with only one field section working in Scotland. It was decided to set up a Branch Office of the Division in Edinburgh which would be broadly autonomous, while following the principles of the division, and ultimately responsible to Chessington.

Before this important step had been taken in 1958 I had made a number of exploratory tours in Scotland and attended the annual summer school in British archaeology which held its meeting of 1952 at Queen's College, Dundee, part of the University of St. Andrews. I also wished to see the field work of F.T. Wainwright, head of the department of History there. This was among the hitherto enigmatic 'souterrains' of southern Pictland. It was at this time that the serious study of Dark Age Scotland was starting to make good progress.

Wainwright was a highly gifted man whose acquaintance I had made at Cambridge when he came to see me during my unemployed period after my demobilisation in 1945. At the time, he was studying the movements of Danish armies in the days of Ethelred the Unready and together we tried to settle some points relating to these along the watershed between the Linton branch of the River Cam and the Suffolk Stour. Later I stayed with him several times in Dundee, where I lectured on the archaeological work of the Ordnance Survey and gathered in some recruits for our system of correspondents. It was in the course of these evenings that I found myself talking to one of the men who had successfully spirited away the Stone of Scone from its place under St. Edward's Chair in Westminster Abbey. I never knew his name. It was a tragedy for British archaeology that Wainwright died prematurely in June 1961, from a brain tumour, a heavy loss to Britain and Scotland in particular.

In 1958 our Branch office was set up as part of the Scottish Regional Office at Rose Street in Edinburgh, with two field sections and the necessary supporting office and recording staff. Rivet, who had now finished his excellent job on the third edition of the Map of Roman Britain, was put in charge. He settled at Corstorphine in the western outskirts of the city.

In the spring of 1961 I made an extensive tour with him in the far north of Scotland to get personal knowledge of the peculiar problems of surveying the antiquities of the region and in particular the remains of the settlements destroyed during the notorious clearances of the first half of the nineteenth century. The one-track roads constructed by the evicting landlords, clan chiefs in fact, like the Duke of Sutherland and Lord Reay, who wanted to introduce the more profitable business of sheep-farming, only had occasional relevance to the distribution over the moors of the old crofting settlements, so that it was almost a day's work even to get to some of them, let alone the fact that much of the country was devoid of any but distant sighting points for survey. There were also some very queasy river crossings on narrow wire suspension bridges. North of Lairg it was possible to travel the whole of the sixty miles to Tongue on the north coast and pass human habitations at only two points, Crask and Altnaharra, with what passed for an inn at Crask and little enough at the other place. That was in 1961. In summer the area is not quite so desolate today with summer caravans along the north shores of Loch Naver.

We made our way from Tongue to Durness over the waste of the Mhoine and round the interminable shores of Loch Eriboll, where we saw the remains of a 'souterrain'. At Durness the doctor who was our correspondent for that part of Sutherland, told us that the only way he could get seriously-ill patents to hospital in Helmsdale away on the east coast fifty miles distant as the crow flies was by helicopter and they might die on the way if sent in an ambulance by road.

We were favoured with good weather and there were compensations such as the great blazing masses of gorse in full bloom and the dominance of the Caithness scene by the humble dandelion growing here in great flowering clumps everywhere. When we spent a night at Melvich, in full view of the Orkneys, we went for an evening stroll down to Strathy Point and found the charming little Scots primrose (*Primula Scotica*) growing in quantity on the short turf.

Going down Strathnaver to the sea we passed a small memorial beside the road. It records that when the Argyle and Sutherland regiment was raised to fight the French at the beginning of the nineteenth century, a muster of a thousand ablebodied men met at this spot at the call of their chiefs as the Sutherland contribution. Fifty years later such a muster would have been impossible because the area was virtually depopulated. Clansmen would follow their chiefs till the time of the clearances, after which they regarded themselves as betrayed by their natural leaders. Thus ended the ancient system which had received its death blow at Culloden Moor.

All this was 6 inch country and so under revision by air method. This was a much faster process than ground survey and as this was very difficult on the Sutherland Moors, and Rivet was a very meticulous person, the rate of this first survey of the clearance sites was slow. The production of the new 6 inch version was thus delayed and although Fox, as Superintendent, who was a very skilled surveyor, devised and suggested quicker methods, Rivet regarded these as sub-standard. He displeased Director-General Dowson when the latter visited this work in the field. I was now only a couple of years away from my retirement and I was not at all sure that Rivet would be my successor in the normal way. He was not in his element in administrative work and I suggested to him that he would probably be happier and more successful in the academic world. He therefore resigned and joined the staff of the University of North Staffordshire at Keele where he was very active and successful in Roman studies, became a Professor, published some very important work and was elected to the Fellowship of the British Academy. Fox moved into his place as Assistant Archaeology Officer, remaining most of the time at Chessington.

As I began to approach my time for retirement the work of the Archaeology Division was running smoothly. We had overcome almost all of our difficulties in the department, my ideas had been accepted and Fox would probably be my successor. I could now take a closer look at foreign archaeological practice.

I held a post of national importance with the Ordnance Survey and I had always been interested in the archaeology of lands outside Great Britain. During my formative period I had taken such opportunities as occurred to visit Holland, North Germany, Denmark and Norway, to say nothing of France. In all of these countries there were features comparable to those in Great Britain, and when I came later to have to tackle the Sutton Hoo excavation I had already seen examples of most kinds of ship burial. My one excursion into the Mediterranean area in 1929 was in a Hellenic Travel Club tour, which helped the development of my knowledge of the archaeology of the central Mediterranean area.

After I had got my division working effectively it became part of my duty to represent the Survey, either officially or more privately, in Europe and elsewhere. In 1953 I had my first introduction to Rome under very pleasant conditions since Margaret was able to accompany me. At the time, J.B. Ward-Perkins was the Director of the British School and was to be there for years to come. I had previously met him at the Sutton Hoo excavation when it chanced that he was staying at nearby Butley Priory with a former headmaster of his old school, Winchester. It was thus that he was able to be present during the weekend in which the main treasures of the royal burial came to light and we had the benefit of his advice and witness.

As a person holding an important post in the British archaeological establishment I found that, provided a room was vacant, I might apply to stay at the school on the specially favourable terms available for students and that this would extend to my wife. I enquired and we were accepted. We set off on June 5, travelling to Rome by the Mont Cenis route through the Alps to Turin, and then to Genoa after which we followed the coastal route past Shelley's tragic shore, Pisa and down the coast of Etruria to arrive at Rome from Civita Vecchia.

The British School was conveniently situated in the Valle Giulia on the ring road which carries the Circolare tram round the edge of the central city. If we wished, we could walk straight across the Borghese Gardens, cross the line of the Aurelian Wall and come out on the high ground at the top of the Spanish Steps. From here there is a fine view of St. Peter's and the Vatican, and we could descend the Spanish Steps into the heart of the old Imperial City. Between them the two routes gave us easy command of all the most important surviving features of the ancient city and at this time it was the pagan rather than the Christian antiquities which received our major attention, but we did not forget to visit and place flowers on the grave of Keats.

Our excursions into the neighbourhood of Rome took us to Ostia Antica, along the Appian Way and to Tivoli for Hadrian's Villa, still undergoing the skilful clearance of its ruins, and to the sensational Villa d'Este. To me, as a working field archaeologist, the most interesting professionally was Ostia Antica. Its ruins, as far as they had been excavated, gave a clear view of the everyday life of folk of those times. It was a place of work and the daily round of commerce, of which the palatial residences were certainly not, however prestigious. Wherever we went we noted the wild flowers, many of which were unfamiliar to us.

The British School was a welcoming place and we greatly enjoyed a fortnight of its slightly austere comfort and substantial and informal meals with plentiful good, cheap wine. But it was unfortunate that Ward-Perkins had to be absent. This was made up for by his deputy, Richard Goodchild, and in view of my journey into Tunisia and Libya the following year, although I knew nothing of this at the time, it was lucky for me that he had just returned from a spell of field work in Libya and was able to give me some idea of the archaeological potential of that region. The last bonus that we received from this first visit to Rome was a cultural one, when we found that a large travelling exhibition of all aspects of Picasso's work was on view within a short distance of the British School, even including some of his excursions into ceramics.

The opportunity to see some aspects of the archaeology of Tunisia and Libya came in the summer of the following year, 1954. Ever since my undergraduate days I had been friendly with T.C. Ravensdale. He had opted for the Consular Service and we regularly kept in touch through his service in Turkey, Iraq and Egypt, his posting when the Consular Service was merged with the Foreign Service. 1954 found him Consul-General in the recently created kingdom of Libya. In the early summer of that year he was obliged to return to London on urgent private business, and during this time he stayed with us at Surbiton. He had come by car all the way and when he returned, he suggested that I should go with him for a short stay at the Residence in Tripoli, and act as co-driver on the journey.

This was an enticing prospect, not least for the long drive across France to Marseilles. We by-passed Paris and made for the upper Loire Valley. Before we crossed the river we spent our second night at Autun, once one of the major cities of Roman Gaul. I had been there for a day in 1950 and we had time to look at the two well-preserved city gates, the theatre and the architectural relics which later inspired the Burgundian style of the Middle Ages and the sculptor Ghislebertus. We continued by Vichy past the Forez for a third night-stop at the fantastic town of Le Puy and the next day we came down past the Cevennes and Mont Lozère into Provence, passing through Nîmes, where we had to be content with a quick look at the outside of the Roman theatre and the Maison Carrée. We spent the fourth night at Arles. We were now quite close to our destination, Marseilles, and after sleeping at a hotel contrived out of Roman baths we had enough time to visit the famous amphitheatre, the crypto-porticus, the strange assembly of sarcophagi in the Aliscamps, and the sculptures of St. Trophime.

At Marseilles the old quarter had been swept away by the Germans in the late war and excavations were in progress in the remains of Greek Massilia before rebuilding took place, but we did not know about this at the time. Next morning, while Tom supervised the loading of the car on to the 8,000 ton boat which was to take us to Tunis, I had just enough time to look round a collection of Toulouse-Lautrec's work which was being shown at the Cannebière. While I was there, a mistral began to blow and we sailed out of a calm port into one of the wildest seas I ever remember. This continued for the rest of the daylight hours and we dined with the greatest difficulty as we neared the west coast of Corsica. The only thing to do was to turn in and we had a fair night because, owing to the distressed condition of a number of cavalry horses belonging to a contingent of French troops on board, the captain decided to pass through the Straits of Bonifacio and continue down the lee side of Sardinia. With the return of light the wind had died down and we reached La Goulette by midday and made our way up to Tunis.

After we had settled into our hotel Tom sought his colleague, Williams, Consul-General for Tunisia, who invited us to supper at his villa, a former residence of the Dey of Tunis, near the site of Carthage. At that time there was little to be seen of the ancient city and we passed a pleasant evening in company with Professor Piccard, Director of the Bardo Museum in Tunis, and his wife. He told us that he was lucky to be alive because earlier that day he had gone out from the local beach in a canoe with his two small sons. Only a short inshore run was intended, but the influence of our storm had not yet died out and he found himself swept dangerously far out to sea. There was no help in sight and it was only by desperate paddling that he was able to regain the shore.

The next day we left Tunis early and made our way southwards by the road which sets off ultimately to reach Egypt after rounding the whole shore of the gulf of the Syrtis. We passed through great tracts of cultivated land from which the harvest had already been gathered and vineyards as far as Sousse, after which we continued for many miles across a vast, arid and featureless tract. After a while the horizon was broken by a large isolated object which looked like a gasometer. As we approached we realized that we were coming to the huge amphitheatre of El Djem. This, second only in size to the Colosseum at Rome and very well preserved, once belonged to a large town which had now disappeared. The present community which huddles near the monument is very humble. In fact, seen from the air, the tract through which we had been passing had been parcelled out in Roman times in a great agricultural centuriation, the complete pattern of which is to be seen on an air photograph. The Emperor Gordian had found it a natural thing to provide this entertainment centre for the formerly immense corn-growing tract so long as it continued to provide bread. This is only one example of the desiccation of good corn-growing land which has taken place in North Africa since Roman times.

Before we left the place I noticed the eroded earthwork remains of what was probably an earlier timber and earthwork amphitheatre of a more modest kind but we had to move on if Tom was to reach Tripoli in time. We went through the port of Sfax and spent the night at Gabes where we began to see date palms in fruit.

Next day we passed into real desert country around Medinine, a sordid little place known for its honey-comb-like dwellings and on round the bend of the Gulf where the total desert was such that we might reasonably expect trouble with drifting sand across the road, but we met with very little and so came to the Libyan frontier. On the final lap to Tripoli signs of human habitation increased steadily as we passed the farms of Mussolini's settlers, where I saw the vivid green of ground-nut crops for the first time. Just inside the Libyan frontier I also saw a cluster of two or three ruined buildings standing in isolation. They were all that remained of the frontier station, the terminal of a railway which was designed by Mussolini to facilitate the invasion of Tunisia in 1939 or 1940. All track and rolling stock had long disappeared and, besides the frontier post, it was the only sign of human life, a melancholy memorial to a vain ambition.

To arrive at Tripoli we first had to pass the site of the old Roman terminal port of one of the routes across the Sahara, Sabratha. This place had received attention from Italian archaeologists who had cleared and carried out the restoration, perhaps too thoroughly, of a fine theatre in the hope of encouraging a tourist trade. It is a beautifully sited structure and I thought that the effort was worth while, with the proscenium intact and the blue Mediterranean as a background. There was much else to see and in many ways the most remarkably preserved feature was a public lavatory with rows of marble seats still in perfect order but lacking the water for their flushing system. As in the other North African sites, many of the visible remains were those of Byzantine buildings and at Sabratha there was a large church of this period whose splendid mosaic floor was in excellent condition, showing a design of a great tree whose foliage was filled with all manner of birds.

Of my actual stay in Tripoli I need say little. Tom lived in the Residency, which was on the water front and once the house of the Italian admiral. The weather was very hot; Tom had to attend to accumulated business in the town, so I visited the well-preserved old Venetian fortress and also a much-defaced Roman triumphal arch standing waist deep in ancient accretions of soil. The town was clean and well laid out with good modern buildings, all Italian work, but the place was in a very torpid state with little in the shops. No doubt the scene is very different now that Libya has struck oil.

On the last day before I left for home Tom took me for a short drive further along the coast east to Lepcis Magna, a much larger terminal port for the cross-Saharan routes than Sabratha and owing its development as a big town to the Emperor Septimius Severus, who was born there. It had quite a large harbour, now almost entirely silted up, and extensive excavations in the town have revealed a large number of ruined temples, Byzantine churches and public buildings the full character of which could not be grasped in a short visit. There was a large protective mole, now badly damaged by centuries of battering by the sea, with the base of a Roman light-house on its end. A long stretch of massively constructed wharf in two tiers remained intact, its upper tier containing large regularly spaced sockets for the timber uprights of cranes. Altogether, it had been a well organised water-front. This was the area which interested me most, but it was obvious that much remained for exploration. Lepcis Magna was the principal port from which exotic wild animals were sent to the circuses of the Roman world.

I flew home from Libya making a night stop at Malta where I was met by Charles Zammit, the director of the Malta Museum, who had been with us at Little Woodbury in 1938. I landed in the early afternoon and in the time available he was able to show me the famous Hypogeum, where I was grateful for the relief from the heat, also the Hal Tarxien temple. I got some idea of the remarkable history of the island, but could see little sign of its latest ordeal in the recent war. I was wryly amused by the well-meant hospitality which offered me hot tea and buttered toast as a refreshment in a temperature well into the 90s.

Next day I left early for home, flying close to Etna over Sicily to land for a short time at Naples in perfect conditions of visibility, continued up the west coast of Italy and then went directly over the Alps, passing close to Mont Blanc. So, still in perfect visibility right across the Lake of Geneva and France, passing north of Paris. It was only as we crossed the coast of the Channel that cloud set in and the next thing I saw was a glimpse of the Star and Garter Home on Richmond Hill as we wheeled round to land at Heathrow.

I had been away for only three weeks, but had greatly enlarged my ideas of the Mediterranean world.

In 1957 my family was beginning to grow up and with my son John at the age of 13 and my daughter Penelope now 10 years of age it was time to introduce them to the educational experience of foreign travel. The English habit of going to Spain for a holiday was just becoming established and our choice fell on Tarragona, an historical city only forty miles from Barcelona on the east coast which combined a good beach life for the children with relics of its ancient importance as an Iberian stronghold, later adopted by the Romans as Tarraco, capital of their province of Hispania Tarraconensis.

We booked some inexpensive accommodation in an inn which was well recommended by our travel agent. We left London on August 27, flew to Beauvais and continued to Paris by bus. We did not stay but went straight on through the night by train to the Spanish frontier at Cerbère. In the early morning we saw the magical sight of the ramparts of Carcassonne lit up by the first rays of the rising sun. After the slow train ride to Barcelona we were rattled at speed down the last forty miles to Tarragona by a Talgo express.

Our accommodation was of the simplest kind in a little inn called the Fonda Marinada, now swept away by modern improvements. Apart from being noted for its cuisine, its position was ideal for our dual purpose of a beach holiday for the children and the examination of the antiquities of the city. In front of the inn one only had to cross a busy road and to go down a long flight of steps followed by a rather casually guarded railway crossing to arrive at the beach. Incidentally, at the foot of the steps were the remains of a Roman theatre on the right hand side, set back into the steep slope which, as in the case of Sabratha in Libya, had a wide vista of the sea beyond the stage. Later use of the site for a Christian church, now ruined, which had been built there to commemorate the successful reconquest of the Balearic Islands from the Moors made it difficult to sort out these two phases, Roman and medieval.

As it happened, the chief advantage to me was that our inn was within a hundred yards of the Paseo Arqueologico, a walk which extended almost half a mile along the surviving part of the ancient city wall and gave a wide view inland across the deep valley intervening between the city and the open country. This wall along the part of the walk nearest to our inn had the most extraordinary character. It was megalithic with, at its base, courses composed of four superimposed blocks of stone at least ten feet long and four feet deep; in all sixteen feet in height and carrying up further with lighter material to a still greater height. This was the Iberian work of the pre-Roman native fortress and its only real parallels seemed to be Inca work in Peru, and it was heavier if not so sophisticated as the work of Herod the Great in the substructure of the Temple at Jerusalem.

It seems that the earlier Iberian fortress, the base of whose megalithic walls were later incorporated by the Romans in their defences, survived only round the north-eastern end of the large flat-topped bluff overlooking the sea on which the fortress stood. Further along the walk, where the megalithic work of the native fortress must have come to a corner and turned to cross the site of the continuing wall, it became entirely an example of Roman masonry, meticulously coursed and with every stone in its composition bearing its mason's mark on the visible side. So it continued, standing practically to its full original height, to the point where it came to the end of the bluff which was the reason for the construction of the fortress in the first place. The subsequent expansion and great prosperity of the city led to the increase of the defences to a length of between two and three miles, but little trace of these remains above ground.

Inside the limits of the older part of the town is a dense labyrinth of narrow lanes and courtyards, the only exception being the open space occupied by the cathedral, its forecourt and approaches. But below the surface there is a whole system of Roman drains and sewers belonging to an original street pattern. This has been the subject of exploration and planning by the local archaeological society.

The problem of water supply must always have been serious at Tarragona, for the product of purely local rainfall must have been quite insufficient for a large population. Here the Romans gave a notable display of their hydraulic engineering as elsewhere in Spain. The nearest source at a higher level than the city was miles inland and any aqueduct would have to cross a deep and narrow valley to maintain a gravitational flow along the contour of a ridge which went another three miles to Tarragona.

This aqueduct is known as Las Ferreras and is a fine two-tiered structure at least three hundred yards long carrying a water channel about four feet wide and two feet deep. I walked out twice to examine this, the second time with Margaret, through large orchards of Barcelona nut trees. We found little trace of the channel as it came to the crossing but the aqueduct itself was in very good condition with beautiful masonry work. A feeble obstruction had been placed at the more visited end to prevent foolhardy people from taking the giddy walk across the abyss but on my first visit I saw a boy walk over in a nonchalant manner. I did not try to follow him.

In the less salubrious parts of Tarragona, now given up to commerce and in 1957 still showing signs of damage in the late civil war there were some open spaces and, examining these, the foundations of Roman shops, side walks and road surfaces could be seen here and there wherever the ground had been disturbed. In late Roman and early Christian times it was clear that the place sank back more or less into its original area and it is then that a big clearance must have been made to accommodate the new cathedral.

Our holiday at Tarragona was a memorable time. The family found a great deal to enjoy and I had my fill of archaeology and am still wondering how the huge megaliths in the Iberian wall were quarried and moved into place. Customs like the daily parade in the cool of the evening and the spontaneous dancing of the Sardana by all and sundry in the Rambla were novel and impressive and the food was good even if our accommodation was austere. The place was not yet spoiled by 'improvements' to attract the hordes of tourists who were soon to descend on the Mediterranean coast of Spain.

We found the Spanish railways very odd and before we left Tarragona our departure was almost delayed by railway trouble. In the early morning two nights before we were to leave, lighter sleepers heard a crash and wondered what it was. Morning revealed that there had been a collision of goods trains in Tarragona station suspending all traffic, and we were all in various degrees entertained that day by watching the rather ineffective staff and a breakdown gang working to clear up a great mass of shattered wagons and spilt cargo, amongst which I noticed large quantities of cork. There was a heavy smell of spilt wine. But the service was back to normal on the morning fixed for our departure and we made our way home by the same route we had come without further incident.

One last point about the Spanish railways. In 1957 and for quite a number of years afterwards it was possible to see old sixwheeler tender engines, mostly of French or Belgian origin, well looked-after and still in remarkably good condition, doing shunting duties. A look at their makers' name plates showed that they were about one hundred years old and still giving good service. There was one at Tarragona.

C.W.P. c.1957

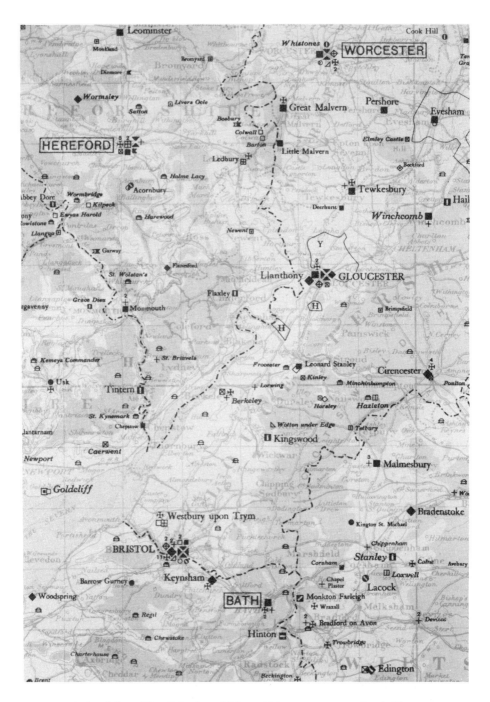

A detail from The O.S. Period Map of Monastic Britain, South Sheet

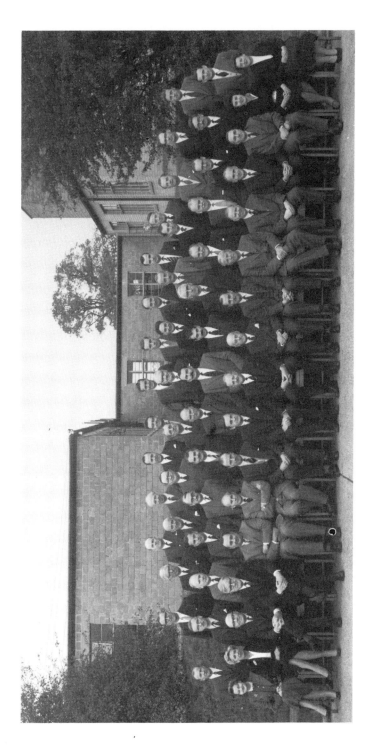

Officers of the Ordnance Survey 1959 CWP is 4th from the left in the front row

The Walls of Tarragona (1957)

C.W.P. at the Dairy, Arundel Castle

Degree-giving at Cambridge, 1965

Majorca, 1965

Charles and Penelope c.1968

At the Cloisters, New York, 1970

David, first grandchild, 1975

The family: John, Penelope, David, James, Margaret, Charles, Beth, Veronica 1983

Last visit to Sutton Hoo: Norman Scarfe, Martin Carver (Director), C.W.P. 1985

Last visit to Sutton Hoo, 1985

Chapter 12

Our holiday at Tarragona in 1957 had no official character and on my side had been the result of my desire to study a site which I had long wished to see while at the same time sharing a good holiday with my family.

Since the last International Conference of Prehistoric and Protohistoric Studies was held in Oslo in 1936 the 1939–45 war had intervened but meetings were resumed at Zurich and Madrid in 1950 and 1954.

In 1958 the Conference was to be held in Hamburg. The Treasury gave its consent for me to attend, and among the proposed excursions to inspect archaeological features of the host country I chose the one which was to visit the uppermost Danube valley, the middle Rhine valley down to the Dutch frontier and then make its way across to Hamburg in time for the opening of the conference.

The assembly point for this excursion was Stuttgart and I made my way there via the Hook of Holland by train to the Rhine Valley, Mannheim and Heidelberg. Stuttgart was now well rebuilt after the hammering it had received in the war from the R.A.F. owing to its unlucky proximity to the chief Mercedes-Benz factory. We were comfortably lodged and the party gathered for the first time at the museum, where I unwisely partook of the local wines, so tempting in the hot weather, and as a result had to sit down quietly and recover on the steps of the Schiller statue outside before returning to my lodgings. Two days after our arrival our first excursion took us southwards to the infant Danube.

We now had two days driving about in the Swabian Jura and our first objective was the Michelsberg. This is a strongly defended site standing on a bluff overlooking the infant Danube not far from Ehigen. It was surrounded by defences which involved the cutting of a truly enormous ditch to cover the side of easiest approach and this was still large enough to contain and conceal a big temporary hut-ment used by the excavators. Along the landward side, away from the steep descent to the river, excavation had revealed a sequence of strongly built rectangular towers or bastions with re-entrants between them and now, at the time of our visit, more work was in progress, revealing similar defences overlooking the river. In the woods nearby were several large burial mounds including the unusually big one known as Hohmichele.

The interpretation of the site was that it was the stronghold of important native rulers of the mid-first millennium B.C. who derived their wealth from the use of this point as a stage in commerce with the Mediterranean down the valleys of the Saone and Rhone to the Greek colony of Massilia. The mounds were their burial places. The quite abnormal defensive details of the site were attributed to the influence of Greek merchants because the tower system had analogies with the Greek practice of the time.

Leaving Stuttgart we moved to Frankfurt and on our way took in Mainz and another visit to a remarkable stronghold in the hill country on the west side of the Rhine, the Donnersberg in the Palatinate near Alzey. This is a large flat-topped hill nearly 2000 feet high which dominated the country round. Our official interest in this site was its general character as a defended native *oppidum* of the period of the Roman penetration into this area. To us it had a more sinister character. The whole of the summit of the hill was occupied as a major American listening post, part of a chain in Western Europe playing its part in the Cold War, then being waged between the super-powers. It was possible for us to see all that we wanted without going into the prohibited area, which bristled with various 'arrays' and detectors but all this made it a depressing place. We came to it in the early evening, tired from a long day's sight-seeing in bright sunshine; now a blight seemed to come over the panoramic view from this commanding height and the sun set among menacing clouds. I was glad when we had completed our journey to our hotel and had settled down for the night.

It was at this stage in our journey that we became aware of the nuisance caused to us by the presence of Monsieur Varagnac, the director of the St. Germain museum who, as the most eminent person in our party, was always called upon to return thanks to our hosts at the various lunches and picnics we were offered along our way. He was a flamboyant personality and in returning thanks he indulged in time-wasting harangues which steadily put us behind with our programme. Long before we reached Hamburg he was demoted as our spokesman by common consent and sulked for the rest of the journey. He met with a final disaster at Hamburg, of which more anon.

We continued down the Rhine towards Cologne and on our way made a detour up the Ahr valley into the Eifel near Andernach and Mayen. Our object was to visit the quarries of various periods from which so much lava stone had been taken in the past three thousand years. The Eifel is a region which, like parts of the Massif Central in France, has been volcanically active within the last ten or fifteen thousand years and it contains deposits of a very characteristic blueish lava which has been used as an abrasive material, chiefly for querns and millstones, for a long time. There is a crater lake, the Laacher See, and the comparatively recent volcanic activity has been proved by the fact that the lava has flowed over the site of a Mesolithic settlement on the shore of the lake. This lava has been used very widely and some was taken into Britain in Neolithic times. We saw many quarries ancient and modern, and then made our way to Cologne for the night.

Like Stuttgart and Frankfurt this city had also risen again from the ashes of the late war. I had been familiar with Frankfurt and Cologne before 1939 and I was shocked by the extent of the devastation and impressed by the large degree of restoration which had been made. We made a quick visit to the foundations of the cathedral to see the traces of the early Frankish church which had been revealed beneath it by excavation, and also to the ancient church of St. Severin where work of the same kind showed the progression from the Roman Christian cemetery chapel through a Frankish phase to the present form. We spent part of the evening visiting the vast remains of the govermental buildings of the Roman city which had been revealed during the rebuilding of their modern equivalent and preserved at great expense for inspection under it. We also went down to see the very fine mosaic pavement which had been found when a great air-raid bunker had been built on the south side of the cathedral area.

When I first visited Cologne as a young man I was impressed by, but profoundly disliked, the vast Hohenzollern road and rail bridge spanning the Rhine near the Cathedral. It was a gigantic castellated affair in the best browbeating Imperial style and loaded with statues of leading figures in the Hohenzollern dynasty; a Wagnerian nightmare. It had survived the 1914–18 war but in 1958 it was gone, blown up in 1945 and replaced by an elegant and functional successor.

After Cologne we continued through the Ruhr district visiting various Roman sites belonging to the ancient frontier system as far as Xanten near Wesel, by which time we were not far from the Dutch frontier. The British forces had crossed the Rhine near Wesel in 1945 and in the course of the fighting the ancient cathedral of Xanten had been much damaged. Our main purpose in visiting this place was to see the remains of an important Roman fort but I was much impressed by the restoration work in full swing at the badly shattered Cathedral. Every opportunity was being taken to find out the earlier history of the structure and to reveal the foundations of various ancillary buildings round the area of the west front. It was here that we were addressed in faultless English by a very young man who was in charge of the work and I have never heard a more lucid explanation of a site. I am sorry that I did not catch his name for I am sure that he had an important future.

Crossing the Rhine we went on to Munster, another war-damaged town. Here we spent the night and our next objective was Warendorf, a classic Dark Age site where the exploitation of sand had revealed well-preserved traces in plan of a large early Saxon settlement with big bowsided houses and numerous lesser structures, including many huts of churls and industrial sites. All had been built of wood and the pattern of the whole site was shown clearly by dark marks in the sand.

It was obvious that our own early Anglo-Saxon settlements in England could only be clarified by extensive work on this kind of ground where the soil conditions were favourable; at this time those which had been found in more restricted minor excavations had consisted of nothing more than the humbler structures. Larger areas must be uncovered upon which these large farmhouses should be discovered and this has proved to be the case, particularly at the important site at West Stow in Suffolk.

We were now entering on the last stage of our excursion and we came to the great expanse of the Luneburg Heath in the north-west of Hanover. This is part of the great belt of heath which stretches right across the whole tract from northern Holland to Poland and beyond, and whose last south-western relic is the East Anglian Breckland with which I was familiar. We visited two megalithic tombs, here constructed from glacial erratics and a rather gloomy interest was added to the occasion when we found that we were quite close to the site of the notorious Nazi death-camp at Belsen. This was partly hidden by a luxuriant growth of gorse among which there were remains of hutments and old barbed-wire fences. Leaving this sinister area we continued north out of the zone of the final Allied advance into the Third Reich and came to the charming and totally unspoilt town of Luneburg. From there it was a short run into Hamburg, the site of the conference.

For me one of its most satisfying aspects was that it marked Gerhard Bersu's full restoration to his proper place in archaeology by his presidency of the conference. He was now an ageing man, had recently been unwell, and it was plain to see that his health was frail, but he got through his part with great success and showed many flashes of his old spirit.

I was still much interested in Fenland archaeology and assiduously attended that part of the Conference which dealt with the terps of north Holland and the many analogous sites of the same kind along the low-lying shore between the Weser and the Elbe. Among the short excursions on offer at the conference was the one which took us by train to a place called Feddersen-Wierde on the coast north of Bremen. Here large excavations were in progress on just such a site, and we also managed to make a visit to the very instructive museum at Bremen.

I took every opportunity to have a good look at Hamburg, a great city which had suffered so terribly in the last war, chiefly because of the large shipyards which produced large numbers of submarines, Nazi Germany's most successful naval weapon. It had also made a remarkable recovery but there were still areas which had not yet been rebuilt.

I climbed the great church towers to look out at the panorama of the city, the Inner and Outer Alster, the crowds of shipping and the estuary of the Elbe running out towards the North Sea. Away to the north, the great bridge crossing the Kiel Canal at Rendsburg was visible which recalled my visits to those parts in 1937. I also did not fail to visit the famous Hagenbeck Zoo.

The conference had its dramatic moments and one of these concerned Varagnac, whose behaviour had troubled us during our journeying before we reached Hamburg. One day there was an emotional scene in the concourse outside the main conference hall, where a large number of members were strolling and chatting before sessions. Varagnac was the centre of this, and the background of the fracas requires explanation.

One of the most famous archaeological finds in France had not long since been made at Châtillon-sur-Seine, at the spot known as Vix where there was much evidence of an important Hallstatt-period centre. This was made by a local schoolmaster called Joffroy, who had been making an examination of this site for some years. During its course he excavated the richly-furnished grave of a Hallstatt princess and amongst other fine objects he found a huge bronze *crater* of Italian provenance which is one of the most remarkable imports from the Mediterranean world to be found in France. The whole enterprise at Vix had been very well carried out and before long Joffroy found himself on the staff of the St. Germain Museum.

I do not know all the details of this affair, but it was obvious from the events at Hamburg that Varagnac had not given Joffroy the opportunity of attending the conference, which might be expected to want to hear more about the Vix discoveries. Suddenly, without warning, Joffroy appeared in the throng at the concourse and presented himself to his chief. After a few moments, a lively altercation began in which Varagnac desired to know why Joffroy had come to Hamburg without his permission. Joffroy replied that he had been sent at the express order of the minister and then the fat was in the fire.

Varagnac expostulated loudly enough for all within many yards to be startled by his outburst, and in the silence which followed he was heard to announce that he would be tendering his resignation. There was a sensation. Varagnac had been accompanied to the conference by a number of ladies and they now gathered round him and they left the scene in a body. I do not know how Varagnac squared matters with the minister for he did not in fact leave the conference, but his humiliation met with no sympathy. Piquancy is added to this episode by the fact that Joffroy succeeded Varagnac as director of the St. Germain museum.

Before I leave the subject of this Conference I must mention that here I first met 'Jo' (John Otis) Brew, then the director of the Peabody Museum at Harvard. He was a member of the party that came up with me from Stuttgart and we soon found that we had a common interest in archaeological topography and mapping. In his younger days he had been a member of the Harvard excavating expedition to Ireland, of which Hugh Hencken (about whom I have written earlier) was also a member, in the late 1920s when I was with the Bristol Society at the Kilgreaney cave trying to establish the presence of Palaeolithic man in Ireland. Later, Brew became a well known worker in the archaeology of the south-western United States and an international authority on conservation work.

This was the beginning of a warm friendship which has continued to the present day. I first saw him at Stuttgart at the reception where the wine flowed freely. When the time came for speeches he was pushed forward to reply on behalf of the visitors and I wondered who he could be, for he was not outwardly an impressive figure and such eloquence as he possessed was rather affected by the good cheer. He spoke, I lent him a map and we have been friends from that day.

Before I close this chapter I must mention an important extension to the temporal scope of the presentation of the topography of things past on Ordnance Survey maps in the early 1960s. It became increasingly necessary to draw attention to the futility of overlooking the fact that there was an increasing number of subjects of real archaeological importance which were excluded from our attention because they were of later date than A.D. 1689. This entirely ignored the fact that the Industrial Revolution of the eighteenth and early nineteenth centuries was now rapidly acquiring an archaeology of its own. This particularly concerned the textile industry and transport by land and water. It was therefore decided to widen the activity of our Division field groups to include this extended field of interest.

In July 1961 I attended a conference at Manchester which made a large number of visits to Telford's canals, early types of textile mills, both water and steam driven, surviving relics of the beginning of rail transport, the early enterprises of the Wedgwood family, the use of iron for structural purposes and much else in the same categories in the counties of Lancashire, Yorkshire, Staffordshire, Derbyshire and Shropshire. Typical features which we visited were the Styal cotton mill, the Pontycsyllte aqueduct, the fulling mill at Helmshore, the Ironbridge complex and so on. At this conference I was accompanied by the Division Superintendent, Mr Fox, so that the field staff could be briefed on the new development. The most recent date for inclusion of any obsolete relic of the Industrial Revolution was finally fixed at 1850.

Chapter 13

Following the Hamburg precedent of 1958 I was permitted to attend the Rome conference in the summer of 1962. It was preceded by a number of optional excursions and I chose the one which was designed to round the coast of Italy from Ancona southwards through Apulia and then across the southern Apennines to the Naples area and so back to Rome.

I left London on the morning of August 19 and went to Paris, where I took the night train for Milan and went on by a train via Bologna to Ancona, reaching the Adriatic at Rimini. From Rimini to Ancona the line runs all the way immediately behind the beaches and I saw the extraordinary spectacle of the swarms of sun-bathing tourists almost continuous between the two places. Half Europe seemed to have spilled out here. The present concern with pollution had not yet set in but one wondered about the state of the water in this landlocked area of the landlocked sea.

The party mustered at Ancona and here most of us had our first experience of a Jolly hotel, one of a chain that had been set up recently in Italy and particularly in the less well-provided areas in the south of the country. They were uniformly good and had the advantage of air-conditioning, which is very desirable when one gets down into the heel of Italy in a hot summer.

The object of this journey was to visit various sites where traces of Palaeolithic man have been discovered, but I do not think that most of those making it were very seriously concerned with this subject; it gave an opportunity to visit a number of areas in the south and south-east of the country which are not otherwise easily accessible.

The first day's journey began with a drive inland into unspoilt Apennine country, where we passed through various small towns like Altiggio, Ripoli and Roseto. We visited a number of sites in the foothills including the grotto of Frassassi and one in particular close to a typical small farm which gave me a good chance to look round and see how the local people managed their affairs. In the farmyard were a number of the local type of medium-sized circular hayricks with thatched conical tops and I was interested to see that several of them had long horizontal recesses about three feet or more deep cut into their sides not far above ground. I learned that these were a sort of bunk bed in which farmhands slept during the hot weather.

There was a profusion of wild flowers in this countryside and darting about among them were large blue bees of rather less kindly aspect than our British bumbles. At lunch time we came to a small village on our way back to the coast. This unexpectedly contained a small spa complete with a miniature pump-room and some associated hotels.

It was here that we lunched at a rustic inn at long trestle tables set out under a beautiful pergola of vines. We had the best lasagne that I have ever tasted. The wine was plentiful and at this point I should say that during the whole of the journey the lunch pauses were well irrigated by the local wines. We were usually the guests of a local archaeological group and they were most generous in this provision. The programme for the latter part of the day often suffered because our hosts were loth to let us go and by the time that we did depart many of the party were in a somnolent condition from the wine and the heat. These usually fell asleep for an hour or two as soon as we had started again while others, who had managed to convey full bottles to the coach, continued their potations and then also joined the sleepers. In the Dickensian phrase they were 'in the arms of Porpoise'. I was one of the few who resolutely kept awake and enjoyed seeing the country.

From the little spa we went back to the coast and continued southwards through a whole succession of villages which once must have depended very much on fishing but were now dominated by the tourist trade. The traffic on this coastal road was very heavy and it was badly in need of being widened. Thus we came to Pescara and turned inland up the valley of the river of the same name and then made the steep climb up to the old Etruscan town of Chieti where we were to spend the night. It is a grimly picturesque old place on a lofty site which commands the whole of the surrounding country. It greeted us with a spectacular thunderstorm and heavy rain.

The next day we went further up the Pescara river, well into the mountains as far as Popoli where we met the only extensive signs of the last war we were to encounter except broken bridges. Here the town had been badly damaged and many buildings on the outskirts had been left in ruins. After visiting a site close to the town which involved much scrambling in mud left by the night's rain we retraced our route part of the way to Pescara and then diverged up a steep and very tortuous road to a small hill village called Bolognano, a most picturesque and constricted place much of which was built on the edge of a precipice. Having heard in the morning about an earthquake which had just destroyed two villages no great distance away it was easy to see how disastrous one could be in a place of this kind of configuration.

Our objective this time was an important one, the Cave of the Pigeons, well down the face of the precipice and reached by a narrow unfenced path overhanging the void. This was very slippery after the rain and, worst of all, there was a gap in the path just short of the cave which had been hastily bridged for our visit by a couple of rather insecure planks. Once over the planks it was also necessary to edge round a rock projection before coming to the cave. It was a very queasy business making this visit, especially when creeping past those who were still coming down the path, but honour required that we should make the effort. I was greatly relieved when we had all gathered for some refreshments offered by the village in a large and beautifully appointed public room which would have done credit to a much more important place. This was a tiny community in a remote cranny of the mountains and one wondered how this had been accomplished. Perhaps it was the result of money sent by one of its sons who had gone to America and prospered.

We made our way back to Chieti and next day continued on the coast road through Ortona, crossing the Sangro and passing through Vasto and Termoli. At Vasto we made a short stop and were surprised to see a memorial in the town square to the Rossetti family of pre-Raphaelite fame whose father had come from this place. We now left the coast and made our way inland to to the town of San Severo at the base of the great Gargano promontory, the spur of the boot of Italy. Here the character of the country changed. This was an area of wide level stretches of agricultural land now cleared of the harvest, dusty and baking under a torrid sun. San Severo seemed to be asleep; everyone was sheltering from the heat and the streets were almost deserted.

After a lunch which was shorter than usual we pushed on quickly because we had to make our way round the great promontory to reach Foggia in time for dinner. We skirted the Varano lake close to the sea and so came to Rodi Garganico, skirted the sea for a few more miles and then turned inland over the centre of the Gargano, which is a great tract of upland reaching nearly three thousand feet in the centre. As we climbed we could look back and see the little Tremiti islands out to sea and so we came to the great beech forest, the Bosco d'Umbra, which fills the centre of the Gargano. This is a magnificent tract of natural woodland which we did not clear till it was nearly dark. To get back to the plain behind the Gargano we had to descend by a narrow road with a good many hairpin bends and we had to thank our driver for his skill in getting the large bus down safely, for some of the bends were so tight that they could only be rounded by reversing, a tricky business in the dark.

At the bottom we passed through the little town of San Giovanni Rotondo which seemed to be very active at that time in the evening, and I remembered that it was a great place of pilgrimage because of its still-living aged priest who had received the Stigmata. After this, all was plain sailing and we arrived at Foggia for a late dinner and bed.

We did not see much of this large town, a major agricultural centre, because we were off very early next morning to the coastal town of Manfredonia on the south shore of the Gargano to see an open Palaeolithic site in its outskirts. Here we were close to the ancient pilgrimage place of Monte San Angelo with its cave shrine dedicated to St. Michael, a cult site which is only a continuation of a much more ancient worship, for discreet excavations in its recesses have shown that it was already a sacred place in the Bronze Age.

We were now in Apulia, with its many monuments of the Norman period and the thirteenth century realm of Frederick II, 'Stupor Mundi', the last of the Hohenstaufen line, who consciously looked back to classical times in his own life and activities.

We continued along the shore of the Gulf of Manfredonia where there are thousands of acres of salt pans and the whole coast is dotted with blindingly white mounds of salt awaiting removal. We crossed the river Ofanto at its mouth and knew that only a couple of miles or so inland was the site of the great battle of Cannae where Hannibal almost broke the back of the Roman Republic. But our objective was Barletta, a few miles further down the coast where we had our lunch. This is a large town of some 75,000 inhabitants and replete with monuments of many periods. Overlooking the port is the vast castle built by Frederick II and modernised later by Charles V in the sixteenth century. Here we had the most memorable meal of our journey on the castle ramparts overlooking the sea, a meal which was prolonged for several hours and during which I was able to slip away and see the famous 'classical' bust of Frederick II in the style of a Roman emperor, one of the most curious artistic products of the Middle Ages. I also visited the twenty-foot high statue of a late Roman emperor which stands in one of the squares. This huge figure was looted by the Venetians from Constantinople when it was sacked during the Fourth Crusade in

1204. It was loaded on shipboard for removal to Venice but the ship carrying it put into Barletta on the voyage and for some unknown reason the statue was jettisoned on the beach. It was taken over by the town and put in its present place.

It stands with its right hand raised above its head grasping a cross and there is an orb in the left hand. I do not know if the cross is an original feature but I think not. It is a most impressive figure of the fourth century A.D. and technically very interesting because it is possible to look up into the inside of the figure from below and see the details of the casting, strengthening struts, et cetera.

Tearing ourselves away from the lures of Barletta we continued down the coast to Molfetta where we made a short diversion inland to see a megalithic tomb in an orchard of olive and carob trees and so we came to the city of Bari after dark. I had hoped to have had a good look at the Norman cathedral but we could only get an impression of its great bulk in the dark and dash into the interior for a few minutes. So to our hotel, in my case the best in the town, where I had a magnificent bedroom but when I came to the bathroom I found only a single jug of water for all my ablutions. I had forgotten that the whole area was drought-stricken and that the great pipeline constructed under Mussolini from sources far north in the Apennines was inadequate to meet the abnormal strain of this torrid summer.

Our evening duty at Bari was to visit the large regional museum housed in the University buildings. These were in fact the old Bourbon royal palace and gave us our first introduction to the almost megalomaniac activity of this feeble dynasty as builders. The palace consists of a group of courtyards in the centre of the city. It does not occupy any vast area but the fortress-like weight of its construction is its striking feature. The individual size and weight of the stones used is amazing and it is obvious that its cost in money and labour must have been a great burden on the country. It was designed to overawe and clearly there was no love lost between the kings of the Two Sicilies and their subjects.

The museum contained a notable collection. It very adequately illustrated the archaeology of Apulia and contained much important Neolithic material, the results of post-war work in that area. This had been largely due to the late J.A. Bradford, who studied the war-time photographs taken over southern Italy with their revelation in remarkable detail of human activity through all phases down to the time of Frederick II.

Next day we did not linger in Bari but set off inland through Capurso, Casamassima, Turi and Petigano where we turned aside for several miles to visit the Castellena grotto. The ground is quite flat and open here but there is a great hole about two hundred feet across and carefully fenced round. Nearby there are buildings which house a large double lift, each cage of which can take fifty people. This descends for about two hundred feet and one steps out into a vast dome-shaped cave with an opening at the top which is the hole seen at the surface. This enormous cavity is flat-bottomed and more than one gallery containing fine displays of stalactites stretches away into the rock at the base of the main cave. It is a most impressive natural wonder.

Leaving the cave we continued on the main road to Alberobello, one of the most curious towns to be seen anywhere. This is the capital of the 'trullo' region where all the buildings are curious one-storeyed dry-stone structures crowned with one or more conical domes also of the same construction. If it is desired to increase the size of a dwelling, another such structure is built alongside and joined to it by a short passage. This type of building is made possible by the way in which the local flat-bedded stone splits into a natural building material without the need for any further dressing. The 'trulli' are whitewashed and the spectacle of a whole town of them is most unusual. Dry-stone construction is common in Apulia for shelters in the fields but it is only in an area about ten miles round Alberobello that it is almost general and specialised in this peculiar manner. In many cases there is a dry-stone staircase at the side of the building which gives access to a walk round the cone roofs for maintenance purposes and the drying of washing. But even here, in a setting which might appear to belong to ancient times there is electricity everywhere and the modern world presses in.

We left Alberobello with reluctance and made our way by Locorotondo to the coastal road at Fasano once more and we went down to Brindisi through Ostuno. The distant pall of smoke and the darting flames at the tops of high chimneys showed that we were coming to another of those Italian ports infested with petrol refineries. In days gone by Brindisi was a point of departure for Romans going to Greece and in more modern times it was a stage on the partly overland route between Great Britain and India. As we approached the town we met a sudden rush of cars going the other way and by their various national markings it was clear that Brindisi's new role as a ferry point for motorists visiting Greece was in operation. The boat from Patras had just come in.

Our business in Brindisi was with the Museum, a well-maintained place where the many extravagant forms of the pottery of Magna Graecia are well displayed. We did not attempt to see the town but there was one inescapable sign of its ancient importance on lines of communication, the two great pillars standing near the waterfront which mark the terminus of the Appian Way from Rome.

As the light began to fail we hurried down the long straight road which brought us to the considerable town of Lecce, capital of the heel region of Italy, the Basilicata, whose name is a relic of its long attachment to the Byzantine Empire. We found the town noisily celebrating the feast of its patron saint, San Oronzo. It was obvious that the architecture of the town was notable but that had to wait till the next day. After a quick dinner I went out to see the festivities, and was drawn to the main square by a great volume of sound. It was packed with people and many were eating and drinking outside the various restaurants. At one end, in front of the Municipio, was a stage and on this a number of singers were giving excerpts from opera supported by an orchestra. They were all good performers but their voices were projected from loud speakers at great volume, a volume which was intensified by the high buildings all round the square. The noise could only be described as stunning but it was greatly appreciated by the crowd which applauded each piece with frenzy. From time to time there were loud reports as fireworks were discharged and fire balloons were sent up into the air which also exploded with spectacular effect. All the streets in the town centre were filled with every kind of stall and I have seldom seen such an animated scene which at the same time was so orderly. I retired to bed but it was a long time before the din from the square subsided.

I got up early next morning and hastened out to see as much of the town as I could by daylight. I found that a lot of the stallholders were still asleep in the open street under their stalls. The fame of Lecce rests upon a preponderance of fine seventeenth century buildings all carried out in stone of a beautiful fawn colour and this was flushed by the early sun as I hastened round looking at some notable churches and admiring the beauty of the scene. In fact, most of the best buildings in the town are the work of a single architect.

From Lecce we went a few miles down the coast to San Cataldo and then followed it closely past the small town of Otranto to our next objective, the Grotte Romanelli. All down the coast we noticed the system of watchtowers standing in prominent positions. They were part of a great number located all round the coasts of the 'heel' and the 'toe' of Italy and constructed by the Emperor Charles V to watch for the approach of Turkish raiders; our own Martello system of the Napoleonic Wars derives from them. Otranto proved to be little more than a large village because one Turkish raid had destroyed the town and carried off most of the inhabitants, an attack from which the place has never recovered.

As we made our way down to the 'heel' at Santa Maria da Leuca the coast line became much wilder, with high cliffs, and when we reached the point from which we were to visit the Grotte Romanelli we found that this could only be done by going down a steep path to a narrow beach and taking to boats which carried us to the mouth of a cave under a beetling cliff. This visit made and our lunch taken, we then struck inland across the 'heel' through the town of Maglie to Gallipoli on the flat coast of the Gulf of Taranto.

This town is placed on a promontory and is flanked on its south side by a splendid beach. It was Sunday and the beach presented a very animated scene. Many hundreds and possibly thousands of local people had come from the villages inland in a vast array of small cars and vans in varying degrees of decrepitude and on motorcycles. Many of these folk were disporting themselves in the sea and the beach was covered with sun-bathers who, one would have thought, already got enough of the sun in their work on weekdays. The beach was backed by an array of ramshackle huts and other flimsy structures offering refreshments and requisites for bathing which reminded me of what we had found at Tarragona in 1957. It was a wonderful scene of relaxation.

Gallipoli had one interesting feature, an ancient stone fountain built for the supply of water to the town. It consisted of a massive wall fronted by a large stone trough showing signs of much wear. The crumbling surface of the wall was covered with the remains of statuary so far gone in decay that it was difficult to make out the original composition. This is believed to be one of the oldest if not the oldest, fountain of its kind in Italy and of Roman construction. It was still in regular use.

From Gallipoli we set out for Taranto, skirting the sea past an ancient castle called the Four Towers and going by Mardo along the Roman Via Valentina direct through Manduria and Sava. The country here is flat and featureless and we came to Taranto in a tremendous heat. It was a relief to find that we were to stay the night in a Jolly hotel with air-conditioning in full action.

Taranto is one of Italy's chief naval bases and most of the town stands on a spit of land dividing two large enclosed sheets of water, the Mare Grande to the seaward side but largely cut off from the open sea by moles based on the Cheradi islands, and the inland Mare Piccolo which contains the naval harbour. The two are joined by a channel crossed by an opening bridge which connects the two parts of the town. We paid a quick visit to the museum which was full of typical Magna Graecia material and then had our dinner. Afterwards I strolled along the waterfront of the Mare Grande and was much struck by the Admiral's official house, a vast structure built in the days of the Bourbons. It was not on the scale of the palace at Bari but in some ways it was even more monumental; the individual stones used in its construction were quite unnecessarily huge and much larger than those which impressed us at Bari. Seen in the dark the great structure looked like something in a Piranesi engraving.

The objective next day was to drive north-westwards right across Italy to Naples and so we made an early start. We followed the shore of the Gulf of Taranto for several miles and then turned inland towards the hilly land of the interior. As we came up off the plain we passed through the town of Castellaneta. At the entrance I noticed a public garden containing a memorial which commanded a wide view back towards the sea and before we had cleared it I realised that we were at the birthplace of Rudolph Valentino. Obviously his fellow citizens were proud of him. The next considerable town we came to was Matera where we paused for a short rest. There had been many centuries of quarrying in its outskirts and we had time to look into more quarries and see that a large number of the inhabitants of Matera were cave dwellers, living in ranges of houses cut back into precipitous slopes.

Continuing northwards we passed for some twenty miles along the westward side of the central upland of Apulia, the dry, open and rolling tract known as the Murge which slopes down on the other side to the Adriatic at Bari and Barletta. Although today many of the more favourable parts have been brought under cereal cultivation, most of the great ridge which rises by easy stages to 2000 feet is still sheep country as, indeed, the whole of it was until quite recently. It is still sparsely inhabited and is traversed by a system of wide ancient tracks belonging to the pastoral life. It was at this stage of our journey that I hoped to catch a distant glimpse of the Castel del Monte, the remarkable castellated hunting lodge built by Frederick II on its summit, but in this I was disappointed as I had also been earlier when we did not visit Lucera, a town near Foggia which contains many relics of his period.

Leaving the Murge behind we travelled for many miles westward, through Spinazzola to Venosa where relics of Paleolithic men have been found. But my interest in Venosa was that it was the birthplace of the poet Horace. As in his time, it is a very modest little place. After we had inspected the Palaeolithic material in the small museum we were offered refreshment by the town and so we were able to see the inside of the Municipio. In the upstairs council room we were entertained to wine and an ice-cream of a vivid green hue and were looked down on by portraits of former notables dominated by a large, entirely imaginary portrait of the poet behind the mayoral chair. He was shown in very jovial mood. There are a few surviving relics of Roman Venosa and one fragment is confidently pointed out as the house of the poet's birth, though this must be very doubtful. Venosa was a staging point on the Appian Way.

From here we went on into the southern Apennines and passed quite close to the picturesque hill town of Melfi but time did not allow a visit and we diverged to have our lunch at a hotel in the beech woods near the lake of Monticchio under the slopes of Monte Vulturo. We were now in wild country with a dense covering of beeches like those we had met with in the Gargano. This lunch was also excellent and very prolonged so I slipped away and wandered in the woods near the lake. This is a perfect example of a crater lake, quite circular and in a perfect setting; an idyllic spot. I lingered there until I thought that the lunch must be over but when I came back to the hotel everyone was still there and the evening was drawing on. When we finally left it was nearly dark and our driver, rather than retrace some fifteen miles to rejoin our road near Melfi, decided to strike across country and join it much further on. This was a bold decision in such remote country and we followed a very minor road in the upper valley of the Ofanto with growing misgivings that we were lost; but we won through and so came over the main spine of the Apennines to Eboli in the dark.

None of this unease affected many of the party who had been fast asleep ever since we left the hotel. From Eboli we came to the west coast by Salerno and, passing across the neck of the Sorrento peninsula and past the site of Pompeii, came to Naples at one o'clock in the morning.

We were housed in a vast unkempt hotel on one corner of the square by the main railway station. In spite of the hour it was still breathlessly hot and the street-life was active. I had a large dusty bedroom, reached through endless corridors and the street noises outside were so loud that I had only a fitful sleep. One longed for a Jolly hotel.

Next morning our first stop was a long visit to the Naples museum where all the riches of Herculaneum and Pompeii make a wonderful display. After that we were driven up to the castle of St. Elmo on the summit overlooking the city and bay, but the more distant view was concealed by heat haze and Vesuvius was not visible. We lunched here and then drove out to Posilipo and it was during this short run that I noticed signs of panic in the crowd in the streets. It was a minor earthquake shock which the motion of the coach prevented us from feeling. As I have mentioned before, there had recently been a severe local earthquake which had badly damaged two villages in the Apennines when we were journeying down the Adriatic coast. This also we had failed to notice though we were at no great distance from the scene and once again the fact that we were moving quickly along the road prevented us from feeling it.

One of the most interesting things at Posilipo was to see the architectural relics of the ancient Baiae visible beneath the surface of the sea, submerged by land movements since Roman times. But we now had to make a quick return to Rome. Crossing the river Volturno we went by the west coast past Gaeta and made a pause at Terracina where the inland high country comes right to the sea and makes a narrow pass. From there we drove straight on to Rome, through Velletri across the reclaimed marshlands and by the Alban Hills. It had been a notably successful tour.

But, sadly, not for one of the party. There was one young man who took many photographs and was loaded down with the necessary apparatus. At one point when we were on our way back from the south the coach was halted by the roadside while the driver made an adjustment and some of the party went out by the back door to stretch their legs. It was during this halt that this man's photographic satchel must have fallen out of the coach because he was sitting near the back door. The loss was soon noticed and we retraced our route to the point where we had halted. There was not much traffic and this was a lonely spot. The lost satchel was a bulky object but no trace of it could be found. It was a sad loss because with it went all the films that he had already exposed. We gave notice of the loss at the next town but I never heard that the lost package was recovered.

For my part the journey was made more pleasant by the presence of Professor Michael O'Kelly and his wife. They were very much in the same class as myself on this occasion, people who came for the ride, were fully aware of the general archaeological and historical interest of the country through which we were passing but were rather less concerned with Paleolithic Italy. Two years ago I learned of Professor O'Kelly's death and this sad news revived many memories of our Italian journey. With his death Ireland lost a very able archaeologist.

In Rome I stayed with old friends of 1959, the Pecchinottis at the Pensione Riposo up near the Janiculum. It was a very successful conference with splendid receptions in the Capitol and elsewhere. I met many old friends. Most of the meetings took place in the newly opened Palace of Science. I spent one long sunny day renewing my acquaintance with Ostia Antica. The most spectacular event followed on the visit of the conference to Hadrian's villa on the last full day. After viewing all the new developments in the work on the villa, which now included the clearance of the Pelusium area and the re-establishment of the artificial basin there, we all moved up to Tivoli where an entertainment for the evening was given at the Villa d'Este. It was a beautiful warm night, the waters were running freely in the famous gardens and they were made even more spectacular by the skilful use of floodlighting. Of its kind it was the most satisfying experience of my life but in the villa itself the struggle to get at the refreshments was extreme and it was a great relief to escape into the gardens. Only relatively few of those present made their way there, most of them preferring the torrid conditions and the uproar in the villa itself. I was forced to the conclusion that many did not really know where they were, but this was to the great profit of those who did.

The conference closed on September 3, and next day I made my way to Florence by an early train. I was thus able to have nearly five hours in that city and visited as many of the famous sights there as possible before taking the night train for Paris. After an uneventful journey I was at home again on the evening of the 5th.

Chapter 14

The most remarkable class of antiquity with which we had to deal in my time at the Ordnance Survey and which had particularly attracted the attention of the founding father of the Survey, William Roy, was the linear defence work designed to exclude the barbarian world from intrusion into the Roman province of Britain.

Roy's biggest piece of archaeological survey had been his work along the line of the Antonine Wall in Scotland between the estuaries of the Forth and Clyde. That was carried out in the mid-eighteenth century; in my time our constant care was the maintenance of the accuracy of our treatment of Hadrian's Wall, 75 miles long between the mouth of the Tyne and the Solway Firth, with frequent new discoveries of various forms of extension down the Cumbrian coast of the Irish Sea. Altogether there were great advances in Wall studies and in 1964, for the convenience of tourists and walkers as well as archaeologists, we published a special map illustrating the latest developments in our knowledge of the defensive complex at the large scale of about 2 inches to the mile, overprinted on the standard 2½ inch map photographically reduced and showing all the modern detail. A similar map of the Antonine Wall was also begun in 1965 but was not published till 1969, by which time I had retired.

Large though our frontier defences were in Britain we were only an isolated province. On the continent of Europe the defence of the northern frontiers of the Roman Empire involved a system extending from the contemporary mouth of the Rhine on the North Sea, stretching in general along much of the course of the Rhine and almost all of that of the Danube right to the outfall of the latter into the Black Sea. In the autumn of 1964 a congress was being held in Germany on the course of the defended frontier or *limes* and it was thought to be an opportunity for me to attend and show the progress we had made in this field of study in Britain and to show the new map.

The congress was to meet at Frankfurt and in the course of a week was to visit many sites along the line of the *limes* from the hills of the Taunus to its terminus on the bank of the Danube in Bavaria. I had a difficult problem to solve in getting to the congress in time because on the day that it opened I was due to give an address on the archaeological work of the Ordnance Survey at the Southampton meeting of the British Association. However, having given my paper I managed to get to London in time to catch the Hook of Holland train from Liverpool Street and by 7 a.m. next morning I was in the Rhinegold Express coming up to Rotterdam and, travelling by Maastricht, München Gladbach and Cologne I reached Frankfurt shortly after lunch.

The congress had gathered at a Lutheran Church Conference Centre at Arnoldshain in the nearby Taunus. I made my way out to Oberursel by local train and shared a taxi with other congress members for the rest of the way. The accommodation at the Centre was excellent, for the place was run by Lutheran sisters and it left nothing to be desired. The programme for the first three days was to be based on this place, with lectures in the morning and short excursions to nearby features of the *limes* after lunch. On September 2 we explored the neighbouring stretch of the *limes* from the Kleine Feldberg fort eastwards for some miles to the well-known Saalburg, the major fort which was completely excavated and restored as far as possible to its original appearance in the early years of this century at the instance of Kaiser Wilhelm II, who was a considerable amateur in Roman archaeology. This was not my first visit to this remarkable reconstruction but it was good to see it with a group of German experts who were able to expound its features thoroughly.

In the afternoon of the next day we drove out to Bad Nauheim some twenty miles north of Frankfurt to see a new fort which had recently been discovered at Rödgen. It was rather a wet day and we went back to Bad Nauheim to spend an hour or two in that pleasant town before we returned to Arnoldshain.

Gerhard Bersu was also with the congress while it was still near Frankfurt. Since his return to Germany after the war he had achieved an enormous amount as director of the Roman-German Commission at Frankfurt and we visited the fine Institute re-planned and extended under his direction in Palmengartenstrasse. But my meeting with him was tinged with sadness, for he had visibly declined in health since the Hamburg Conference of 1958 where he had been president. We were able to have some quiet talks about old times before 1939, but, as I said goodbye to him, I wondered if I should ever see him again. My fear was justified. Before the following Christmas he was dead.

The next day, the congress took to its buses and made off southward through Darmstadt into the Odenwald to visit sites on the line of the *limes* running down the east side of that feature and we paused for lunch at Amorbach, where we had an opportunity to visit the fine baroque church. By the end of the day we had made our way as far as the picturesque town of Schwabisch Hall where we spent the night.

On the following day we moved on down to Aalen near the great eastward bend of the *limes*. On our way we visited several sites and were then entertained to a festive lunch by the Aalen municipality after we had inspected excavations near the town and taken part in the opening of a very creditable new museum. It was pleasant enough but, as with many German meals, overlong.

We now turned eastwards along the north side of the juvenile Danube in keeping with the great eastward swing of the old Roman Rhaetic frontier and before we reached Nordlingen we saw two famous sites on our left, the isolated hill fort known as the Ipf on its conical hill top near Bopfingen, and the Goldberg nearer to Nordlingen where Gerhard Bersu did much to show the feasibility of winter excavation because the greater dampness of the soil was then more favourable for the tracing of organic remains.

The whole of this day consisted of a run through beautiful country, and the various sites we visited gave us many glimpses of German country life. We met many local types who conducted us across the fields to the sites. It was now autumn and so many of the fields were dotted with autumn crocuses, very beautiful in bloom, but otherwise a pernicious weed, nearly ineradicable from pastures and often fatal when eaten by cattle.

Passing through the fine open town of Nordlingen we came down to the Danube at Donauworth and crossed to the other side. At Nordlingen we were within ten miles of the battlefield of Blenheim and we continued eastwards through Rain as far as Neuburg, where we crossed the river again to the north side and made directly for Eichstatt, our destination. Shortly before we reached this town we saw a large marquee by the road surrounded by an assembly of country folk. This was a bierfest in full swing and would probably be a lively place as the night drew on.

Before we settled in for the night we went some six miles north of the town over open agricultural country to see the line of the *limes* at Petersbusch and Eckertshofen; it was quite obvious, with a large spread bank with a ditch to the north. Here I walked alone for more than a mile along its line into the depths of a large pine wood and saw one of the large monumental stones put up by King Ludwig of Bavaria, one of a series set to keep the line of the *limes* in memory. Night was fast drawing on as I retraced my steps along the track through the silent forest. I was conscious of being a long way from home and I was not sorry to regain the open country and return to a much-needed dinner at Eichstatt.

The next day was Sunday and we resumed our course eastwards, first visiting the site of an important Roman fort at Pfunz which gave support to the *limes*. It had been excavated a long time before and one of the village ancients was much in evidence, the last survivor of those who had worked in the excavation on that occasion.

We were now coming to the point where the *limes* comes to the north bank of the Danube and ends. Here the last twenty miles or so of it are known as the Teufelsmauer. We kept along the north side of the river, passing Vohburg and so through Pförring and Marching until we came to the spot where it runs down a gentle slope to the river on the north side of the Schwaberg. After walking along its last half mile and inspecting a commemorative monument we continued to Kelheim, a small town which stands at the eastern end of a minor gorge through which the Danube passes. Here we went to a restaurant where Sunday lunch was in full swing with many of the local folk enjoying a good meal, though on this occasion ours was less substantial. Leaving this cheerful scene we recrossed the river and retraced our way along the southern side of the passage to Eining where we all walked down a lane to the monastery of Weltenberg. This lane passes along a narrow ledge of land between the river and a line of cliffs. Cut and dated on these cliffs were the records of a number of floods for a hundred years back and we noted that at the highest recorded flood our lane must have been at least fifteen feet under water and the village of Haderfleck on the other side of the river almost completely submerged. Here the Danube is flowing fast, with a width of several hundred feet and the amount of water passing on that occasion must have been enormous. We reached the monastery which is sited in the end of a small valley coming down to the river and our particular object was to see the fine baroque interior of the church. It was a very unrestrained example of the style and one of its features was the *trompe l'oeil* painting of a balustrade overlooking the central space. It was very cunningly done and closer inspection showed the head and shoulders of a man looking down from it into the church. This was said to be a portrait of the church's architect. The whole monastery was placed at a level which must have made it very liable to be flooded.

From Eining we made our way to Abensburg and then made a direct run for Regensburg. But direct run is an overstatement for, while we were making our way in a continuous stream of weekend motorists, we had a breakdown a few miles from the city. In the end we were carried in by taxi to our hotels.

In the evening and the following morning I was able to have a good look round the fine city of Regensburg, once Castra Regina and a major fort on the Roman Frontier. There were many surviving records of this phase and we were fortunate because excavations were in progress along a long stretch of the Roman city wall. The phase we saw exposed was a late one when the fort was increasingly threatened. These foundations were made of massive architectural fragments from important Roman buildings, Roman funerary monuments and a fair number of pieces of broken statuary. Everything large and heavy had been pressed into service. This was on the side of the fort furthest from the river but round on the riverside there were the remains of a very massive Roman gateway, which in its original form must have been very like the Porta Nigra at Trier. These remains are today buried in a number of later buildings but, even so, they are impressive. The great gate of the medieval wall along the river front is intact and from it a fine old bridge crosses the Danube with the help of a small island. The bridge had been damaged in the war and was still only in a temporary state of repair. There is also a good cathedral with a single tall tower.

I had to be back at the office on September 10. I left by a midday train for Nuremberg where I changed into a direct train for the Hook of Holland. As we neared Nuremberg we passed the vast remains of the Marzfeld stadium where the notorious Nazi rallies were held before 1939. It was a melancholy sight of total dereliction. As seen from the train, Nuremberg showed no signs of the destruction of the late war. In the first few miles of my journey onwards past Furth I reminded myself that we were travelling over the first short stretch of railway line opened in Germany. We entered the valley of the Main and passed Wurzburg, where there is a fine view of the old episcopal city from the train and went on past Aschaffenburg and the site of the battle of Dettingen to Frankfurt. From there the route went down the Rhine Valley, reaching the Hook through Emmerich, Arnhem and Utrecht, an unexpected diversion from the direct route by Cologne and Rotterdam. After a comfortable crossing I was in London again after breakfast.

Chapter 15

As we moved into the middle of the 1960s the time for retirement drew on. I had come late to archaeology, which, in my youth, was still partly the concern of the leisured and financially independent members of society. It took me from 1924 to 1939 to work my way into a more favourable situation and by then I was half way through the normal life span. In 1939 I was thirty-eight and at this point the 1939–45 war broke out and archaeology had to take a back seat for its duration. Then in 1947 I had the good fortune of my unexpected succession to the Archaeology Officer post at the Ordnance Survey when I was on the verge of forty-six. I could not hope for more than fourteen years at the Survey before my retirement but in fact I was permitted to stay on after my sixtieth birthday because, as I was fit, my continued service was thought to be beneficial. It was also decided to gave me an extension to make up as many years as possible for the improvement of my pension and to count in my four years of war service.

In the early summer of 1964 I began to plan my retirement and it was agreed that the end of March 1965 would be an appropriate time. Plans were now well forward for the completion of the Survey's new Headquarters on the Crabwood site at Southampton and it was expected that the place would be ready for occupation in 1966. Various delays postponed this until the summer of 1967 but it was obvious that the days of the temporary office at Chessington were numbered. I decided to let a successor make a fresh start.

The Archaeology Division now contained a number of persons whose competence in field archaeology and survey procedures was of a high order and it had been thought quite proper to allow our Superintendent, Fox, to succeed to the Assistant Archaeology Officer post when Rivet departed. Fox was not a graduate but he had been elected to the Society of Antiquaries, no mean distinction in the mid-20th century, and he had played a great part in organising the Division for Survey purposes in relation to archaeology. The rest of the country's archaeological establishment did not, to my certain knowledge, contain anyone liable to be a candidate for the post better fitted to make a success of it. In the normal course of events Fox would have had ten years' service before him as Archaeology Officer.

In the event my advice was not taken and when the post was advertised the graduate requirement was made very plain. The whole business was an affair of some delicacy and the reason why this course was taken was never given. It was true that Fox was very competent and active but his personality was not fully acceptable to everyone. Sometimes he was lacking in tact in dealing with others but I was aware of nothing serious enough to justify passing him over for the post, only of much to recommend him.

So the advertisement went out when the field of choice was smaller than usual and I expected that the successful applicant would come from the staff of one of the Royal Commissions. I was right in this, for the only applicant who looked anything like filling the bill was one of the more senior members of the Scottish Commission sited in Edinburgh. I had met him a few times in the past at Cambridge and elsewhere and I knew that there was no doubt about his competence as a field archaeologist.

I went to Edinburgh to sound out this candidate and found that he was quite prepared, not to say anxious, to move south and the arrangements went forward to a point at which it was irrevocable. His technical qualifications were good but had the Survey authorities known more about his personal background he would not have been acceptable to them. I had no inkling about this till I reached Edinburgh, where I found the Secretary of the Scottish Commission, Kenneth Steer, much embarrassed and annoyed by these complications.

It was an unhappy time and I take leave to doubt whether the Director-General would have accepted the candidate if he had known what was happening in Scotland in time. The last months of my period at the Office were made uneasy by the certainty that these affairs had made a bad impression and that the new Archaeology Officer would be starting his career in the Survey on the wrong foot. The mistake of not appointing Fox was to become only too apparent in the coming years.

I parted from the Ordnance Survey with sadness. It could be an exasperating body, still full of anomalies, but it had been my great fortune to be able to spend eighteen years doing congenial work, building on the foundation laid by Crawford and organising a really effective archaeological side for the Survey as well as providing a less-intensive archive for the use of the country as a whole.

Of course, all this was not all my own work for I had some very able assistants. The early years had been hard, with difficult conditions of life and many vigorously contested battles to secure the effective performance of our part of the general revision. As I left the shabby old temporary buildings by the side of the Leatherhead road on that March evening, it was as well that I did not foresee the difficult years which the Division would once more have to face under the nerveless direction of my successor.

It is a common experience that those who retire after an active life in archaeology fairly soon find themselves encumbered by even more and more varied work than they normally encountered during their time of official employment. The various societies and other bodies to which they have belonged, or with which they have had contact, knowing that they are now at leisure, hasten to seek their help with tasks and projects some of which can be very large indeed.

There were still some uncompleted projects relating to period maps which remained to be completed or carried out when I retired. The first of these, which was well forward in the spring of 1965 was the completion of the second edition of Crawford's Dark Ages map, on the compilation of which I had been engaged intermittently for several years. Since the Survey had not yet departed to its new building at Southampton and I continued to live at Surbiton I could easily make the run up to the Chessington office at any time, and so the new edition was completed and published in February 1966.

I also wanted to complete the run of period maps covering the era between the

Roman and Norman Conquests by compiling a final map dealing with the late Anglo-Saxon period from the accession of Alfred to the throne of Wessex in A.D. 871 to the Battle of Hastings. This was begun in 1966 as soon as the preceding Dark Ages map's second edition had been published and I was working at it on and off till it was finished in 1973. This involved fairly frequent visits to Southampton and also to Scotland where I received a good deal of help from Professors Duncan and Nicolaisen and Dr Ian Cowan.

Special efforts were made to show the impact of Scandinavian settlement and influences all over Britain and also the topography of the political and ecclesiastical history of the time. By now the Survey's interest in period maps was flagging and although it did full justice to this map it was probably the last of its class that will be published except for new editions of the earlier maps already produced since 1924. In keeping with the inflationary trend of the time its cost to the purchaser was £3 by contrast with the modest prices in shillings and pence which held good down to the 1950s.

Although the Survey had been in existence for some hundred and seventy years no attempt had been made to publish an account of its progress to any date, except by Colonel T.P. White R.E. of Edinburgh in 1886, and this, though useful, was quite insufficient. In 1960 the first proposal to attempt a full account came from a group of cartographers and geographers outside the Survey in which the prime movers were W.A. Parsons, Keeper of Maps in the Bodleian Library, F.B. Marley and J.H. Andrews, a lecturer in Geography at Trinity College, Dublin. The history was to be a private production by a commercial publisher.

This proposal came in 1961 when Major-General Dowson was Director-General. His first reaction to the project was favourable but he soon changed his mind and wished to bring the enterprise under closer control. I had been approached by the original promoters to contribute a chapter on archaeology in the Survey and so I was one of those invited to meet a representative of the Director-General at a meeting at the Royal Geographical Society. Brigadier R. Gardiner attended to put the views of the Director-General and the meeting had not gone far when it became clear that the idea of an independent publication not directly controlled by the Survey was viewed with disfavour. So an official history was proposed by the Survey, which was to contain fourteen chapters to be written by a mixed team of Survey and other contributors in which the original proposers were to figure. Dowson was about to retire and he was to be editor.

Considering the number of years it had been in operation, the Survey did not possess any considerable archive of its work, a deficiency partly attributable to the considerable losses caused by the fire and bomb damage at the old London Road headquarters in Southampton in November 1940. The many officers who had served with it over the years had left little in the way of accounts relating to their time and the largest body of material consisted of old War Office records, Annual Reports and the actual results of the work in the form of many published maps. The period between 1824 and 1846 in Ireland was well represented because the records of the Phoenix Park office in Dublin escaped damage in the 1939–45 war. A full account of the Survey in Ireland in the nineteenth century was already under preparation by J.H. Andrews and was to be published at Oxford in 1975.

A good deal was known about the early director, Sir Thomas Colby, but there was no great amount of published reminiscence or kindred material. The two more recent directors-general, Sir Charles Close and H. St. J.L. Winterbotham had done some work in this field. Sir Charles Close wrote his *Early Days in the Ordnance Survey* but it was only for private circulation, and Winterbotham gathered material at the time of the sitting of the Davidson Committee in the early 1930s.

During my own eighteen years in the service I noticed no particular official interest in preserving such early records as still survived. From time to time long lists of various out-of-date material considered to be superfluous were circulated to the officers, who could indicate whether they recommended the destruction or preservation of the various items. Of course most of them were genuinely expendable but sometimes valuable record material figured in the lists and seemed to attract few if any signatures for preservation. On one occasion I recall rescuing an eighteenth century map of an estate in Somerset. Major Martin, the Director-General's personal assistant, was another one who, in my presence, carefully hid away and so retrieved records belonging to the early stages of the large-scale survey in Scotland, which were listed for destruction.

Earlier in this book I have also mentioned my own rescue of the original drawings belonging to the first 1 inch survey, three hundred-odd in number, and their accompanying hill-shading material, all finally deposited in the Map Room of the British Museum with the help of A.C. Bickers and Brigadier M. Collins.

The history which was now to be written between 1960 and 1980 should have been a second edition of an earlier one written round about 1900, soon after the completion of the first large-scale survey of Great Britain. Much original material probably survived at that time and people were still alive who could have recalled much of interest, now gone beyond recall.

As soon as I was approached by the original proposers of the work I began to write my chapter on the history of archaeology in the Survey, and by the time the new arrangements were made it was well on its way to completion. Thus it came about that only a few months after my retirement in March 1965 it was ready in its original form, though in later years I was to expand and modify it from greater knowledge. It was the first completed piece and the preparation of the history was to be such a sluggish business that twenty years were to elapse before its publication.

Dowson's editorship was of short duration and he was followed by R.A. Skelton, the able Superintendent of the Map Room at the British Museum. It was he who really planned the work in its original form, indicated sources and dealt with contributors until 1970, by which time little progress had been made and he wanted to give up the editorship. In that year he lost his life while driving down to Southampton to a committee meeting at which he was to offer his resignation.

This work then devolved upon Major-General Edge and the task of writing the chapter on the Ordnance Survey in the Second World War came to me, including others describing the various special services performed by the Survey outside its ordinary line of duty. The writing of the 1939–45 chapter was a delicate business, owing to the complicated relationships between the Army and the Survey in the critical summer of 1940, something from which the Survey and, in particular, Brigadier M. Hotine, emerged with much credit. The other chapter involved sorting out a very miscellaneous bag including various surveys of the Channel and other offshore islands, Palestine, Jerusalem, Sinai and many other assigments. But although Edge was active, and contributions began to come together his own involvement with Ministry of Transport Enquiries made it impossible for him to continue, so finally Colonel W.A. Seymour, a retired Survey officer, undertook to complete the work. It was decided to abandon the scheme of a number of chapters on specific subjects and substitute a more continuous narrative treatment combining them all.

This difficult task was very successfully performed by Seymour and eventually the work was published by William Dawson Ltd of Folkestone in the spring of 1981. It had been a long period of gestation and the official history appeared at a significant time, when the Survey had finally abandoned the part-military part-civilian system under which it had worked for nearly two hundred years.

As a postscript to this account of the official history I must mention the independent action which I took with the archaeological part. During the course of my association with the preparation of this history I had done a great deal of work on other topics besides archaeology all of which, including my archaeology chapter in its original form, was abandoned when the continuous narrative form was adopted.

It seemed a pity that anyone wishing to know the history of the archaeological part of the Survey's work would have to spend £30 on the whole book when a complete chapter written entirely on this subject already existed. I therefore approached the Council for British Archaeology to see if they would be interested in adding it to their list of publications. They readily agreed and so, late in 1980, a sixty-four page brochure was added to their list at the price of £3.95 and entitled *Archaeology in the Ordnance Survey, 1791–1965*.

The affairs and the interests of the Ordnance Survey and the Royal Geographical Society have much in common and an interesting product of this was the Society's *Fenland Memoir*, which was published in 1970 and of which I was the editor. It cost me a great deal of work in my retirement. Its full title is *The Fenland in Roman Times. Studies in a major area of peasant colonisation with a Gazetteer covering all known sites and finds*.

The origin of this publication goes back to the appearance of the third edition of the Survey's *Map of Roman Britain* in 1956. General Sir James Marshall-Cornwall was then President of the Society and he queried our failure to show the contemporary Roman coast line on this map. We were able to demonstrate the impracticability of this, but Sir James was not entirely convinced and decided to set up a Committee and the Society voted the sum of £500 to employ a qualified person to carry out the necessary research.

The Committee held a number of meetings at which Sir Mortimer Wheeler and Sir Ian Richmond were present. The only applicant for the work was plainly not competent to do it and it was pointed out by me that even an approximation to a good result could only be obtained by the convergence of studies in a number of disciplines, and would require a research organisation costing vastly more than the sum which had been voted.

During the course of these meetings I was surprised by the reluctance of both Wheeler and Richmond to admit this and finally the project was laid aside. But Sir James was determined that the Society should promote an important piece of historico-geographical research on a Romano-British topic and so I introduced the study of the Fenland in Roman times which, after much progress had been made, was left incomplete by the failure of the Cambridge-inspired Fenland Research Committee to survive the 1939–45 war. I knew that, in spite of the demise of the committee, a number of individuals like Mrs Sylvia Hallam and J. Bromwich were still working in this field. I pointed out that a desirable and realisable project would be an examination and cataloguing of all good photographic cover in the Fenland area to make sure that all parts of it had been adequately covered in this way. I knew that there were still deficiencies and that all work on the Romano-British exploitation of the Fenland must have this coverage, and without delay, because war-time ploughing had gravely damaged much of the evidence which was plainly visible from the air before 1939. The normal wastage of peat under cultivation would soon complete the wiping out of what remained.

The committee approved the idea and I was commissioned to find a suitable person to do the work. As a result, Dr Peter Salway of Sidney Sussex College was put in charge and it was not long before we had linked up with Mrs Hallam and Bromwich. I think I have already mentioned before how, after Mrs Hallam had completed her studies at Newnham, she applied to me for advice about a subject for a Ph.D thesis and as she was interested in archaeology and was living at Spalding I had suggested a field study of the many Romano-British settlements in that area and this she had undertaken. John Bromwich was a member of the English Faculty at Cambridge and was also very interested in the Roman phase in the Fens. His particular interest was the most southerly tract between the Isle of Ely and Cambridge, a specially important peripheral area which he was studying intensively.

Having set this matter going I considered that I had done my part and turned to other matters. Time passed and in the period 1960-65 the Royal Geographical Society Committee, which was supposed to be directing this work, never met to my knowledge. In these five years much work was done by Hallam and Bromwich and in the case of Salway it was mainly concerned with an important excavation on the eastern verge of the Fens at Hockwold in Suffolk. Other geologists and palaeobotanists were completing studies relevant to the work of Hallam and Bromwich; a massive gazetteer of all known Roman Fenland features was also being prepared, going back to the earliest sources of information, mainly in the early eighteenth century.

I was unconcerned with this phase of the work, though accounts of its progress were casually encountered. It was the responsiblility of the Royal Geographical Society to publish the results if it wished to do so and at some stage Salway had become its co-ordinator, to be succeeded by Bromwich when Salway moved to a post away from Cambridge. In the early part of 1965 Bromwich began to have trouble with his eyes and a successor was required. I retired from the Ordnance Survey at the end of March and meanwhile, the Geographical Society had decided on the publication of a memoir, Number 3 of its Research Series, which would contain seven papers by contributors as well as the gazetteer, bibliography, index and distribution maps.

The society asked Sir Ian Richmond to edit this. He accepted the commission but before he could do anything his sudden and untimely death occurred. So the wheel came round full circle and I was asked to take his place in November 1965. The results which had come from my suggestions five years earlier were very different from what I had expected, but they were very substantial and I had to deal with them.

In general, the contributions of the geologists, soil scientists and palaeobotanists gave little trouble. They were designed to elucidate various aspects of the work of the main contributors on the field archaeology side. Salway wrote a general historical consideration of the probable role of the Fenland area as an Imperial domain. Bromwich's own study of his own area was meticulous and made a large contribution to our understanding of the fluctuating fortunes of the Fenland in Roman times. Mrs Hallam's part ran to 113 pages out of the 176 occupied by the seven contributors and was a hard nut to crack. The text of the memoir was completed to its full complement of 337 by the gazetteer and the index of topographical names, which occupied 180 pages.

The Hallam section was a record of a monumental piece of field work among the sites in the silt areas south of the Wash and those mostly covered by peat in the Spalding area and the Witham and Deeping Fens of South Lincolnshire. She also supplied 158 notes in 12 pages of small print. It was an extremely difficult piece of work to read and later, when the memoir was published, Professor S.S. Frere plainly refused to review the work because of its density. It was finally reviewed by Sir Harry Godwin. There was no doubt about its value but the inevitably repetitious account of hundreds of peasant sites was daunting.

A troublesome feature of the editorial work was that Mrs Hallam and her professor husband removed to Western Australia before I took over. I was thus involved in a great deal of correspondence. One of the most difficult tasks was the preparation of the necessary supporting maps showing fluctuations in the settlement pattern over the four centuries of the Roman occupation. This required a lot of supervision and cost me a good many visits to Kensington Gore, but the patience and skill of the Society's drawing staff under Mr Holland brought everything to a successful conclusion. A visit by Mrs Hallam to Britain in the spring of 1968 finally ironed out the various difficulties, but nothing could prevent her work from being a prolonged wet-towel exercise, as anyone who attempts to master it will find. The work weighed heavily on me for five years until the memoir was finally published in the autumn of 1970 while I was in America.

While I was working on this memoir, the Royal Geographic Society honoured me with the award of its Victoria Gold Medal in March, 1967, for services to archaeological and historical cartography. I appreciated this very much because Crawford had been its recipient before me. I think that on the whole I had earned it.

Chapter 16

There have been other ways in which I have tried to make myself useful during my retirement. I made an index for volumes 6 to 10 of the Society of Medieval Archaeology's *Proceedings*, but these contained some very technical matter on medieval carpentry which rather defeated me and I do not think this was a success. I was also variously associated with the Council for British Archaeology. For a number of years after the 1939–45 war it had been publishing a regular calendar setting out the details of forthcoming excavations and summarising the results of completed ones. The post-1945 rush of interest in field archaeology had greatly increased the number of excavations in progress and the Council set up this regular publication as a guide to the large number of volunteers willing to take part in them.

In May 1966 Miss de Cardi, the Council's Secretary, asked me to take on its editorship and I continued in this capacity until 1971 when her retirement, coupled with a large change in the control of the Council relieved me of this useful but sometimes exacting task by quietly ceasing to send me any more material. The work had been no sinecure and, needless to say, was unpaid but I was rather surprised at the cavalier way in which the Council dispensed with my services without any thanks; for this Miss de Cardi was certainly not responsible.

When I was still in post in Chessington one of the pleasures of my situation was that, within reason, I could supply the needs of young persons for maps of much larger scale if they could show a genuine interest in archaeology and had some specific objective in mind such as a vacation project with archaeological possibilities. I well remember being visited by a bright young man named Jones, still at school, who, with several friends, wanted to verify the course of one of the Sarn Helens (Welsh for Roman roads) across moorland country in South Wales. We got out the relevant map cover and discussed it together. I issued him the maps because he showed clearly that he knew what he was about and useful new information for map revision might accrue to the Survey. It was not very long after when I began to hear the name of G.D.B. Jones associated with various Roman investigations. From these he went on from strength to strength and is now Professor in charge of the Department of Archaeology at the University of Manchester.

I was also in a position to give encouragement, as in the case of Martin Biddle, whose name is well known in archaeology today on both sides of the Atlantic. He was at Merchant Taylors' School in Hertfordshire in the mid-1950s and had already excavated the More at Rickmansworth before being completely free of school. Later he turned his attention to the site of the fantastic country retreat of Nonsuch, built by Henry VIII near Ewell in Surrey and not more than 3½ miles as the crow flies from the Ordnance Survey Office at Chessington.

In this case maps were not required but I went over with my son John as volunteers to see how things were progressing. We were there in the long summer evenings and saw a very well-excavated plan of the palace. It was never a large building. Many of its foundations contained stones with Romanesque decoration which must have been brought from Merton Abbey, then recently dissolved and demolished only a few miles away, and we were also shocked by Henry's callous behaviour in sweeping away all but the lowest traces of the medieval parish church of Cuddington because it coincided in part with the site chosen for Nonsuch.

Biddle was in charge of everything but when I got to know him I found that he was much in need of encouragement because he thought he was not coming up to the standards of Sir Mortimer Wheeler as an excavator which, on Biddle's own showing to date, was nonsense and I told him so. In the following year, 1960, the off-lying banqueting house nearer to Ewell village was excavated and in 1961 the need to increase modern hotel accommodation at Winchester conveniently situated for the cathedral led to the excavation of the new Wessex Hotel site. This began so extensive an excavation in the cathedral precinct that it became a matter of national importance. Biddle planned and carried out all this and in 1962 the whole was transferred to the Winchester Excavation Committee, which aimed at elucidating the history and the development of the city, England's first capital, from Iron Age times well into the High Middle Ages. Later Biddle was appointed to direct a museum of major importance in America.

The Prehistoric Society's excavation at Little Woodbury in 1938 and 1939 had shed a lot of light on farming in the Iron Age on the chalk lands of southern England but, as is so often the case, it raised as many questions as it answered. At the time of my retirement, the closer study of ancient agriculture in Britain generally was being mooted, including the possibility of making a practical study of early agricultural and pastoral method by experiment on the ground, and the study of early methods of food storage, particularly the use of grain pits. This was inspired by work in progress in Denmark and a committee was formed to carry this on under the chairmanship of Professor W.F. Grimes and much encouraged by Professor G.W. Dimbleby. The first Hon. Secretary, Dr Wood, left for Australia and I was asked to take his place. This I did for three years, during which important experiments were made with grain storage pits in the valley of the river Ebble near Salisbury and a site for an experimental farm was acquired at Butser Hill in Hampshire.

Finance, and the acquisition of sponsors and a site were constant preoccupations with the committee, and once the Butser project was progressing favourably, I found it time to resign the secretaryship to a more professionally qualified successor.

So my retirement at Surbiton was far from idle. As well as those activities described above, I was also assisting my wife with her scholarly activity as a student of the life and work of Erasmus and his times. In the autumn of 1970 I accompanied her to the United States where she had an appointment for a semester at Cornell University. I also took the chance afforded to visit my brother for a month in British Columbia. While at Cornell I was able to have informal discussions with students on archaeology in Britain and I gave a public lecture at the University on the Sutton Hoo excavation which was largely attended. Before coming home we also visited Boston and stayed with friends at Harvard. I was able to attend the annual dinner of the American

Fellows of the Society of Antiquaries of London and renew much past acquaintance.

My wife and I also made a series of car and coach journeys between 1965 and 1974 which took us to such diverse regions and places as Touraine, the Balkans, Spain, Greece, the Cevennes, Palestine, the Jura, the Pyrenees and Turkey, both in Europe and Asia Minor. In all these journeyings we were both concerned with the historical, literary and archaeological associations of the many places visited. One of my most memorable experiences was to climb the great Roman ramp at the desert fortress of Masada and look down on the marvellously complete vestiges of the lines of the Roman investment of the place.

But from 1971 onwards no doctor on our panel seemed to be able to give a name to the cause of the increasing lassitude which began to oppress my walking although, fortunately, not my mind. I had a persistent dull pain in the small of my back and found it very wearisome to walk up even a gentle slope. It was no longer possible for me to keep our large garden at Surbiton in order.

My son was now curator of the Greater London Council's large collection of maps and prints at County Hall and on returning from the United States in 1970 I had undertaken to catalogue the prints one day a week. The journey from Surbiton to County Hall just outside Waterloo Station was a very easy affair, but before the end of the 1970s travelling to London was becoming an exhausting business for me.

Finally we resolved to give up the big house at Surbiton and move into a more modest home in Teddington. Shortly before the move in June, 1979 my wife was due to receive the degree of Doctor of Letters at Oxford. Naturally I accompanied her but I was too exhausted to get out of the car to go to the Sheldonian Theatre for the ceremony and had to remain in the car park.

I was obviously ill, but it was only in April 1981 that my real trouble was diagnosed as kidney failure at Northwick Park Hospital at Harrow. This was the beginning of a very difficult year in which I was in the West Middlesex Hospital for a week at the beginning of August and ended up at Charing Cross Hospital where I was on the kidney machine twice and from which I was sent home in a greatly improved condition on September 18.

But my luck was out. On September 30 I had a fall in my bedroom and broke my right hip. I had a replacement operation at the West Middlesex Hospital the same day and was then removed to mend the break by a spell in Teddington Memorial Hospital, only a quarter of a mile from home.

I came out from there with two legs but severely impaired mobility which has steadily improved from walking frame to two sticks and then one, and though I go for modest daily walks in Bushy Park close by, I resign myself for the most part to corresponding with old friends, reading the current archaeological publications and perfecting the stamp collection which has been my hobby for most of a lifetime.

Envoi

It was a sad day when I had my fall for its consequences have proved to be irreversible. Although I am quite well in myself, it is no longer possible to have easy contacts with former colleagues or to move about freely to see what is going on in the field. I am reduced to the position of a mere spectator of the astonishing expansion of archaeology in Britain in recent years.

When I went rather unexpectedly to Cambridge in 1919 after a difficult early life, the archaeology of Britain had really only just begun to emerge from its early stages and the limited number of universities offered little opportunity for its study. Today, universities proliferate in all parts of the country and Faculties of Archaeology are frequent. Highly specialised new techniques have developed which can squeeze the last drop out of any excavation and no doubt there is much more to come. With the aid of large sums of money, special attention is now being paid to enterprises such as the salvaging of the 'Mary Rose' at Portsmouth and the York Archaeological Trust's Coppergate excavation with its elaborate and imaginative organisation for public inspection and education.

After the lapse of over forty years the Sutton Hoo site has received new attention in a project which is designed to make an intensive study not only of the site at Woodbridge but also of the whole East Anglian kingdom, an enterprise promoted by the Society of Antiquaries and the British Museum, and ready to spend a sum of money in seven figures and to continue if necessary for a decade. There can be no better demonstration of the progress of archaeology in Britain than a comparison of the necessarily improvised excavation at Sutton Hoo in 1939 and the present highly-organised enterprise.

Earlier in this book I described the process by which prehistoric studies were placed on a firmer footing in Britain by the reorganisation of the pioneer Prehistoric Society of East Anglia in 1935. A national Prehistoric Society emerged from this and celebrates its Jubilee in this year 1985 in which I now write, and one of the great satisfactions of my life is to remember that for the first twelve years of its life I was privileged to act as its Honorary Secretary.

A measure of the vast development of public interest in archaeology is the ironic situation which has now arisen in which it is becoming necessary to protect famous monuments like Stonehenge, not from vandalism so much as from the sheer wear and tear to which they are exposed even when they are visited by eager crowds under proper control. No one would have dreamed of this development when in 1918 I wandered over the litter-strewn site, then completely without any real form of protection and on which gypsies quite recently camped.

At various times in my career I have been involved to a greater or lesser degree with a number of excavations which have, in different ways, marked new departures in this branch of archaeology and, in particular, those at the Trundle, Shippea Hill in the Fens, Giant's Hill in Lincolnshire, Little Woodbury in Wiltshire, Sutton Hoo in Suffolk and Star Carr in the East Riding of Yorkshire.

Sutton Hoo was an altogether exceptional experience, although each one was a landmark in its own right. But I am convinced that my most important contribution to archaeology in Britain was the organisation of the Archaeology Division of the Ordnance Survey, with the assistance of some very able members of my staff. The application of the right degree of archaeological detail to maps of different scales was an obvious duty which we performed and I think that my more diplomatic approach to my superiors was a means by which we often got better results than Crawford, whose prickly temperament sometimes tended to lessen the effect of his undoubted genius as a field archaeologist.

Where I and my staff scored heavily was in devising and perfecting our less intensive record of all known or suspected monuments, sites and finds over the whole of Great Britain. The Serpell Committee which reconsidered the organisation of the Survey in recent years, and completed at long last the full civilianisation of the staff, abolished the Archaeology Division which was a sad day for me in my retirement. There was quite a lot of public protest and most of the Division staff were distributed to work with the Royal Commissions in England, Scotland and Wales. But a saving feature has been the retention of this less intensive record which continues to grow using, I believe, computerised methods and this is a continually growing record to which anyone can have access.

It now seems that by the end of the present decade computerised digital maps will be available from the Ordnance Survey over most parts of Great Britain, as they already are over much of the Birmingham area today.

By that time I shall probably be dead, having already lived beyond the Biblical span of life, but I hope I shall be remembered as one who did something to promote the general advance of archaeology.

Appendix I

C.W. PHILLIPS (1919–23, Fellow: 1933–47)

C.W. Phillips came into residence in 1919 holding an entrance Exhibition. He read History and was awarded a scholarship on being placed in the First Class in Part I of the Tripos. Having taken his B.A. degree in 1922, he spent a fourth year reading Law. He continued to reside in Cambridge working as a College supervisor in History, and it was at this time that he developed his interest in field archaeology, being much influenced by O.G.S. Crawford, the first archaeology officer of the Ordnance Survey, at whose suggestion he began in his spare time to revise the field archaeology of Lincolnshire.

He was appointed College Librarian in 1929, a post that he held till 1945, and in 1933 was elected to a research Fellowship. In 1940 he joined the RAFVR holding the rank of Flight Lieutenant and was engaged on special duties at the photographic interpretation centre, where much of his time was spent in preparing detailed gazetteers of G.S.G.S. maps of Europe. After the war he returned to Cambridge for a year, and was then appointed Archaeology Officer at the Ordnance Survey, the third holder of that post. The next fifteen years saw a great increase in the revision of large scale maps, and Phiillips was able to build up the Archaeology Division until it had a staff of some sixty employed in updating and improving the representation of antiquities on Ordnance Maps, as different areas of the country came to be revised. After retirement his connexion with the Ordnance Survey continued as he was engaged in writing its history.

Beside his official work, C.W.P. contributed much to British archaeology, when progress in the subject was still largely a matter of private enterprise. His survey of Lincolnshire in the late 1920's led to his discovery and excavation in 1933–4 of the Giants Hills Long Barrow near Skendleby, the first excavation of a northern long barrow carried out to modern standards. He was an active member of the Fenland Research Committee, established in 1931, and was one of the first to appreciate the extent of the Romano-British exploitation of the Fenland. This led much later to his editing a monograph *The Fenland in Roman Times*, published in 1970 by the Royal Geographical Society. A honorary secretary of the Prehistoric Society during the first ten years of its existence he played an important part in establishing the Society on a national footing, and the great increase in membership during that time owed much to his efforts. He took an active part in the Society's excavation of the Iron Age site at Little Woodbury, near Salisbury, in 1938–9, and will always be specially remembered for his supervision of the excavation in the Summer of 1939 of the Sutton Hoo ship burial, for which he was able at short notice to assemble a party of the most highly skilled archaeologists to help with the work. This is perhaps the most remarkable archaeological discovery ever made in Britain: the delicate work of recording the structure of the ship largely revealed by stains in the soil and by the distribution of the iron clench-nails, and the recovery of the extraordinary assemblage of grave-goods was not made easier by the fact that at the time the country was under threat of war. The results of C.W.P's later fieldwork are preserved in the maps and records of the Ordnance Survey, and he was largely responsible for the revision of the third and fourth editions of the O.S. booklet *Field Archaeology in Great Britain*

C.W.P.'s major contribution to the College was the rearrangement and cataloguing of the Library after removal of the books in 1929 from their temporary home in the court to the War Memorial building approached from C staircase. This work took four years, and at the same time many of the old books, mainly from the Cooke and Wheatley-Balme bequests, were cleaned and rebound.

From the time of his election as a Fellow Phillips made a point of dining in hall frequently during term. The Fellowship was then small – only eleven – and the Fellows knew each other well. In 1936 Phillips presented to the Society a loving-cup, chosen from an exhibition of silver hall-marked in the jubilee year of King George V. Before the outbreak of World War II Phillips had already become an institution. He was a large man who uttered all his statements with weight and a confidence which defied any trace of doubt or contradiction. He had a wonderful gift of being able to describe a commonplace and ordinary incident by the use of a single word which was precise and correct and at the same time, to his audience, utterly unexpected. The total effect might produce a hilarity which enlivened many an evening after hall. Dr Durrant recalls an occasion when C.W.P. was speaking of his car, at that time a large and powerful Ford, which had come to rest in Jesus Lane and refused to start. Assistance was obtained and, as explained by the owner, 'the engine started again with the noise of a *fieldpiece*'. On another occasion he entertained the SCR with an account of a poor meal he had had in a country hotel. A guest had complained of the portion of meat with which he had been served. C.W.P. observed that he was amazed at the *fortitude* with which the waiter carried away the rejected portion. Phillips's thumb-nail character-sketches were memorable: he once described an unpromising pupil as 'a very old, very cold suet pudding, abondoned on a foreshore'.

It became a ritual on Saturday evenings in term time that Phillips delivered a meditative monologue about the state of the world in general and Cambridge in particular: he saw it in the darkest colours. These monologues came to be known for this reason as 'phillippics'. They were distinguished by shrewd insight as well as by forceful and picturesque language, and were better than anything available on the wireless at the time. They had something of the penitential exercise about them, by assisting at which one felt one somehow acquired merit. They were attended mainly by the younger members of the Society.

In the vacations when Phillips could devote himself entirely to archaeology, he used to report on his progress. The long vacation of 1939 was particularly memorable, for that was when he was engaged on the excavation of the Sutton Hoo ship burial, against time – for he saw very clearly the approach of war, which indeed was a recurring theme in the 'phillippics'. The Society was privileged to enjoy a week-by-week explanation in vivid terms on what is now regarded as a classic excavation. One detail: the woodwork of the ship was preserved only as a discolouration of the sand in which it was buried. It was uncovered not by spadework but by the careful removal of undiscoloured sand using soft brushes. This is the sort of detail that he conveyed – the romantic attraction of the remarkable finds of gold and silver objects seemed in comparison of minor importance.

The British Cartographic Soc.

Cartographers as well as archaeologists will have noted with deep regret the death on September 23rd of Charles Phillips. Born on 24th April, 1901, he won a history scholarship at Selwyn College (of which he later became a Fellow and served as its Librarian), but from an early age he was most interested in field archaeology and its proper presentation on maps. Before the war, besides carrying out some important excavations (most notably of the Neolithic long barrow at Giants' Hills in Lincolnshire and of the Anglo-Saxon ship-burial at Sutton Hoo in Suffolk), he ranged widely over the country and from 1926 onwards was closely associated with the work of O.G.S. Crawford, the first Archaeology Officer of the Ordnance Survey. After serving in the R.A.F., both at its Central Airphotographic Interpretation Unit and at the Directorate of Military Survey, he was in 1945 appointed a successor to Crawford. This was of immense benefit to the country, for he had both the experience and the ability to direct and build up the Archaeology Division of the O.S. to an adequate strength to deal with the historical background to the resurvey of Britain that was then beginning – something that involved not only fieldwork but also the progressive construction of a national index of archaeological sites. He also revived the series of Period Maps and personally compiled both the second edition of the *Map of Britain in the Dark Ages* and the first edition of that of *Britain before the Norman Conquest*. The latter appeared only after his retirement in 1965, as did *The Fenland in Roman Times*, which he edited for the Royal Geographical Society, but it was also in retirement that he saw with distress the step by step reduction and downgrading of the Division that he had created. Fortunately it had not been completely destroyed by the time of the Serpell Committee and on their advice the surviving members of its staff and the archive that had been developed have been transferred to the Royal Commissions on Historical Monuments. So his work lives on and he has left an invaluable legacy to Britain.

Antiquity Vol. LX. No. 228 1986

Charles Phillips' career at the Ordnance Survey lasted for 20 years and the work he did there is, for many, the thing for which he is best remembered.

Phillips came to the Ordnance Survey in 1945 in the confused aftermath of the war. The post of Archaeology Officer, which he took over, had been created in 1920 (the archaeological tradition of the OS was, of course, much older) but the staff was miniscule and the organisation rudimentary. During the ensuing years he built up the Archaeology Division to some 60 strong and made it into an organisation which was the envy of foreign visitors.

He joined the Department at exactly the right time. The post-war resurvey was just starting and the various developments, such as new towns, which are potentially so destructive of archaeological sites, were about to get into top gear. An organisation was clearly needed which could harness the new survey potential to the task of recording the sites which were threatened and surveying them with an archaeologist's eye before the bulldozers moved in.

Few could have had the energy, initiative and organising ability, as well as the necessary expertise, to tackle such a job. But Charles Phillips was fully equal to it.

In the past the relations between the archaeologists and the surveying staff had not always been harmonious but, under Phillips's guidance, all this changed and the recording and surveying of antiquities went steadily ahead so that, by the time of his retirement in 1965, the task was largely complete and a card index had been built up which has proved of enduring value to archaeologists all over the country – and, indeed – the world.

At the same time the production of the Ordnance Survey's incomparable period maps was energetically pursued, to give pleasure and instruction to millions.

A few years after his retirement the Government made a fierce onslaught on the Archaeology Division and virtually eliminated it. This greatly saddened Phillips who fought to save his old organisation. His efforts were in vain but the work that he did can never be wholly lost.

His records and maps remain and the standards of archaeological cartography that he and the Ordnance Survey set will endure as will the reputation of this very great archaeologist.

Major-General R.C.A. Edge

Appendix II

Archaeological and Historical Maps published by the Ordnance Survey between 1870 and 1978.

1870 Facsimile of the fourteenth century 'Gough' map of Great Britain.
1914 Facsimile of Philip Symonson's map of Kent, 1596.
1924 Map of Roman Britain. 1:1,000,000, 1st. edition.
1928 Map of Roman Britain. 1:1,000,000, 2nd edition.
*1930 Seventeenth Century England. 1: 1,000,000.
*1933 Neolithic Wessex, 1 inch to 1 mile.
*1933 Map of the Trent basin showing the distribution of long barrows and megaliths, 1/4 inch to 1 mile.
1936 Map of South Wales showing the distribution of long barrows and megaliths, 1/4 inch to 1 mile.
1937 Earthworks of Salisbury Plain, Amesbury sheet, 2 inches to 1 mile.
1937 Earthworks of Salisbury Plain, Old Sarum sheet, 2 inches to 1 mile.
1938 Britain in the Dark Ages, North sheet, 1st. edition, 1 : 1,000,000.
1939 Britain in the Dark Ages, South sheet, 1st. edition. 1 : 1,000,000.
1939 Scotland in Roman times: Forth, Clyde and Tay area, 1/4 inch to 1 mile.
*1950 Monastic Britain, South sheet, 1st. edition, 1:625,000.
*1950 Monastic Britain, North sheet, 1st. edition, 1:625,000.
*1951 Ancient Britain, South sheet, 1st. edition, 1:625,000.
*1951 Ancient Britain, North sheet, 1st. edition, 1:625,000.
*1954 Monastic Britain, South sheet, 2nd. edition, 1:625,000.
*1954 Monastic Britain, North sheet, 2nd. edition, 1:625,000.
*1956 Map of Roman Britain, 3rd. edition, 1:1,000,000.
*1962 Southern Britain in the Iron Age, 1:625,000.
*1964 Hadrian's Wall, 1st. edition, 2 inches to 1 mile.
1964 Ancient Britain, South sheet, 2nd. edition, 1:625,000.
1964 Ancient Britain, North sheet, 2nd. edition, 1:625,000.
*1966 Britain in the Dark Ages, 2nd. edition (single sheet). 1:1,000,000.
1960 The Antonine Wall, 21/2 inches to 1 mile.
1972 Hadrian's Wall, 2nd. edition, 2 inches to 1 mile.
*1974 Britain before the Norman Conquest, 1:625,000.
1978 Monastic Britain, North and South sheets, 3rd. edition. 1:625,000.
1978 Map of Roman Britain, 4th. edition, 1:625,000.

* Denotes the author's complete or partial responsibility for compilation.

Appendix III

Various publications by the author or to which he has contributed.

C.W. Phillips. 'The Excavation of Merlin's Cave at Symond's Yat in the lower Wye Valley', *University of Bristol Spelaeological Society's Proceedings*, Vol. 4, 1929–35, pp. 11–33.

C.W. Phillips. 'Field Archaeology in Lincolnshire', *The Lincolnshire Historian*, Nos. 1 to 5, 1948–50, pp. 41–54, 92–99, 117–127, 187–195.

'Excavations at the Trundle, West Sussex', *Sussex Archaeological Collections*, Vol. LXX, 1929.

C.W. Phillips, 'The Excavation of the Giants' Hill long barrow at Skendleby, Lincolnshire', *Archaeologia*, Vol. 85, pp. 37–106.

C.W. Phillips. 'The Excavation of the Sutton Hoo ship burial', *The Antiquaries' Journal*, Vol.22, April, 1940, pp. 149–202.

C.W. Phillips. *The Historian's Guide to Ordnance Survey maps*, National Council of Social Service, 1964, 'Period Maps of the Ordnance Survey', pp. 35–41.

C.W. Phillips. *Field Archaeology, some Notes for Beginners* issued by the Ordnance Survey, H.M. Stationery Office, 1947, pp. 40.

C.W. Phillips,   "   "   "   "   "1951

C.W. Phillips, A.L.F. Rivet, and R.W. Feachem,"   "1963.

Notes for Correspondents of the Archaeology Division, 1958, O.S. Office at Chessington, by C.W. Phillips, pp.8.

C.W. Phillips. *Archaeology in the Ordnance Survey, 1791–1965*, The Council for British Archaeology, 1980, pp. 1 – 63.

ed. W.A. Seymour. *A History of the Ordnance Survey*, 1980, William Dawson and Sons Ltd., Folkestone, Kent.

Index